REVENGE

REVENGE

HOW DONALD TRUMP WEAPONIZED
THE US DEPARTMENT OF JUSTICE
AGAINST HIS CRITICS

MICHAEL
COHEN

MELVILLE HOUSE
BROOKLYN • LONDON

REVENGE: HOW DONALD TRUMP WEAPONIZED THE US DEPARTMENT OF JUSTICE AGAINST HIS CRITICS

First published in 2022 by Melville House
Copyright © Michael Cohen, 2022
Afterword copyright © 2023 by Norman Eisen and E. Danya Perry
All rights reserved
First Paperback Printing: August 2023

Melville House Publishing
46 John Street
Brooklyn, NY 11201
and
Melville House UK
Suite 2000
16/18 Woodford Road
London E7 0HA

mhpbooks.com
@melvillehouse

ISBN: 978-1-68589-074-2
ISBN: 978-1-68589-055-1 (eBook)

Library of Congress Control Number: 2022944371

Designed by Beste Doğan

Printed in the United States of America

1 3 5 7 9 10 8 6 4 2

A catalog record for this book is available from the Library of Congress

To Laura, Samantha, and Jake:
You three are my life and inspire me
every day to be my best.

AUTHOR'S NOTE

I want to thank Brian Karem, without whom I would not have been able to get the insider information that was essential to get this work completed. He conducted many of the interviews included here. I knew of him peripherally as one of the reporters covering the White House who occasionally sparred with Donald Trump. But I knew he was the guy I wanted to help me on this book after he stood up to Trump and beat him in court three times to keep his press pass. When he asked the important question of Trump, "Will you accept a peaceful transfer of power," and Trump became the first president in history to say no, I also knew this was a guy who got it and understands the dangers of Donald Trump and the Department of Justice. I also knew that people wouldn't necessarily want to talk to me at the Justice Department, but would more likely open up to someone who was known for honoring confidences. That, as it turns out, is invaluable among those on the inside who want to see the Department of Justice reformed.

INTRODUCTION

WHY WON'T THE MANHATTAN DISTRICT ATTORNEY hold Donald Trump responsible? Why won't anyone? You've been told it's my credibility. I call bullshit. Put me on the stand and let me loose.

No problem. That's not the reason Donald isn't being held accountable. I propose that it's because placing me on the witness stand will reignite a firestorm of media attention that will ultimately focus on the improper and illegal actions of members of the FBI, the Southern District of New York U.S. Attorney's Office, the former president, the Department of Justice, former Attorney General William Barr, and all of those who lied, manipulated, and cheated to get their win while deflecting from their own culpability.

It's 2022 and the fetid stench of the Trump administration lingers on even as the Manhattan district attorney backs out of charging him for the crimes we all know he committed. If we don't get it together and fix the problems of justice in this country, then we could be looking at the end of democracy.

We should all be worried about our government. Because if you're not, then what happened to me could happen to you.

For example, when you go to sleep at night, do you have night-mares about FBI agents raiding your home, searching your furniture, going through your closets, ripping through your clothes—including your daughter's underwear drawer—and leaving with boxloads of your belongings?

Do you have nightmares about knocks at your door—two dozen federal agents with guns standing in the hallway holding a warrant and demanding entry into your home for crimes you were falsely accused of committing?

Have you ever feared that the president of the United States wants you dead, wants to destroy you and your family, your reputation, and even your children's future?

Do you break out in a cold sweat just thinking about those things?

I didn't—until it happened to me.

How would you like it if the craziest and most powerful person in the world spent his every waking narcissistic moment trying to use you to deflect from his dirty deeds. I once said Donald Trump wanted me dead. I now know he did everything he could to make that happen.

As you will see in these coming pages, that is not hyperbole.

That thought came to me as I sat sweltering in a hotbox in up-state New York, isolated and nearly forgotten. My family and closest friends refused to give up and tried desperately to save me before I suffered a stroke or a heart attack as they tried to secure my release from federal prison.

I thought about it as I watched government agents in the Bureau of Prisons and the Department of Justice lie about me and force me back into prison once I was released.

"Say hello to Bill Barr," I told the government agents as they re-arrested me and forced me into handcuffs and shackles prior to shipping me back to the upstate prison from which I'd just been released.

It should come as no surprise that reporters at the White House apparently knew I was going back before this all went down.

I realized five minutes after I met with Adam Pakula and his supervisor Enid Febus, two government officers, at 500 Pearl Street in Manhattan—the Federal Courthouse—that something was awry. I was supposedly getting fitted for an ankle monitor so I could begin my in-home incarceration. Instead, I was to be sent back. The moment they handed me and my lawyer a two-page document which blatantly violated my First Amendment rights and demanded that I cease writing and publishing my first book, *Disloyal*, I recognized the fingerprints of the president's newest chief fixer, Bill Barr—because I had once been that guy.

However, the goal of this book is not to cry about my lot in life. I chose my own path when I sided with the slime of humanity. I know what I did and I continue to have nightmares about it to this day. Making amends for it is one of the driving forces of my life.

But, let's not forget: I'm not the only one who worked for a scumbag. We seem to be rich with them in this country. If everyone who worked for a scumbag quit, there'd be a lot more unemployed people in this country. And don't forget, I was never part of the Trump presidential circus. I didn't work for the campaign. I dealt with a petty tyrant who ran a small family company. He wasn't yet an international pestilence. And the bottom line is he fooled a lot more people than just me—74 million, to be exact, who voted for Donald in 2020. He also didn't do it alone. Over the years, both the left and the right paid for his ride into the White House. Some of them clung to him when he got in trouble. He sacrificed others—like me —causing many former allies to become enemies. Mitch McConnell is the sad sap who falls into all three categories.

The goal of this book is to open your eyes to the danger to the country when you have a deranged president who weaponizes the Department of Justice for his own benefit. If I have to smack you in the face to do it, so be it. After all, Trump isn't unique. I want to help us all change the government so the authoritarians don't ultimately win and destroy democracy.

Yes. I have suffered. And, yes, my family has suffered too.

But in pointing this out, I'm trying to show you what can happen to *you*—to everyone not in power or a friend of the powerful. We are in danger of losing this country to fascists who are destroying our democracy and the rule of law and replacing it with something unseen since the dark days in Europe prior to World War II. Donald Trump was just a practice run. If those who think like him are allowed to take control of this government—like they tried to do during the January 6 insurrection—then we're all fucked, and my suffering will become the nation's suffering. As I helped create this Frankenstein's monster and let it out of its cage, I feel it is my moral duty, or if you prefer my *penance*, to make sure we re-cage the beast.

This book was not easy for me to write. As a result of this experience I suffer terribly from PTSD. While writing *Revenge*, and interviewing individuals with first-hand knowledge of my prosecution from the federal government, and of what I put my family through by my association to Trump, no one could believe I'm not on medication.

I'm not.

I've spoken at length about Trump in my previous book, *Disloyal.* In this book I want to talk about a deeper problem that affects all of us.

I'd like you to put aside whatever you may think about me personally—from what you've read or seen in the media. Simply evaluate the facts. You don't have to believe me. All I ask is that you follow the facts.

We have a serious problem in this country that goes beyond Donald Trump and beyond our vitriolic day-to-day politics.

There is a deadly cancer plaguing our justice system.

The Department of Justice has become the Department of *Injustice.*

We must fix this immediately.

Donald Trump wasn't the cause. He was a symptom. But, Donald is also a master craftsman at using the system to benefit himself and destroy those he wants to crush. In that fashion he exposed the system for what it has become—an instrument of those who have power to wield against those of us who have none. But none of this could have happened if our elected officials hadn't already perverted the system, giving Donald the opportunity to exploit it.

If we are to be a nation of laws, then those laws have to apply to everyone, rich or poor, and no matter what race, religion, creed, or color. All of us have to be equal under the eyes of the law.

That is not the case, and while we don't say it out loud, in our hearts we know it to be true.

What this book will do is outline the road map to the problems and offer solutions.

While I do use my own experience to outline the problem, what I want you to consider is what can and *does* happen to anyone when they fall under the scrutiny of the Department of Justice. My privilege gave me an edge in getting out of prison before my health problems killed me. Others don't have that opportunity and the government just does not give a shit. If the Department of Justice wants you, then they will use any means available to achieve their goal. Hence the adage often discussed in judicial circles: "The Department of Justice could indict a ham sandwich if it chose to."

Consider this: What if government investigators used the most highly sensitive financial database (FINCEN) on the planet not legally, but illegally? And not to prosecute you, but to belittle, denigrate, and disparage you? We're talking about a database that is used to hunt terrorists and money launderers and mobsters. In my case, it was used to smear me, and in so doing, hurt two people I didn't know— but who unfortunately share my name. The government agent who illegally used the planet's most secure economic information system received a mere slap on the wrist—a lesser sentence than I got for paying off a porn star for playing with the president's "mushroom penis."

How safe do you think your private financial records are now? And don't say, "Well, I have nothing to hide, so why would they bother me?" I didn't have anything to hide, either, and neither did the people whose only sin was sharing my name. The government did it anyway.

What if the prosecutor in your case refused to speak with you for months despite your volunteering to help them? What if your prosecutor saw your case as merely a means to an end of climbing a career ladder? And what if you were prosecuted for aiding and abetting a federal crime, but the individual who directed it and benefitted from the act was never prosecuted?

I mean for God's sake, Sammy (The Bull) Gravano got better treatment from the government than I and he was a confessed assassin for the mob!

As many of the people who've known me the longest pointed out, this life event irrevocably changed me. I honestly wanted to help.

I still do.

When it came down to it, I went to prison because I paid off the president's paramour *for him!* It wasn't virtuous, but illegal? Come on. When I was confronted with *omissions* (a lack of information) on my income tax returns I was ready, willing and able to fix it and attempted to explain how it should have been a civil and not a criminal matter. I was directed *not to*—by the government—and then faced bogus charges of income tax evasion when I never faced an audit, never got a delinquency notice, never filed a late return, never requested an extension, and paid every tax dollar my CPA determined that was due and owed. At each step along the way the government contrived to ruin my reputation, crush my soul, and destroy my family—for the sake of an orange-faced piece of shit who ran roughshod over the Constitution. As of this writing he remains unindicted and free, and I've had to pay the price for illegal activities he perpetrated, planned, and directed.

At least Sammy the Bull got to testify against John Gotti, who was ultimately charged and convicted. Trump has never been charged and every attempt to do so, so far, has been thwarted. It turns out he's truly the "Teflon Don."

This is what the American public has to understand. There *are* two separate types of justice in the United States. One is for those who have the power. They don't pay for their illegal actions. The other is for the rest of us—and we pay too damn much. One of my sins was thinking I was a member of the class of protected individuals: those who are able to get away with anything they want.

I'm not.

Now, make no mistake, I've sinned. I've paid for my sins and I continue to do so.

But my eyes have also been opened in this process, and I know damned well that those who are prosecuting the sinners are not only sinners themselves, but in the process of committing their sins they have corrupted our Department of Justice.

What you will find in these pages is not just that those who are perpetrating this injustice in our country have no problem doing so—it is that some of them think they're actually doing their job and protecting the country. Many of the people who spoke to me for this book are still employed by the Department of Justice. They are heroes who fear losing their job or worse, being improperly prosecuted as I was. That is why many of them spoke to me "on background" only, which requires that I don't identify them. I want to thank them for speaking with me and helping to provide their insight and concerns about what's going on inside the DOJ. It is what they have to say that sheds a light on this dark and evil chapter in American history.

As for the rest of them—and I'm referring to the dirty ones who prosecute high profile cases and are hell-bent on obtaining convictions for their own benefit, for better job offers, higher pay and higher status—for these animals, appearance has become their reality. These individuals become enslaved to the powerful who are to be protected at all cost because that's just the way justice works. In their warped perception they believe might makes right because they got a pay raise.

If we're ever to live up to the ideals of our Constitution, this must change.

And if I have anything to do with it, that change starts now.

REVENGE

CHAPTER ONE

THE BULLSHIT BEGINS

IT WAS JANUARY 10, 2017, and I was sitting in the bright sunshine of the IMG Academy ballpark in Bradenton, Florida, watching my son play baseball. I'd traveled there from New York with my son, who was a teenaged lefty pitching phenom with Hank's Yanks, the high school travel baseball team for the New York Yankees. He'd drawn interest from a few minor league teams with ties to MLB clubs and there were a lot of scouts present. It had us both excited. It was a proud day for father and son—and a rare time away from Trump world for me, where I could just enjoy being with him. He was 16 years old, a fair-haired athletic youth with a lot of potential. Standing six foot two, proudly wearing number 11. I was your clichéd proud father indulging in the dream that his son might have a future as a major league ballplayer. I sat in the crowded stands enjoying the sun, happy to be away from work for a day, watching my boy, daydreaming about his future . . .

And then my cell phone rang. I tried to ignore it but it kept on ringing. And it wouldn't stop ringing for many days thereafter.

That initial call was from Rosalind Helderman and Tom

Hamburger, two reporters with the *Washington Post*. They wanted to know about accusations against me found in an unpublished opposition research paper focused on Donald Trump, a research paper that would soon come to be known as the "Steele Dossier."

They began asking me questions about eleven specific allegations—ugly allegations about my work with Trump and my alleged business associates. I was caught off guard, but I was able nonetheless to quite naturally deny all of the allegations, because none of them were true.

But that was just the start.

As the shitstorm got underway, I simply couldn't believe the questions and smarmy insinuations based on the Steele report that were thrown at me by reporters and journalists of every stripe. Did I travel to Prague? Did I meet with Russian oligarchs and act as a go-between for Putin in Russia and Trump in the United States? Did I hack the Clinton server? Did I hack the DNC computer? Did I pay off Russians to clean up Paul Manafort's mess? Did my family own a dacha in Sochi directly next door to Vladimir Putin's house?

It wasn't just patently absurd; it was fucking ridiculous. And soon, more than 1700 stories about me in the mainstream media painted me as a combination of John Wick, Jason Bourne, and Ray Donovan, skulking around trying to make deals with shady Russians for Donald Trump. The only thing it seemed I wasn't accused of was working as a liaison with Ernst Blofeld.

Take, for just one example, the accusation that I'd made a secret trip to Prague to conduct some clandestine negotiation with Putin's people about stealing the election. I tweeted out on January 10, 2017 that I'd never been to Prague, because I'd never been to Prague.[1] That didn't stop anyone in the media from drawing the conclusion that I had definitely gone to Prague and that I acted as an intermediary between the Russians and Trump. I received more than 800 phone calls from journalists asking me questions about traveling to Prague, and the speculations that it's true continue to this day. Now, don't get me wrong—I fixed a great many things for Donald Trump, did some despicable things for him, and Trump is a truly horrible human being. But the Steele Dossier and its allegations against me was another matter entirely.

It would subsequently turn out that, while a small amount of what it said about other matters eventually proved factual, everything that the Steele Dossier had to say about *me*—everything—was false. All of it was later proved to be falsehoods based on innuendo, rumor, and conjecture. I proved it then and I can prove it now.

But don't take my word for it. Ask the members of the Robert Mueller investigation. Ask the FBI. You can even ask the federal prosecutors who hate me. It was all lies. Each of these agencies subsequently proved all of these outrageous allegations against me were false.

But by then it was too late. My lot was cast.

In January 2017, I was up to my eyeballs in the cult of Donald J. Trump. I'd worked for him for ten years, and my relationship with him had never been better. I helped get him elected president. I was his apex predator, his "fixer"—first as executive vice president of the Trump Organization and special counsel to Donald J. Trump, then as the personal attorney to the president of the United States. Over the years he had screwed people over, manipulated them and used them, and I helped him do it. But, in my naiveté, I never thought any of that would happen to me.

Why did I think this? Because I was the one who threw people under the bus for him. I had bailed him out of too many jams. I had helped his kids and his family out of numerous difficult situations—most of them engineered by their own stupidity and thoughtlessness. I was a trusted confidant and I had earned that trust with loyalty, so I believed there was no way he would betray me.

But he soon would, and with an ease that was startling—and I'd seen him do some very startling and fucked-up things during the previous decade. It was a decade filled with a lot of work, because Donald Trump requires a lot of work. Don't get me wrong, there were some good times too—going backstage at concerts, "The Apprentice" and the Miss Universe pageants, and lots of events and parties and gatherings where I had the opportunity to be with people I otherwise never would've met. But with Trump it was always, first and foremost, about work—even when I attended these events. And the biggest part of my job was covering for his fat ass.

And after years of doing it, I had settled into a bland, daily routine. I got up at 4:30 a.m. every morning, immediately showered, dressed, picked out a tie and jacket, made myself some oatmeal and a cup of coffee, black, no sugar. I'd spend my early mornings watching the news on FOX, CNN, and MSNBC, flipping through the stations indiscriminately while I ate, usually settling for an extended period of time on a story that had an impact on the Trump world. Over the years that world expanded greatly and there was a time when I was ecstatic to be a part of it. After I watched the early morning news, I'd brush my teeth, put on the tie and suit jacket, kiss my wife and children goodbye and walk the two blocks from my home to Trump Tower. I'd generally be in the office by 7:30 a.m. and stay until at least

7:30 p.m. dealing with Donald's shit. That was my world. That was my life. Looking back, though, it was more like a nightmare.

The job, though, is why I've been accused of knowing "where all the bodies are buried." I've been compared to a mafia don's consigliere—and while in some respects that is a proper analogy, it should be understood that Donald Trump never let *anyone* know *everything* that was going on in his world. You knew what he wanted you to do by what he didn't say as often as what he did say. A nod. A wink. A statement like "Well, it would be bad if X, Y, or Z happened," indicating that's what he wanted to have happen. A man like that simply doesn't tell anyone where all the "bodies" are buried. At least he sure didn't tell me.

So at first, I could not understand why everyone thought I knew more about Trump than I did. I thought it was just a natural assumption that since I was in constant contact with him I knew everything. I had used my proximity to Trump to gain access to people myself, so I could understand that assumption. But, as it turned out, it was something far darker and more dangerous—and the first hint of what was really behind it all came when the Steele Dossier was published.

For those who don't know about it, the mess that came to be known as the Steele Dossier was originally an opposition research paper financed by the Democrats and written between June and December of 2016. It contained allegations of misconduct, conspiracy, and cooperation between Trump and the government of Russia prior to the election in 2016.[2]

Let's go through that timeline quickly, so we understand why and how the Dossier came to be, and its relevance to what happened to me.

It was first reported the DNC had been hacked in April 2016. By

June, the DNC had hired Fusion GPS, a commercial research and strategic intelligence firm, tasked with probing Trump's alleged ties to Russia. Fusion hired Christopher Steele, a former British intelligence officer and James Bond wannabe, to do the research. Steele submitted his first report at the end of June and said in it that Russia had cultivated Trump for five years and had compromising material from a previous visit Trump made to the Ritz-Carlton Hotel in Moscow around November 2013.[3]

According to the Dossier, this is where the so-called infamous "pee tape" was recorded—the incident whereby Trump had supposedly watched while a bunch of Russian hookers he'd hired urinated on the bed in the hotel's presidential suite, because former President Barack Obama had slept there once. That's some real sick shit, and there's no denying Trump is filled with real sick shit. But this claim is totally false—as I stated in front of the House Oversight Committee.

It's true, though, that Trump—a real, old-fashioned racist—certainly did have a warped fixation on Barack Obama. He couldn't get over Obama roasting him alive at the 2011 White House Correspondents' Association dinner, an annual gathering where a comedian usually hosts a fairly gentle "roasting" of the President in front of the press corps—a kind of "make nice" event. But that night, it was the president who did the roasting, and it was of Donald Trump—and it wasn't that gentle.

Let me be clear: Donald Trump hated Barack Obama from the get-go. It's a visceral hatred. He hates him because he's black. He hates him because he's successful and he hates him for being everything Donald Trump knows he himself is not: smart, talented, urbane, witty, and charming.

But what he hates Obama for more than anything else is poking fun of him in public that night. Some say, and rightly so, that that was the night Trump decided to run for president—just so he could obliterate everything Obama did. That night, April 30, 2011, Trump became a man on a mission.

Of course, you can't blame Obama for making fun of the man. Trump was the guy behind the birtherism narrative saying Obama wasn't eligible for the presidency because he wasn't born in the United States, which the right had used like a cudgel to question the legitimacy of the Obama administration. That prodded Hawaii to release Obama's "long form" birth certificate and "hopefully that puts all doubts to rest," as Obama said at that Correspondents' dinner. Trump, who was there, sat stoically as Obama ridiculed him mercilessly that night. No one was happier, Obama said, that the birther hoax was behind us than Trump, because now, Trump could concentrate on the things that really matter, "Like, did we fake the moon landing."

Despite his claims to the contrary, Trump took that very hard. Never forget that Donald Trump is a thin-skinned, frightened little man with a massive ego. To him, having thousands of people in a room and countless more watching on television laughing at him was the single greatest humiliation he could imagine and experience. He was—and remained—seething in anger at Obama, and consequently the Democrats. Let's face it, that's why Donald ran as a *Republican*. He wasn't a dyed-in-the-wool Republican. Never was. He was Donald Trump and most of his thoughts about politics, if he had any genuine ones, lined up with Democratic policies—especially when it came to abortion. He was not a poster boy for the GOP.

But our national trajectory was set that night in 2011, fueled by the fire in Trump's shriveled soul for being made fun of—and worse, by a black man!

So while the Steele Dossier was wrong about the pee tape, it's true, at least, that Trump was resolved to piss on Obama in any way that he could.

Another thread of the Dossier that dealt directly with me had to do with Felix Sater, who had been a casual acquaintance of mine when we were both kids. When I met him again as an adult, some 40 years later, he was far different from the boy I'd briefly known.

I met with him in September 2015, to consider a real estate opportunity for a Trump-branded tower in Moscow. Sater, who was born in Russia, was a longtime Trump fan who once spent a year in prison for stabbing a man with a broken martini glass. He was suspected of money laundering and stock manipulation in 1998. He got a pass from the United States because later he became a CIA informant. Now, he claimed Russian connections that could help us get funding for a real estate deal in Moscow, to help us build Trump's long-desired hotel in Moscow.

In October, Sater told me that his associates would meet with Putin to discuss getting funding from VTB Bank, and Trump signed a letter of intent, according to Buzzfeed, later that month. Yes, I talked to Sater. He also emailed me in November saying, "Buddy our boy can become president of the USA and we can engineer it. I will get all of Putin's team to buy in on this, I will manage the process."[4]

To be clear, I knew he was full of shit. That's why in January I was still willing to try to make the deal for the Trump Tower in Moscow and, giving up on Sater, emailed Kremlin spokesman Dmitry Peskov directly. But I didn't go to Russia. In fact, I have never been to Russia. From the onset of my discussions on this project, I always maintained three specific requirements that needed to be filled before I would even *consider* traveling to Russia. I called them my "Three-Prong Test":

1. Identify and provide proof that the potential licensee either owned or controlled a piece of property that would be acceptable to Mr. Trump;
2. Be shown proof they were capable of obtaining the necessary licensing and zoning permits to build a building in Moscow the size of the project we were contemplating;
3. And finally, be shown proof they had verifiable commitments for the funding of the project.

Sater was never able to get past the first prong, let alone all three, so in June I met with him in New York to put an end to the countless requests asking that I go to Russia to work on the Trump Tower deal. Meanwhile, I briefed Trump ten times on the status of the Trump Moscow deal (though I later told Congress it was only three . . . my big lie that I pleaded guilty to under duress of the Southern District of New York). But I didn't go there. I didn't encourage Sater to talk to Putin. I had no contact with anyone other than for business purposes—and the Mueller investigation subsequently proved it.

As was widely reported, in August 2017 I submitted a written statement to the House and Senate Intelligence committees which said the effort "to build a Trump property in Moscow . . . was terminated in

January of 2016, which occurred before the Iowa caucus and months before the very first primary." That wasn't true. But I lied because Trump told me to. And I maintained *that* fiction while in reality the last conversation I had about a Moscow project was in *June* 2016. That gave Trump the ability to tweet out, in July 2016, that, "For the record, I have ZERO investments in Russia." It was true—but it wasn't for a lack of trying. He had worked hard to drum up something to invest in, and I had assisted him.

Throughout Trump's run for the presidency, the Democrats had no idea what they were up against. It was as if they simply could not believe what they were seeing—the sheer hate-filled anger, the maniacal level of lying, and the single-mindedness of Trump. That was part of the reason for the research that led to the Steele Dossier. The Democrats wanted to know who their opponent really was.

The "pee tape" incident was one of 16 pre-election reports, plus one post-election report, which composed the Steele Dossier. It was designed to tell the Democrats, as Paul Harvey would say, "the rest of the story" about The Donald.

The day after Independence Day in 2016 Steele met with an FBI agent in London to reveal his initial findings, and two weeks later Steele submitted a report to Fusion that stated that an adviser to the Trump campaign named Carter Page (who can be seen in the videotape of the WHCA 2011 dinner sitting near Trump)[5] met with senior officials from Russian oil giant Rosneft, including Rosneft chief Igor Sechin (the former Deputy Prime Minister under Putin), and senior Kremlin official Igor Diveykin, during the Moscow trip. Page, a former American petroleum industry consultant, downplayed that meeting when he later had to testify before Congress. He described it as merely "a brief, less-than-10-second chat with Arkadiy Dvorkovich," Russia's deputy prime minister.[6]

But when the House Intelligence Committee released the full transcript of Page's testimony, it did validate some of the Steele Dossier. For example, as one report noted, "Page revealed during his testimony that he met with members of Russia's presidential administration and the head of investor relations at the Russian state-owned oil giant Rosneft during his trip to Moscow in July 2016."[7] It was enough to provide a thin veneer of credibility to an otherwise ridiculous and erroneous document. And ask a reporter who worked at the White House at that time. Most reporters thought it signaled the end of Donald Trump.

Initial reporting heated up the effort to trace conspiracy theories about cooperation between Trump associates and the Kremlin, so, naturally, as one of Trump's closest associates, I was tossed into the sack of people that would come under extreme scrutiny for being involved in a conspiracy that didn't exist, or in my case, that I wasn't a part of. I never was. I never would be. It's easy to see why some people didn't believe it. I lied for Donald Trump—mostly on minor issues. But my credibility was compromised and I paid a heavy price for my mistakes.

But I never made the mistake of betraying my country.

It is easy to understand why Page fell under scrutiny though. He is the founder and managing partner of Global Energy Capital, a one-man investment and consulting firm which specializes in—wait for it—Russian and Central Asian oil and gas.[8]

He had previously professed his love for Russia and Vladimir Putin, publicly and quite often. In 1998, Page joined the Eurasia Group, a strategy consulting firm, but he only lasted there three months. In 2017, Eurasia Group president Ian Bremmer said on Twitter that Page's strong pro-Russian stance was "not a good fit" for the firm and that Page was its "most wackadoodle" alumnus.[9]

Political scientist Stephen Sestanovich later described Page's foreign-policy views as having "an edgy Putinist resentment" and a sympathy to Putin's criticisms of the United States.[10] Over time, Page became increasingly critical of United States foreign policy toward Russia, and more supportive of Putin, with a United States official describing Page as "a brazen apologist for anything Moscow did."[11] Page at the time was often quoted on Russian state television and often credited as being a "famous American economist."

Wackadoodle, perhaps, but it all tended to lend some credibility to accusations that those associated with Trump were plotting with Russian oligarchs or even Putin himself.

But whatever sins Page committed, Trump did his associates far worse when, on July 27, 2016, he went out in a press conference to plead with Russia to hack into Hillary Clinton's emails. "Russia, if you're listening, I hope you're able to find the 30,000 emails that are missing, I think you will probably be rewarded mightily by our press," he said.

It was later revealed that Russia launched their attempt to hack Hilary Clinton's personal and campaign email servers that same day.[12]

In other words, he put a target on my back and the back of everyone else who worked with him by openly courting Russia in a press conference. That's the irony of all of this nonsense—the DOJ searched high and low for nefarious plots. They accused me of surreptitious activities like I was an undercover spy. But they never acknowledged what was right in front of their faces. For God's sakes, Donald spoke it into an open mic on a stage, live, with cameras recording the whole outlandish event. Who needs undercover operatives? Trump isn't smart enough for such plotting. He's just a bloviating asshole who shouts in public what he wants and people react to it. The Russians took him up on his offer. Go figure.

Meanwhile, Christopher Steele was still looking for nefarious plots with me involved. George Papadopoulos, a neophyte who had little to do with strategy, bragged to an Australian that he knew the Russians had dirt on Clinton. Papadopoulos was just another blowhard with little real use other than making himself feel important. But for a moment, at least, he was a player, thanks to the Steele Dossier.

And of course it was reported in the Steele Dossier that the Kremlin was happy with U.S. divisions about our upcoming election. I'm sure they were. That much is certain. Putin would love to weaken our democracy. It's obvious he did his best to try and do so. But as the Mueller Report later showed us, Trump was too inept to be of any use in that effort.

Still, Steele kept on digging—and writing. In late August he reported that Putin met on August 15 with former Ukrainian president Viktor Yanukovych. The Ukrainian president confirmed that Paul Manafort, who chaired the Trump presidential campaign from June to August, received significant kickbacks while working as a political consultant in Kiev. But he also assured Putin that no documents existed to corroborate the payments.

By September 2016, Steele said he had uncovered information that Trump paid bribes for possible business deals in Russia—and that's when my name came up. It was natural, I suppose—Carter

Page talked to Sechin the oil oligarch in Russia and emphasized my importance for any deal with Trump. To be honest, I *was* Trump's fixer, but that doesn't mean I was an undercover agent. I was his fixer. I was his blunt instrument. But I never had the influence over Trump that many thought I had. No one did—or does! But of course, Steele either didn't see it that way, or more likely didn't want to. His report leaned heavily on my participation in dealings with Russia. It was all later disproven by the Mueller Report, but that was still to come, and meanwhile Steele was reporting that I was assigned to "clean up the operation from the Trump side" with Manafort and Page.

Meanwhile, although Steele's report wasn't known yet to the public, it was the worst kept secret in Washington D.C. And that says a lot since no one in D.C. can keep a secret—especially politicians and reporters. They trade on innuendo and dark secrets that are usually little more than supposition. Thus was precisely the case with the Steele Dossier. Reporters were openly discussing it over beers at local restaurants, as were staffers in the halls of Congress and in the offices of the West Wing.

It was later reported[13] that at least *a dozen* national media organizations had a copy of the Dossier before it became public. One reporter friend of mine said the thing was passed around "like a bottle of booze at a frat party." Everyone saw it. Everyone spoke about it—to each other. While it was unvetted information, most of the press bought the premise: Trump was courting Putin and everyone around him was selling out their country. By the time I heard about it—in that phone call from the *Washington Post* reporters—dozens, if not hundreds of reporters, had discussed the Dossier for months. And, of course, the more the stories circulated, the worse they got.

Some theorized that as a result of all the speculation and innuendo, a surveillance court approved a wiretap on Page on October 21. The FBI was apparently looking, at first, to make Page the key scapegoat. They screwed the pooch there and overreached.

As was reported in the *Washington Post* later, "The Justice Department has conceded to a secretive intelligence court that the available evidence about Carter Page, a former Trump campaign adviser, wiretapped by the FBI during the Russia investigation, was legally insufficient to justify the last several months of his continued surveillance in 2017."[14]

On Halloween of 2016 the *New York Times* reported the FBI didn't see a clear link between Trump and Russia—which apparently angered Steele, who then took his ball, ran home, and stopped cooperating with the FBI.

But by November Senator John McCain knew about it. That's where it gets interesting.

I respect John McCain. He was a patriot who cared for his country and Donald Trump shat all over him and his legacy. Why? For similar reasons to his hatred of Obama—because Trump was jealous of McCain and knew he would never be as well respected as McCain was—a respect that extended to McCain even by his political opponents. That really bothered Trump.

McCain was a war hero. He was a man of character. When McCain ran for president an audience member once suggested his opponent Barack Obama was less than American. McCain immediately corrected her, stood up for Obama and said while he had a difference of opinion with him, he still respected him. Trump, of course, would never do that. It isn't in him. He only knows how to belittle people.

Perhaps most infuriating to Trump, McCain stood against him long before anyone else had the balls to do so. That angered Trump as much as Obama making fun of him, and so Trump hated McCain with a passion rivaling that of his hatred of Obama, and insulted him at every opportunity.

Now, I'm not going to insult McCain. But I will say that McCain had his own seething anger toward Trump—who wouldn't, given the circumstances?—and it's obvious he saw the Steele Dossier as a way to embarrass Trump. To be fair to McCain, the Dossier had a thin veneer of respectability—it covered the bases (barely), looked at some already infamous people like Carter Page, and was written by a former member of British Intelligence. McCain, a military man, could respect that.

So, in a January 11, 2017 statement McCain said about the Dossier, "Upon examination of the contents, and unable to make a judgment about their accuracy, I delivered the information to the director of the FBI." At the time that was James Comey. "That has been the extent of my contact with the FBI or any other government agency regarding this issue."

McCain should've seen through the Steele Dossier for what it was, and my fear is that maybe—probably?—he did and passed it along anyway to stick it to Trump. The thing is, I paid for it.

By then McCain was nearing his own end. On July 14, 2017 he underwent a minimally invasive craniotomy for a blood clot above his left eye at the Mayo Clinic in Phoenix. But he returned to the Senate less than two weeks later to cast a deciding vote allowing the Senate to begin consideration of bills to replace—rather than kill—the Affordable Care Act, thwarting Trump's attempt to wipe out perhaps the most major accomplishment of the Obama legacy. He also delivered a speech criticizing the party-line process used by the Republicans, urging a "return to regular order" utilizing the usual committee hearings and deliberations. Of course that played against Trump and his emerging Trumplicans who want to rule by bending others to their will. McCain was no fan of fascism. Trump bathed in it.

Soon afterward, McCain was also facing scrutiny for his handling of the Steele Dossier. McClatchy reported that he faced two lawsuits.[15] In one, launched by a Russian oligarch named in the Dossier, and filed against Buzzfeed for publishing the Dossier, it was revealed that a long-time associate of McCain's named David Kramer (a former State Department official who ran Arizona State University's McCain Institute for International Leadership) was the source of the leak to Buzzfeed.[16]

Of course after McCain died Trump had a field day tweeting about it and his connection to the Dossier. "So it was indeed (just proven in court papers) 'last in his class' (Annapolis) John McCain that sent the Fake Dossier to the FBI and Media hoping to have it printed BEFORE the Election," he posted on March 17, 2019. "He & the Dems, working together, failed (as usual). Even the Fake News refused this garbage!"

Nonetheless it's fair to point that the concerns of John McCain and David Kramer in passing along the Dossier were not just about political payback. The concern with Russian collusion was real—and founded on facts. Many in our government were well aware how dangerous Putin is. So, it's understandable they took the action they did.

However, the fact that the Steele Dossier was a complete piece of fiction is why the FBI couldn't bag Trump. If experience teaches us anything, Trump will squirm his way out of anything that isn't sewed up tight. The DOJ is used to threatening people and getting them to plea bargain, out for fear of a longer and harsher sentence. But Trump has been fighting these battles since he was out of diapers. The DOJ overestimated their own power and underestimated that of Donald Trump. They still do. But I'm just a mere mortal. They got me.

Trump is another matter, and what happened after the Dossier came out proves it. The upshot is there are a lot of people still pissed off that Trump remains free. Steele, who penned the Dossier, is one of them.

As late as October 2021, he still wouldn't admit he'd made mistakes, about me or the Dossier as a whole. In an interview with Steele, George Stephanopoulos said, "Michael Cohen has completely turned on Donald Trump. He's accused him of all kinds of things, he's gone to jail. It defies logic that if he did this he wouldn't say so now?" Steele insisted, "I don't agree with that . . . it's self-incriminating to a very great degree.' Stephanopoulos asked him if his obstinancy about my supposed involvement "hurts your credibility," and Steele replied, "I'm prepared to accept that not everything in the Dossier is 100 per cent accurate. I have yet to be convinced that that is one of them."

He's been spinning the same yarn for five years, but it doesn't make it true.

But to give the devil his due, reporters knew from the beginning that the information was unvetted. They knew there was no corroboration for most of it. The very thing that journalists claim they hold dear—reporting vetted, factual information—they sacrificed to print spurious, scandalous and prurient information within the Steele Dossier. The race to be the *first* reporting it overcame the desire to get it *right*. Today the press rarely does anything else. It's even rarer that a member of the press *thinks* of doing anything else.

The Steele Dossier may not have been the sole source of the "Russian Collusion" storyline. After all, Hillary Clinton called Trump a Russian puppet to his face in one of their debates; and Trump's blatant ass-kissing of Putin and certain oligarchs is even addressed in the book by his former press secretary, Stephanie Grisham. But because the Dossier turned out to be mostly fiction, it gave Trump the ability to scream "fake news" and further muddy the waters.

Meanwhile, the Dossier-inspired tumult—especially about me— continued unabated throughout the spring of 2017, on into the next year. As early as January 11, 2017, the *Wall Street Journal* had reported, "Mr. Cohen has family ties to Ukraine and a history of business dealings with Ukrainian immigrants to the U.S. There is no apparent connection between those people and the Russian government or cyber-hackers."[17]

That's the truth, but everyone fixated on that story line anyway, especially the idea that I had clandestine meetings with Russian agents in Prague. Even after I went so far as to show pages from my passport to reporters to prove I hadn't been there—or anywhere in the region—Buzzfeed published an article under the headline "This Is The Inside Of Trump's Lawyer's Passport."[18] It also left open the possibility that I had somehow managed to sneak into Prague unseen:

> . . . The stamps indicate he traveled abroad at least four
> times in 2016: twice to London, once to St. Maarten,
> and once to Italy in July. The Italian trip is the most
> intriguing, because it places Cohen in what's known as

the Schengen Area: a group of 26 European countries, including the Czech Republic, that allows visitors to travel freely among them without getting any additional passport stamps.

Upon entering the Schengen Area, visitors get a rectangular stamp with the date, a country code, their port of entry, and a symbol showing how they entered—such as an airplane or a train. In Cohen's passport, that mark appears on page 17, with a date of July 9. The mark is too faint to be fully legible. The exit stamp, similar but with rounded edges, is also light, but the letters "cino" are legible, indicating he flew out of Leonardo da Vinci–Fiumicino Airport in Rome. That stamp is dated July 17.[19]

The Schengen Area? It seems crazy, but it wasn't. For me, it was even more dangerous than I knew at the time. As a source in the Department of Justice later told us, "Even if the information about Michael Cohen and Prague was fictional, it was usable in his prosecution. It gave the thin veneer of respectability to his investigation and prosecution."

The McClatchy news service seemed to have it in for me in particular. "The U.S. special counsel in the Russia probe has evidence that President Donald Trump's personal lawyer Michael Cohen traveled to Prague in 2016, refuting Cohen's claim that he never visited the Czech capital and bolstering an intelligence dossier that first described the trip,"[20] they reported in May 2017.

As late as April 2018, more than a year after the first reports came out about the Steele Dossier, McClatchy was claiming I was lying and had visited Prague—but this time *Vox* cleaned up their mess:

> That such a meeting happened is one of the most specific claims in Christopher Steele's dossier alleging collusion between the Trump team and Russia to influence the 2016 election—and because, since the very first day that dossier was publicly released, Cohen has adamantly denied taking any such trip, and Trump's team has relied on that denial to dispute the dossier's accuracy. "I have never been to Prague in my life. #fakenews," Cohen tweeted on January 10, 2017, hours after the dossier was posted.
>
> Yet a new report from McClatchy's Peter Stone and Greg Gordon claimed that special counsel Robert Mueller has evidence that Cohen did, in fact, enter Prague through Germany at the height of the 2016 campaign, in "August or early September."
>
> The McClatchy report is based on anonymous sources, and we don't yet know what the purported evidence is. It could still prove to be mistaken. Cohen himself reiterated his denial again Saturday morning, telling CNN, "No, I have never been to Prague," and sending this tweet rebutting the story: "Bad reporting, bad information and bad story by same reporter Peter Stone @McClatchyDC. No matter how many times or ways they write it, I have never been to Prague. I was in LA with my son. Proven!"[21]

You can blame reporters for getting the story wrong, and I do, but that doesn't have anything to do with how screwed up the Department of Justice treatment of the case was, from the beginning to the end. They have the power of subpoena. They are the court of record. They should've known better, and I think they did know better. Nevertheless, as I subsequently found out, they obtained access to my Gmail account, my family's iCloud account, and my telephone call register, and proceeded to investigate me.

It never led to information used in the eight counts to which I ultimately pleaded guilty.

In any event, it wasn't until April 19, 2019 that *Newsweek* ran a headline "Report claiming Trump's attorney lied about Prague Trip contradicted by Mueller findings."[22] Finally.

But by then it was too late.

The nightmare kicked into high gear with something that seemed innocuous—one of those innocuous but annoying living-in-New-York-City things: A flood in my upstairs neighbor's apartment had led to a flood in my apartment, causing a lot of damage. We had to move into a hotel for a few days while repairs were made.

So at 7:00 a.m. on the morning of April 9, 2018, my wife and I were sitting together having breakfast in the Loews Regency Hotel, when there was a knock on the door. Nobody knocks on your door in a hotel unless you call for room service. We hadn't.

I walked to the door in my shorts and T-shirt, looked through the peephole, and saw what must have been two dozen men and women in black suits standing in the hallway. No one was smiling. It was pretty obvious who they were but I had no idea what they wanted.

So, I opened the door and said, "Can I help you?"

The lead agent was central casting: standing about six foot two, broad-shouldered, well-manicured. Over his right shoulder was one of the biggest men I've ever encountered. He was at least six inches taller than the lead agent, and actually had to step sideways to pass through the doorframe. He didn't say a word; he didn't need to.

We didn't know it at the time, but meanwhile, simultaneously, 48 other agents converged on my apartment that was undergoing renovation due to the flood, as well as my law office and our safety deposit box at TD Bank.

The lead agent handed me a federal warrant, issued by the Southern District of New York U.S. Attorney's Office, dated 4/08/2018 and signed by U.S. Magistrate Judge Henry B. Pitman at 7:54 p.m.—not even twelve hours before. The warrant said my home, hotel room, and offices were to be searched for evidence related to conspiracy, false bank entries, false statements to a financial institution, wire fraud, bank fraud and illegal campaign contributions.

The agent asked me to unlock and hand over my cellphones, and step into the hallway.

Knowing that I was a licensed firearm owner, he asked me if I had any guns with me. I told him I had two, on the night table in the bedroom—a Glock-43 and a Glock-27. The agent asked me if they were loaded, to which I responded that they were. He then asked if the guns were chambered. I responded that they were not. We stepped back into the room as they secured the firearms for the duration of the search. Upon conclusion, they returned them to me.

Despite the president's later allegations that they had busted down our doors and ransacked our properties, I want to emphasize that that wasn't true. They were very cordial, very professional. They had even waited for my son to leave for school before coming up to the room. We offered them tea or coffee. They didn't want any.

They spent five hours going through our rooms. They went through the sofas, looked behind curtains. They looked on top of and beneath cabinets, and even removed, checked, and photographed all of my daughter's stuff in her underwear drawer. They photographed everything—even going through pillowcases. To this day, I still don't understand the need to photograph my college-aged daughter's underwear.

To make matters more disturbing, in the middle of it all, in walks my daughter herself, meaning to surprise us with a visit from college. Instead, the surprise was on her. She sat with us for the duration of the hours-long raid, watching the spectacle unfold. (She would later tweak the agents on social media about their examination of her underwear drawer, noting that all they'd found was a pack of cigarettes she'd been hiding from Laura and me. "Busted," she tweeted.)

Each of the bedrooms had a safe and I was directed to open them. In the master bedroom the safe contained some assorted jewelry as well as an envelope containing nine thousand dollars. On the outside of the envelope was written "Real Real."

The agents had laid out everything they found on the master bedroom bed and fanned out the $9000 found in that "Real Real" envelope and photographed it as if it were Pablo Escobar's millions in his safe house.

They asked why we had the cash. Laura told them, "This is my 'Real, Real' money."

One of the FBI agents turned around and said he didn't understand, "Do you have money that isn't real?" Maybe he thought I was a counterfeiter too, who knew?

Laura calmly explained "Real, Real" was a high-end consignment shop that sells merchandise like shoes and dresses. She had been saving over the course of six months to shop there.

I couldn't tell if they were disappointed not to find the 10 million in cash that Steele claimed I possessed to pay off the Russians for Manafort's deals and mistakes.

Interestingly enough, as Laura and I sat on the couch watching television while the agents continued to search our hotel room, a commercial for the "Real Real" came on and I yelled at the agent in charge to come take a look. "Hey, the 'Real Real' has a commercial on, come take a look," I called out.

Throughout, we didn't get upset. Not in the slightest. There was nothing that we had done that would have caused us any worry.

So I was beyond surprised when they walked out of the hotel apartment with a dozen boxes.

As I said, the raid—or rather, raids, as they raided the hotel room, our apartment, my office, and our safety deposit box—came up with nothing, other than 16 pages of shredded documents they found in my law office.

Asha Rangappa, a former FBI agent and CNN analyst, tweeted, "This is not going to end well for the defense."[23] No kidding. But how it ended had nothing to do with what they found in the raid, and certainly nothing to do with the shredded pages of useless garbage.

Just so you know where your tax dollars are being spent, the FBI sent the shredded material to Quantico for reassembly. Those documents, they found, included "pages from rambling letters that don't seem to have a connection to the current investigations by the Office of Special Counsel and Southern District of New York," Buzzfeed and other news organizations noted.[24] Some of the shredded information included an odd, unsolicited letter from a woman who listed celebrities she hadn't met—like George Lucas, Harrison Ford, Steven Spielberg, and Michael Jackson, who at the time I received the letter was already dead. I'd never read the letter and had no idea why she wrote to me. I'd thrown in the shredder because my wastepaper basket was full.

Of course that still made huge headlines, and the innuendo about what they found was fodder for several news cycles. Despite some of the documents being reassembled, because the information had no probative value—and probably should have just remained the garbage it was—no press releases were issued by the prosecutors. Who knows? Maybe they shredded them.

In the end at least some media reports questioned the significance of the raid on my home and the information that was seized:

> It remains to be seen whether any of the reconstructed documents are of use to federal prosecutors from the Southern District of New York in their ongoing probe into Cohen, whose home, office, and hotel room were raided by the FBI in April. They are among nearly 4 million individual paper records or electronic files discovered on more than a dozen cellphones, computers,

and other devices. Some of the devices—including old cellphones, cameras, and laptops—belonged to Cohen's wife and children.[25]

Elsewhere, though, after the raid, the scrutiny on my non-existent trip to Prague intensified. The *Washington Post* on April 14, 2018 brought it up again. "Cohen's visiting Prague . . . is concrete. Over the course of three of the Dossier's 17 reports, the claim is outlined—but we hasten to note that all these allegations have not been confirmed by the *Washington Post*."[26]

Well, if they weren't confirmed, then what the hell were they doing being reported as "concrete"? The *Post* and others wanted to say I took over management of the relationship with Russia after Paul Manafort was fired and that I secretly traveled abroad to do so. Not only did the old lies get repeated, they got *enhanced*.

The *Post* undermined its own reporting though by saying, "If he was not in Prague, none of this happened." No shit. I wasn't on the moon then either.

But according to Greg Miller of the *Washington Post*, his colleagues at the newspaper "literally spent weeks and months trying to run down" my alleged visit to Prague to pay off Russian hackers. "We sent reporters through every hotel in Prague, through all over the place, just to try to figure out if he was ever there, and came away empty."[27]

There were claims otherwise, of course—a McClatchy story in April 2018 reported that the Mueller investigation "has evidence" I'd gone to Prague in 2016.[28] A December McClatchy story reported my cell phone had connected with cell phone towers in Prague.[29] (A story in *The Nation* took McClatchy to task, noting that more than two years after the Mueller Report had come out and said I hadn't gone to Prague, McClatchy had left the story about adding "a tepid editor's note, rather than a retraction." [30])

It was the BBC—not the American media, but the freaking BBC—that was the first to point out something meaningful about the raids—how "there's basically no precedent for this sort of action in modern U.S. presidential politics."[31]

But, other than the poor reporting from the press, life returned to some sense of normalcy for a while after the raid. Reporters still diving into the Steele Dossier and the allegations against me slowly began to see how baseless it all was—at least in my case. So, I went back into the Trump fold, believing there was nothing to the federal investigation and that it would eventually all just blow over.

Immediately after the raid on my home and office, Trump himself had called and told me not to worry. He told me to "stay strong." He told me it was all bullshit and the investigation was going nowhere. Our conversation was about five or ten minutes long. He told me three times there was no Russian collusion. He told me not to worry, stay strong and that nothing would happen because he was the president. I was still in his good graces, or so I thought.

Less than two weeks after the FBI raid, Trump slammed a report in the *New York Times* that said his legal team was bracing for me to "flip," and he went wild on Twitter:

> The *New York Times* and a third rate reporter named
> Maggie Haberman, known as a Crooked H flunkie
> who I don't speak to and have nothing to do with,
> are going out of their way to destroy Michael Cohen

and his relationship with me in the hope that he will 'flip.' Sorry, I don't see Michael doing that despite the horrible Witch Hunt and the dishonest media![32]

In retrospect, a mob boss does the same thing Trump did. You mollify and pacify the guy you're going to whack so he never sees it coming. That's what Trump did. As for me, I was stupid enough—at first—to believe him. And since I didn't hear from the DOJ at all—despite four months of repeated attempts to reach out to them—I mistakenly thought all was well. The whole thing seemed to fall flat . . . until the creation of the special counsel into Russian collusion.

It became apparent to me what was really going on when Rudy "Colludy" Giuliani was named legal advisor to the president in early May of 2018, adding incompetence to corruption and bullshit on the Trump team. I knew then where the relationship was headed between Trump and me.

On June 15, 2018 Trump confirmed that I wasn't his lawyer anymore. He also said on Twitter that he always liked me and that I was "a good person," and then lied saying the FBI "broke into" my home and office. (As I've already said, they were polite and professional.) Trump also called the investigation into my activities an "attack on our country," and briefly thought about firing Robert Mueller.

But he didn't. What he did do was begin to take stock of what was going on and figured the best way to deal with the problem was to, instead of firing Mueller, get rid of me. Getting rid of Mueller would risk causing his own downfall. Getting rid of me gave him additional ability to deny he had anything to do with the activities he had everything to do with—while looking like he was happily punishing me in the name of justice.

The raid let Donald Trump play the victim role. It gave Trump the ability to throw me under the bus and distance himself from his own activities. It gave him the appearance, again, of being even more victimized by the DOJ while he quietly controlled it—often without the players knowing they were being played. It had everything to do, I firmly believe, with Donald Trump allowing circumstances to develop so that I became the focus of an investigation instead of him.

In July, even before I was charged, Giuliani said he advised Trump not to discuss the possibility of a pardon for me. Why would they discuss a pardon? I hadn't been charged with anything yet. Sure, they may have thought I could be, but Giuliani also said, "Michael Cohen should cooperate with the government. We have no reason to believe he did anything wrong." Confusing? Sure it is. But that's how Trump's brain works . . . circular reasoning.

Anyway, I knew the signals. Giuliani and Trump were setting me up. Trump was afraid I would talk to prosecutors, so once again he was setting himself up as a victim. If I did anything wrong—he didn't know about it. And if I talked about anything Trump did wrong? I must be lying because he had no reason to believe I did anything wrong because HE didn't do anything wrong. Hell, he even encouraged me to talk to the government. So, if Trump did that then how could he be guilty of any wrongdoing?

That's the convoluted circular craziness that lives in Trump's head. That's how he works his con. Work everything around so Trump is the victim being taken in by the corruption of others. But Trump is the master of the deception. He's the heart of the corruption—and all of us who worked for him cooperated, sometimes knowingly and sometimes unwittingly, in furthering his corruption.

What's more, Trump, I was starting to see, was doing the same with the DOJ. And despite whatever reputation the FBI and "G-Men" have, the truth is they are humans who are just as vulnerable to Trump as anyone else.

I know that, as the BBC noted, the raid on my private home, hotel room, law office and even my safety deposit box was rare. Every lawyer knows that, since prosecutors are also lawyers, the raiding of a lawyer's office is a very rare event—especially when the lawyer is the personal attorney to the president of the United States. Law offices are often considered inviolate—almost sacrosanct. And when a lawyer's office is raided, he is looked upon as a pariah. I can't tell you the number of people who've said "Well, you must be into some very bad shit if the Department of Justice raids your law office." At the very least, raiding a lawyer's office almost always signifies such a high level of confidence by the DOJ in their case that conviction become a self-fulfilling prophecy. Worse, the stench of impropriety has trickled down to my family, with my closest family members also wearing the stain of my activities. That's another by-product of being associated with Donald Trump.

But the fact is that little found in the raid of my home and office led to the charges to which I later pleaded. In fact, if the judge and prosecutors had looked at the seized documents, they never would've brought charges against me. Their allegations were simply lies.

In short, the DOJ under Trump—knowing how things would

look—conducted a raid they didn't need to conduct, and it was done specifically to destroy my reputation. The raid was predicated on the fact that we all assume the DOJ has the public's best interest at heart when it conducts a raid like this. But in this specific case, the interest was in protecting Donald Trump. The investigators and lawyers conducted themselves improperly and, if not against DOJ standards, then against the ideals of justice. I'm questioning those closest to the president who had his best interest in mind instead of the country's. I am also questioning how they manipulated standing procedures to make sure I took the fall.

As is obvious to everyone by now, Donald Trump has a preternatural ability to avoid consequences for his actions. In my case, the standards and procedures of the government were already set up—once they decided to investigate me—to bring about my fall. Prosecutors are more interested in conviction rates than justice and once they had me in their sights, they needed to close. I am merely pointing out how someone who is seriously twisted and who wields the power of the presidency—like Donald Trump—can take advantage of the situation to benefit himself even when most of the people who are doing his bidding think they're doing the right thing. After all, they're "just following orders"—the historic mantra of the thoughtless taught by the fascists.

Then again, everyone who participated in my prosecution has profited from it. Some have joined the boards of prestigious companies. Some have gone on to greater fame and glory as criminal defense attorneys. And while such careerism, in and of itself, is not so unusual, what is unusual is the methods the DOJ used—which I think bespeaks the motives some members of the DOJ had in prosecuting me. Again, under the guise of conducting a fair and impartial investigation, many of the DOJ attorneys—even those who weren't knowingly serving the whims of Donald Trump—personally profited from my prosecution.

Here's how: The investigative zealots who came after me did so to punish Donald Trump. They mistakenly thought I held the secret key to Trump's kingdom and believed if they squeezed me, I could provide information they wanted—information, as it turned out, I didn't have. Sure I cooperated with them. I visited the prosecutors many times. I testified in Congress against Trump. I told everything I knew—but still, Donald Trump remains unindicted for the crimes he orchestrated and had me commit—*for his benefit.* If the DOJ hierarchy had actually done their job and prosecuted Trump then, I would be fine with whatever they did to me. But they didn't. They stopped with me. Some thought that prosecuting me sent Trump a message that he was vulnerable.

But it had the opposite effect. It told Trump he was *in*vulnerable, because once again he got away with it. The man has never faced any accountability his entire life. He's had people like me protect him constantly. And now he's so used to getting away with things that he just assumes it will go on forever.

I testified before Special Counsel Robert Mueller soon after the raids, in June 2018. At first I agreed to provide testimony because I thought the counsel would do something about Trump—I certainly didn't think I'd be the only "major" player indicted. Hell, in the scheme of things, I was barely a minor player. I didn't work at the White House. I had *nothing* to do with government. But . . . I didn't work for myself, either. I worked for Donald Trump.

So I went to Washington with the three lawyers representing me at the time, Guy Petrillo, Amy Lester, and Philip Pilmar. When we arrived at the special counsel's office, we were escorted into a barren room that contained a twelve-foot plastic fold-up table. There were four plastic chairs on one side, and approximately a dozen on the other. They didn't even have the classic water bottles at each seat.

Then Mueller's team came in as a collective force, carrying file folders, yellow pads, and notebooks. They were a well-dressed group and each of them had the classic twelve-mile stare of a soldier ready for combat.

After signing a series of documents, the questioning began . . . and went on for about eight hours.

One of the most memorable lines of questioning dealt with Roger Stone's phone call to Donald Trump advising him that he had just gotten off the phone with Julian Assange of WikiLeaks. Stone told Trump that in a few days there was going to be a massive drop of emails that would destroy Hillary Clinton's campaign. The emails he was referring to were the now-infamous Podesta files.

When it was over, they requested a follow-up that would be in New York. I guess the information was so relevant, and so vital to their investigation, that they'd decided on the spot that it would be worthwhile to come to me. Little did I know, I would meet with them another half dozen times.

I know when the Mueller investigation began there was little talk of me. I also know that after the Steele Dossier fell into their hands I became a "Person of Interest." I found out about the Steele Dossier in January 2017 and the Mueller investigation didn't begin until May 17, 2017. Rod Rosenstein appointed Special Counsel Robert Mueller on that day to look at the Russian government's efforts to interfere in the 2016 election, any links between Russia and the Trump campaign (which I was never a part of), and in that ominous language that eventually snared me, "any matters that arose or may arise directly from the investigation."

From the beginning it should be understood that Trump always had control of the Mueller investigation. Technically, Mueller was not independent. He could be fired, the way Nixon fired Archibald Cox. But that didn't work out so well for Nixon—in fact it turned out to be a fiasco known as the Saturday Night Massacre—and it would have fared even worse for Trump. So you can bet that instead of firing Mueller, Trump was protecting himself by closely monitoring what went on with me.

In any event, subsequently, his report would exonerate me. As *Vox* reported:

> Mueller's sentencing memo for Cohen . . . suggests that the special counsel is investigating this—and that he found Cohen's information useful. Mueller wrote:
>
> "Cohen provided relevant and useful information concerning his contacts with persons connected to the White House during the 2017-2018 time period."
>
> "Cohen described the circumstances of preparing and circulating his response to the congressional inquiries."[33]

Mueller also said something in the report that would directly affect my life—and bring Trump down on me:

There is evidence that could support the inference that the President intended to discourage Cohen from co-operating with the government *because Cohen's information would shed adverse light on the President's campaign-period conduct and statements.*"[34]

If Trump was of a suspicious nature—and he most certainly is—that statement alone would set me on a path toward destruction within the Trump world and enable him to sacrifice me easily—which he did.

How did it go downhill so fast?

A timeline published by *Axios* in November 2018 fills in some of the blanks and shows how it went down. How it all kicked off:

Adult film star Stormy Daniels claimed she had an affair with Trump in 2006 and received a $130,000 payment from Cohen to keep quiet.

Following Daniels's allegations, federal investigators in New York raided Cohen's home and office in April. As a former U.S. attorney told *Axios* at the time, "Here's what must have happened: Mueller bumped into evidence of criminal conduct that was beyond his scope, so he referred it to the Rod," meaning Deputy Attorney General Rod J. Rosenstein.

A court ruling after the raid meant that Trump's team lost first access to items that were seized, and the secrets of "the only person on earth intertwined in Trump's professional, political, personal, legal and family life" were available to federal investigators.

The scope of the government's investigation widened in May after it was learned that investigators had monitored Cohen's phones.

Cohen broke his silence in July in an interview with ABC News' George Stephanopoulos—seemingly indicating that he'd be willing to cooperate with the feds: "I will not be a punching bag as part of anyone's defense strategy. I am not a villain of this story, and I will not allow others to try to depict me that way."

Cohen's lawyer, Lanny Davis, released a tape to CNN detailing Cohen's conversation with Trump about paying off Karen McDougal, a *Playboy* model who alleged an affair with the president, later in July. Davis promised there was "more to come."

Soon after, Cohen told CNN that Trump knew ahead of time about the 2016 Trump Tower meeting between some of his top campaign officials and a Russian lawyer promising dirt on Hillary Clinton.

Cohen's family taxi business soon came under scrutiny, prompting tweets from Trump in late July.

In August, news broke that federal investigators were looking into related tax and bank fraud.

Two days later he pleaded guilty to eight counts including tax fraud, excessive campaign contributions, and more.[35]

In short, there's indication that little or no actual investigation came from the Justice Department prior to them raiding my New York home and offices—or just enough to justify the raid—which was very little. There's plenty of indication there was an investigation afterward—though how much investigating could they actually do on the hundreds of thousands of pages of material they took from me in April until I pled guilty in August of 2018? Although I offered to speak to them, the federal government turned down all the offers from my attorney at the time.

Of course, through much of this time Christopher Steele and his Dossier were still seen as canon in the press. I was depicted as the dirty scumbag lawyer who paid off girlfriends and traveled to Prague so Donald could have golden showers and play with Putin. Steele later was found out to be wrong on almost every count . . . but all of that happened after the damage was already done to me. The Southern District of New York felt obliged to investigate me further. Those who have done so have also done very well for themselves after the fact. But that's been the way of the DOJ for years—prove yourself a capable prosecutor; make your bones in the Federal mob and you get rewarded after you leave government with a fat corporate salary—often for little work. It's the reward. But in this case the rewards were given merely because they prosecuted me, did little work in the process, but in that process proved themselves to both Trump lovers and haters.

Let's take a look at what the government hung its hat on.

There were five charges of tax evasion. Not one. Five. Why five? Because it made for better press. It also had the effect of giving Trump the ability to distance himself from me and *his* illegal activities by claiming my case had nothing to do with *him*; it was about me. Coincidence? Hardly. The other three charges against me? I lied to get a home equity line of credit, and I paid off Stormy Daniels and Karen McDougal.

Let's take the last accusation first: The Karen McDougal charge. I never paid any money to Karen McDougal. My participation in the McDougal matter occurred after David Pecker, the *National Enquirer,* and its parent company American Media Inc. (AMI), entered into a business relationship with the former *Playboy* Playmate for the sum of $150,000. I had no involvement in the negotiations between McDougal and Pecker (I know, a funny last name, under the circumstances). I became involved after the fact to ensure that Trump's interests were fully protected, as well as to deal with Pecker's desire to be repaid by Trump for the $150,000 outlay. Pecker suggested Trump pay the paper $125,000, which would constitute the life rights portion of the non-disclosure agreement with McDougal. The remaining $25,000 would represent a business arrangement between the paper and McDougal to appear on two covers of *Men's Health* magazine, and to have her name appear as an author on 24 articles that would be ghostwritten by someone else and appear in various magazines owned by AMI.

The purpose of the payout was a classic "catch and kill." Pecker caught the story. Pecker owned the story. Out of loyalty to Trump, Pecker would never print the story. I merely reviewed documents on the deal for Trump to make sure his interests were protected. Still, Pecker—who actually had made the payment to McDougal—somehow would later get immunity from SDNY for his grand jury testimony against me.

Pecker ultimately abandoned the request for Trump to repay the $150,000—a debt Trump had just ignored—because of McDougal's popularity on the cover of *Men's Health*, which helped sell more than $350,000 worth of magazines. Pecker could then leverage the large outlay of money and justify it as a worthy investment.

As I say, Pecker and the *Enquirer* ultimately entered into a plea deal with the government, but that was subsequently put into jeopardy by allegations that the *Enquirer* had tried to blackmail Jeff Bezos. (On February 9, 2019, the *New York Post* ran a headline "Hard Times For Pecker" after the Bezos story came to light.)[36]

The only legitimate charge against me was my participation in the payment to Stormy Daniels, the infamous porn star who said she had an affair with Donald Trump and that he had a mushroom appendage. (That's the allegation, by the way, that pissed off Trump more than anything else. According to Stephanie Grisham, he pulled her aside on Air Force One just to deny the accuracy of that story.) I have stated over and over that I did this—and I have proof that it was done at the direction of and for the benefit of Donald J. Trump.

The sixth count against me was for the home equity line of credit (HELOC) loan. Of all the charges brought against me, this is the most duplicitous. Gary Farro is the senior vice president of First

Republic Bank, and the banker who produced my HELOC documentation—the document the SDNY stated I falsified.

I long suspected the government forced Farro to cooperate. When my team tried to reach out to him he refused to talk and accused us of harassing him by even making a call. What kind of nonsense is that? I'd known the guy for years. We were friendly. I gave him referrals for his business. I was a highly respected client of his at First Republic Bank for years. I maintained large accounts and had more than enough equity in my home to justify the line of credit—I had 80 percent equity plus more cash in the bank than the mortgage and the HELOC combined. And yet, after my prosecution I was persona non grata with the bank and the guy who produced the line of credit application. If I did something wrong, isn't the guy who facilitated the loan application at least partially responsible? If I didn't meet the margins or requirements would the bank have even made the loan? And if they did, why aren't they liable for breaking the rules? The fact is I have never defaulted or even been late on any loan obligation to the bank. It's all a shell game.

Anyone who has applied for and received a home equity line of credit knows how the process works. In my case, the application was produced upon request and sent to me by Gary Farro. I had previously provided my personal tax returns and corporate tax returns as part of the process for the first and only mortgage on my home. Some of those returns were also some of those used in the indictments for income tax evasion—I'll speak to that shortly. The prosecutors claimed that the information in that application was inaccurate. Specifically, they claimed I did not disclose information on my New York City taxi medallion loans and thus placed the bank in jeopardy.

Judge William H. Pauley III failed and failed miserably in his role as a judge to be fair and impartial. He didn't note that all the corporate returns were accurate and reflected outstanding mortgages on each of the corporations. Moreover the corporate returns are irrelevant as the HELOC is collateralized by the real estate asset it becomes attached to. In essence, it's a second loan which is predicated on being given a line of credit based on your home's equity.

The allegation that I'd put the bank in jeopardy was stupid and bogus. It defies logic and reason. In fact, I presented Christopher Paragammo, the pre-sentencing coordinator, with three separate appraisals of my home's value over a nine year period showing I had 80 percent equity in the property. Not only did Paragammo ignore the documents, he claimed that if I presented them, it demonstrated that I am not showing remorse and would not receive what are known as downward departure points, which could reduce my time in prison.

So, I want to ask Gary Farro: Did the prosecutors threaten you or the bank? Did they tell you what to say to avoid any further review of the bank? I am going to suggest that the answers to these questions are "Yes."

When we spoke to members of the DOJ on background, they said there were some anomalies in how I was prosecuted. In fact, though my prosecution wasn't unique, it was extremely unusual in that it was done not in furtherance of the law but contrary to it.

Finally, there are the five counts of income tax evasion, to which I pleaded guilty. Regarding this, I need to be crystal clear on how disgraceful I believe the prosecutors at the SDNY acted. They knew that I never in my entire life filed a late tax return until 2017, when this mess first erupted. I had never filed for an extension. I kept and still keep meticulous records in three-ring binders tabulated with headings and notes. I have never been audited. I was never once told by the IRS that I had a deficiency. I never received a letter from any IRS agents which is standard protocol afforded to all taxpayers. There are some key elements, as shown in the Paul Manafort case, that indicate income tax evasion. None of them exist in my case.

Below is the checklist used by IRS agents to prove income tax evasion. As you can see, I do not fit into any of the line items; what it shows is a tax omission—not an evasion. That's a big difference as a tax omission is handled civilly, not criminally. Of equal importance is the question of how many first time offenders are thrown in prison? DOJ records show that *very* few are. Percentage-wise, it's less than one tenth of one percent of all taxpayers. So, of course, I was.

What is necessary to bring an income tax evasion case:

GOVERNMENT:	Michael Cohen
1. Failure to file tax return.	NO
2. Cash transactions.	NO
3. Overseas business transactions.	NO
4. Overseas banking transactions.	NO
5. Fake invoices.	NO
6. Fake wire transfers.	NO
7. Hiding assets.	NO
8. Overseas bank executor.	NO

At this point, would it shock you if I told you that Andrea Griswold of the SDNY did not want my matter resolved prior to the plea? At least it seemed that way when she responded to an email query from my new accountant, threatening that if I filed amended returns rectifying the five years' worth of open tax issues, which would have included all penalties and interest—meaning I would have paid everything— then the IRS would potentially scrutinize the amended tax returns, and potentially increase my financial liability. In essence if there was a screw-up, it was my former accountant Jeffrey Getzel who made it.

I was not involved in tax fraud. Getzel simply screwed up. There was no tax evasion. It was a tax *omission*. I did not lie on the returns, hide money overseas, or hide cash domestically like Manafort did. In fact, every dollar was deposited in Capitol One Bank—which happened to be located at the base of the building I live in. Moreover, I provided every single bank statement proving it in an organized and tabulated three-ring notebook to my accountant, Getzel, whose sole job was to reconcile my accounts and prepare my returns. Later, I provided these records to the IRS, too. Some genius, first-time mastermind tax evader I am. Nevertheless, I paid dearly for Getzel's bungling, while Getzel himself received immunity from the SDNY in exchange for his testimony against me before the grand jury.

And once again I am required to pay for other's mistakes. I didn't mind paying the money that I owed, which I did *in-full* prior to sentencing. The loss of my freedom is another thing entirely.

It's not as if I hid money or took someone else's money and spent it on luxury items for myself—like Avenatti or Manafort. My scenario is the epitome of a tax omission. Millions of these cases occur annually and are resolved between the taxpayer and the IRS without incarceration. I fucked up in that I trusted my CPA, never reviewing the 1800-page return. Why, you may ask? Truth be told, I can no more understand my tax return than I can read a Chinese newspaper or hieroglyphics. I know I didn't deserve prison time. But, again, I acquiesced to the SDNY's demands to plead guilty because my wife was on those joint income tax returns, and they threatened to indict her as a co-conspirator to the hush money payment to Stormy Daniel's payment. That's the key. The government knew it. That's why they played it the way they did. Rough and dirty! They wanted to say they caught a dangerous and felonious member of Donald Trump's inner circle. To do so, they leveraged my wife as the bait. Fortunately they didn't ask me to confess to the Lufthansa heist or the Lindbergh baby kidnapping because I would have pleaded to those charges also to protect the love of my life from these animals.

Here's a fact you can easily check on Google: In 2016 H & R Block did a report on the number of people who were indicted and served prison time for tax evasion. The report showed 150 million tax returns filed and with 861 people being charged, prosecuted and receiving prison time—all of them but me were repeat offenders.[37]

Later, my attorney Lanny Davis called it *disproportionate sentencing.* The late judge William H. Pauley III abandoned his better judgment and his oath as a judge to be fair and impartial by simply ignoring the facts.

As a matter of established fact, if you look at page nine through ten from the Petrillo sentencing memo, information we provided to Judge William H. Pauley III in review of my case clearly notes that I paid more than five million dollars in taxes during those years with a tax deficiency of $1.39 million or $260K a year. Certainly not the sophisticated tax cheat the government claimed I was.

This might be the most unsophisticated tax avoidance scheme in history.

Finally, as for the Russia stuff—as we now know by others who were in Trump's orbit, including Stephanie Grisham—Trump was indeed Putin's puppet. But I wasn't. Never had been and wouldn't be. And I never dreamed prosecutors would go after me for some of the things I was accused of doing. Sure, I paid off Stormy Daniels. But that doesn't make me Sammy the Bull Gravano to Trump's John Gotti. Trump isn't that smart and I'm not Sammy. I dealt with campaign issues. We stiffed contractors. I fixed a CNBC poll to assuage Trump's fragile ego. I paid off Stormy Daniels—for Donald Trump. So, yes, I paid off a porn star so my employer and Republican presidential candidate could avoid embarrassment and destroy the little hope everyone had in the general election. Those are the shitty things I did. Trump may have sold out his country, because Trump has no loyalty to anyone but himself. He doesn't care what happens to any of us. I was stupid for hitching myself to that wagon—but it's a far cry from messing over a bunch of contractors to being a traitor to your country. Trump told me to "stay strong" because he could protect me and knew I wasn't guilty. And the whole time he was using the circumstances to arrange the act of throwing me under the bus to hide his own culpability. He was a useful idiot for Russia—not a mastermind of deception. Putin was and is much smarter than Trump. It's a toss-up as to who is more conniving. Putin has great survival instincts, but Trump has the survival instincts of a New York sewer rat.

Me? I got caught in the squeeze, and in the end, common sense and justice did not prevail. Here's the point—it couldn't. It never had a chance. If the DOJ, as they told Lanny Davis, had no interest in pursuing a case against Donald Trump, who was the actual perpetrator of the crimes I helped facilitate by paying hush money to a former lover, then I was going to be where the buck stopped. On my head, and that's where it landed.

I pled guilty on what some called the "worst day for Trump's presidency so far," and it came minutes after Paul Manafort was found guilty on eight felony bank and tax fraud charges in Virginia. The next day, Trump tweeted sympathy for Manafort:

"I feel very badly for Paul Manafort and his wonderful family. 'Justice' took a 12 year old tax case, among other things, applied tremendous pressure on him and, unlike Michael Cohen, he refused to 'break'—make up stories in order to get a 'deal.' Such respect for a brave man!"

As for me, he tweeted that anyone looking for a "good lawyer" should not "retain the services of Michael Cohen!"

So, because people were nonetheless speculating, I had Lanny Davis make something clear: That I "would never accept" a pardon from Trump. "He considers a pardon from somebody who has acted so corruptly as president to be something he would never accept," Davis added.[38]

I've written about the case extensively in *Disloyal*, but have not, until now, touched on the corruption inside the Department of Justice that was behind it all—that is, that the DOJ was working as an extension of Donald Trump, as his new fixer. You can take my word for it. I know exactly what the DOJ did for Trump, because I was Trump's fixer for a decade. Let's be honest, when Trump became president he felt comfortable enough trading me in because he expected the DOJ to do just that—protect him.

And Trump, as everyone knows who's ever been around the man, is extremely adept at manipulating, maneuvering, and exploiting people. He was very good at manipulating bureaucrats in the DOJ, and later he created the perfect ally in Bill Barr.

William Pelham "Bill" Barr was the ultimate inside lackey. He served as the 77th and 85th U.S. attorney general. From 1973 to 1977 he was employed by the CIA. He worked for a year inside the Reagan administration and is a longtime proponent of nearly unfettered presidential authority over the executive branch of the government. In Barr's mind, the president is American royalty. In 1989, as the head of the Office of Legal Counsel, he justified the invasion of Panama just to arrest Manuel Noriega. He authored a report in 1992 called "The Case for More Incarceration." His father was Jewish, but Barr was raised a conservative Catholic. He has a history of scandal in his past and Texas Congressman Henry B. Gonzalez called for Barr's resignation as AG citing "repeated, clear failures and obstruction"[39] by the Department of Justice.

He's had questionable business dealings,[40] while allegations of misfeasance[41] and malfeasance[42] have plagued him his entire career—a career which somehow kept going despite the numerous scandals. He was involved in the Iran-Contra scandal,[43] accused of possible illegal phone surveillance,[44] and *New York Times* writer (and former Nixon staff writer) William Safire referred to him as "Coverup-General Barr."[45] This was before he ever got involved with Donald Trump. Some have called Barr a fascist,[46] others just claim he's corrupt.[47] But his fondness for strong-armed executive branch leadership combined with his questionable ethics[48] made him a perfect choice for attorney general when Trump had an opening to fill.

He was political flotsam with a questionable resume who took over the Justice Department with just one thing in mind—do what the previous AG, Jeff Sessions, would not do, which was run interference for Donald Trump. Sessions recused himself from the Mueller investigation. Barr attacked it.

Once Barr became attorney general—right about the time of my sentencing—he could easily have given the DOJ plenty of leash to investigate The Donald—knowing that in the end Donald Trump would never face recrimination for any of his alleged illegal activities. Barr could see to it. But he never encouraged any investigation into Trump. In fact, he stopped them before they started. That's when we all knew Barr had become Trump's new fixer.

Which would soon prove bad news for the old fixer.

When the Southern District of New York's U.S. Attorney's Office announced on Tuesday, August 21, 2018, that I had pleaded guilty in Federal court to eight counts, including criminal tax evasion and campaign finance violations, U.S. Attorney Robert Khuzami said, "Michael Cohen is a lawyer who, rather than setting an example of respect for the law, instead chose to break the law, repeatedly over many years and in a variety of ways. His day of reckoning serves as a reminder that we are a nation of laws, with one set of rules that applies equally to everyone."

With all respect to Khuzami . . . If the rules applied equally to everyone, then I'd be writing a book about the prosecution and conviction of Donald Trump.

But whatever else it did, prosecution crushed me. Imagine working for an organization, getting prosecuted for it, and when you talk to prosecutors about who was behind it they don't go after the boss? Rudy Giuliani made his reputation on busting and going after the heads of the Five Families. I offered the equivalent of the "Valachi Papers," which authenticated the crimes Trump committed and had me commit, and instead I got greeted again with what Robert Khuzami said about me. *His day of reckoning serves as a reminder that we are a nation of laws, with one set of rules that applies equally to everyone.*

Others also weighed in on it.

FBI Assistant Director-in-Charge William F. Sweeney Jr. said:

> This investigation uncovered crimes of fraud, deception and evasion, conducted through a string of financial transactions that were carefully constructed and concealed to protect a variety of interests. But as we all know, the truth can only remain hidden for so long before the FBI brings it to light. We are all expected to follow the rule of law, and the public expects us—the FBI—to enforce the law equally. Today, Mr. Cohen has been reminded of this important lesson, as he acknowledged with his guilty plea.

IRS-CI Special Agent-in-Charge James D. Robnett said:

> Today's guilty plea exemplifies IRS Special Agents' rigorous pursuit of tax evasion and sends the clear message that the tax laws apply to everybody. Mr. Cohen's greed to hide his income from the IRS cheats all the honest taxpayers, and we should not expect law abiding citizens to foot the bill for those who circumvent the system to evade paying their fair share.

And then there's the IRS. President Joe Biden is famous for saying the top corporations in this country pay "zero" in income tax—yet I'm the big fish for what I did, which was what?

Meanwhile, the biggest joke is that Trump has been defrauding the government for years. In February of 2022, his own accountant abandoned him and claimed you couldn't believe anything the man said about his finances. As was reported worldwide, Trump's accounting firm admitted that "ten years of financial statements are unreliable."[49]

However, I'm the bad guy. They ignored that I was never late filing my income taxes. I never once asked for an extension. I paid millions in taxes over those years. In fact, I had never been audited in my life. I made one simple mistake—I hired the wrong accountant—but here's what the government's charges said I did:

> As a further part of his scheme to evade taxes, CO-HEN also hid the following additional sources of income from Accountant-1 and the IRS:

> A $100,000 payment received, in 2014, for brokering the sale of a piece of property in a private aviation community in Ocala, Florida.

> Approximately $30,000 in profit made, in 2014, for brokering the sale of a Birkin Bag, a highly coveted French handbag that retails for between $11,900 to $300,000, depending on the type of leather or animal skin used.

More than $200,000 in consulting income earned in
2016 from an assisted living company purportedly for
COHEN's "consulting" on real estate and other projects.

In total, COHEN failed to report more than $4 mil-
lion in income, resulting in the avoidance of taxes of
more than $1.4 million due to the IRS.[50]

Now allow me to give you the real facts. Those bullet points in the
DOJ document referred to above—They are all 100 percent inaccurate and, more importantly, SDNY prosecutors knew it. To reiterate,
all of those funds were deposited in Capital One Bank, were identified
on bank statements and provided to my accountant Jeffrey Getzel,
whose sole job was to reconcile my bank statements. This is a classic
case of a tax omission which would normally require payment of the
amount owed along with a possible financial penalty. I want to make
it clear that I paid the tax omission prior to sentencing and I received
no benefit for that action when I was sentenced by Judge Pauley.

The long and the short of it is: While I did not engage in tax fraud,
I had to plead guilty to it in order to protect my wife and family. That's
right. I was given 48 hours, from a Friday at 5:30 p.m. to the following
Monday at 9 a.m. to plead guilty or the SDNY threatened to file an
85-page indictment against me *and* my wife. Again, I take responsibility for what I did—though I contend most of the charges against
me—as I've proven with these tax charges—are inaccurate. But what
about "Individual 1," as referred to in the charging documents?

Trump faced nothing. But again, this isn't all about him—no
matter how much he'd like it to be. This is about the Department of

Injustice, and how when they want to go after someone—in this case me—they do so with a cavalier attitude and no mind to adhere to the rules they say they are defending.

Looking back on it, on April 5, 2018, just days before the raids, I should have known where it was all going to go for me. While Trump spoke to reporters on Air Force One he denied knowing about payments he directed and authorized me to make to Stormy Daniels. "You'll have to ask Michael Cohen," Trump said when asked why I would make a payment from my own money. "Michael is my attorney."[51]

That was the slap in the face that woke me up.

I could feel the wheels of the bus going round and round as Trump drove over me. It is NO coincidence that the FBI raided my home, office and hotel room just four days later. I know how Donald Trump works. What he told reporters on April 5 was a challenge to the DOJ to conduct a surgical strike, deliver a bullet to the brain pan, to sacrifice me so he could live to fight another day. Again, the FBI was very professional and polite as they raided me—they were just doing their job. But remember, as much as Trump denied the payoff to Stormy Daniels, it has been proven that he reimbursed me for the money I spent to protect him and his lies. He knew what the FBI would do. By saying "Ask Michael Cohen," he indicated that I had information worth obtaining. He might as well have opened the door to my home himself and told the FBI to walk right in.

Remember, on September 6, 2017, *Vanity Fair* quoted me saying I would "take a bullet" for Trump. I said this as I was preparing to appear before the House Intelligence Committee regarding my alleged ties between the Trump campaign and Russia. I also attacked the idiot Steve Bannon, who claimed I was a "leaker."

"I'm the guy who stops the leaks," I said. "I'm the guy who protects the president and the family. I'm the guy who would take a bullet for the president."

In retrospect Bannon's proclamation was another wakeup call. A Trump minion pointing his finger at me. Doesn't matter if it were true. It only matters that it was said. Trump could use that as a deflection point in the future. And, of course, he did just that.

In January the *Wall Street Journal* reported that I had arranged the payment to Stormy Daniels—whose real name is Stephanie Clifford. The report noted that ahead of the 2016 election, Daniels signed a nondisclosure agreement which prevented her from speaking about their tryst. In February of 2018 I told the *New York Times* I made the payment to Daniels out of my own pocket—"Neither the Trump Organization nor the Trump campaign was a party to the transaction with Ms. Clifford, and neither reimbursed me for the payment, either directly or indirectly." The disgraced attorney Michael Avenatti—a man destined to wear an orange jumpsuit for a long time—sued Trump and me. "To be clear, the attempts to intimidate Ms. Clifford into silence and 'shut her up' in order to 'protect Mr. Trump' continued unabated," the lawsuit claimed.

I know reporters who spoke with Avenatti before an appearance on CNN in New York, that Avenatti said he was sure I was the "mastermind" behind all of Trump's illegalities and I was as guilty as Trump—if not more so. That bullshit didn't help either. Avenatti was full of shit and deflecting all of his illegal acts on me. He truly deserves everything he has received and what's coming to him. (As of this writing, he's been sentenced to four years in prison, and still faces further charges.)

But it was when Trump said "You have to ask Michael Cohen" that I knew what was coming at me. I hired Lanny Davis, who had been one of Bill Clinton's impeachment lawyers, as my personal attorney. I knew the corrupt DOJ was gunning for me. I knew Trump was behind it. I knew that if you weren't a friend of Donald Trump then you were an enemy and he would use the corrupt DOJ to hound me to the gates of hell.

So in the last week of July, my attorney went on the offensive against Trump:

> July 24, 2018—Cohen's attorney Davis sets off a firestorm when he releases a secretly made audio recording to CNN of Trump and Cohen discussing the payment to McDougal.

> In the recording, which Cohen secretly taped as Trump was running for president in 2016, Trump and Cohen discuss buying the rights to her story. The tape was one of 12 seized in the raids on Cohen.

> Cohen tells Trump "we'll have to pay" for the story. Trump is heard saying "pay with cash," but it is not clear from the audio whether Trump is suggesting Cohen pay or not.

> Giuliani says the tape is "powerful exculpatory evidence" that the president did no wrong.[52]

I've taken a lot of grief for recording my client, but remember who that client was and these specific circumstances in which he had once again stiffed someone. He was always stiffing someone. This time I was called on to deal with it, and we were dealing with his "long-time friend" (whatever that means), David Pecker of the *National Enquirer*. I didn't record Trump just to record him. It wasn't about me. It was about David Pecker being furious because Trump wasn't paying him back for the McDougal payout. To be clear, this was the *one and only* recording of Trump I ever made. The reason I taped him was to prove to Pecker that Trump was going to pay him back. If you listen to the tape, you clearly hear Trump asking me if we can pay in cash. I say "No," and then you hear us both agree that it must be made via check.

Of course, that's not where it ended with Trump either. He lied about knowing about Pecker's payment to McDougal—which was the primary reason I produced the tape. And, he had the nerve to suggest that me talking to *the prosecutors* should also be illegal. As Fox and NBC reported, "Trump, in a Fox News interview after Cohen's plea, denied knowing about Cohen's payments until 'later on.'" Later in the interview, Trump reacted to Cohen's plea bargain with prosecutors by suggesting that it should be "illegal" for people facing criminal charges to make deals with the government. "It's called flipping and it almost ought to be illegal," Trump said. "It's not a fair thing."[53]

That, in a nutshell, is how I ended up with a case in the Southern District of New York.

As the *New York Intelligencer* later noted,

> The Steele Dossier was a case study in how reporters get
> manipulated.[54] The aim was to dig up dirt on Donald
> Trump, especially regarding any ties he might have to
> Russia. Steele delivered, alleging a long-standing con-
> spiracy between Trump and the Kremlin and offering
> details that proved to be as unfounded as they were
> spectacular: a meeting in Prague between Trump law-
> yer Michael Cohen and Russian officials in 2016 . . .

In January 2021, *The Nation* published a story called "The Rise and
Fall of the Steele Dossier," with the subtitle "a case study in mass
hysteria and media credulity." The article noted that

> Trump launched his political career by spreading the
> "birther" lie about President Obama, and then became
> Obama's improbable successor with an anti-immigrant,
> anti-Muslim presidential campaign. Upon losing the
> White House four years later, Trump, true to form,
> blamed his ouster on a vast election fraud conspiracy
> aided—according to flunkies Rudy Giuliani and Sid-
> ney Powell—by "communist money," "Venezuelan vot-
> ing machines," as well as Chinese and Iranian hackers.
> The right-wing mob that attacked the Capitol to thwart
> the certification of Joe Biden's victory was the apotheo-
> sis of Trump's unhinged bigotry.[55]

But the article also noted that the Democrats and their allies challenged Trump's 2016 victory with a "xenophobic conspiracy theory of their own"—that Russia had installed Trump in the White House in an elaborate plot working with the Trump campaign.

The article blamed the Steele Dossier for being the root cause of this and it has a point. Donald Trump is caustic enough. Stick to the facts of his racism, sexism, xenophobia, cronyism, corruption and you'll do fine. But adding the Russia collusion to it was a mistake. Duped by Russia? Yes. The Mueller Report showed that beyond a doubt Trump was a useful idiot. But it was not collusion.

As the article also points out, Buzzfeed was given the opening it needed to publish the Steele Dossier after it leaked out that James Comey had briefed Trump on the report. That was the legitimate news hook that happened during the transition to give the story legs. And the article also noted that

> The conspiracy supposedly escalated during the 2016 campaign, when then–Trump lawyer Michael Cohen slipped into Prague for "secret discussions with Kremlin representatives and associated operators/hackers."
>
> This purported plot was not just based on mutual nefarious interests but, worse, outright coercion. To keep their asset in line, Steele alleged, the Russians had videotaped Trump hiring and watching prostitutes "perform a 'golden showers' (urination) show" in a Moscow Ritz-Carlton hotel room. This *kompromat* meant that the leader of the free world was not only a traitor but also a blackmail victim of his Kremlin handlers.[56]

Corporate media went crazy for the story and everyone fell for the fiction. They wanted to, which says something for the education in this country that we often fall for fiction rather than facts. It certainly explains Donald Trump's appeal—and the love of the garbage Steele Dossier.

I am far from a perfect person. I acknowledge that. I've made mistakes—grave ones to be sure—but the mistakes made in the Steele Dossier are as grave as anything I've ever done, if not more so. It hoped to trap Donald Trump. It didn't. It gave Trump fuel and ammunition precisely because it was crap and Trump, the ultimate purveyor of crap, recognized it for what it was and used it to falsely proclaim his innocence.

The Steele Dossier is simply the biggest mistake ever made by one political party to try and uncover the corruption of the other. Rather than taking their time and getting things right, it blew up in the Democrats' faces because they didn't bother to vet their facts. They are guilty of the very thing Trump is accused of—disseminating and spreading fake news. I take no pride in saying that. It is merely a fact. Donald Trump is the largest piece of shit ever to be dropped on the American public, and the rest of us, including the Democrats, suffered.

Christopher Steele is an architect of the continuing belief in conspiracies from both party extremes. As early as 2019 *The Hill* reported that the FBI had "put a stake" through the heart of the Steele Dossier. "It's mostly useless," John Solomon said in an opinion piece.[57]

I will disagree with that to some extent: It made us aware of Trump's nefarious activities and it brought attention to Trump's cuddling up to Putin—even if most of the accusations were wrong.

But in a very real sense, it wasn't useless. It was worse than useless.

The Steele Dossier helped to destroy lives.

It helped to fuel the fire of conspiracy.

It helped to land me in federal prison.

It was simply one of the worst pieces of opposition research ever written, bought and sold by an unsuspecting electorate to bring down a tyrant when the simple truth would've sufficed.

For that we must never forget the Steele Dossier and its author Christopher Steele. We must learn from it, or we're doomed for another visit in the White House by Trump—or more likely someone worse: a Donald J. Trump 2.0.

CHAPTER TWO

THE "SOVEREIGN DISTRICT" OF NEW YORK

OUR CRIMINAL JUSTICE SYSTEM IS BROKEN—that's the key theme of the recently published book *Why the Innocent Plead Guilty and the Guilty Go Free,* by Jed S. Rakoff, a senior judge of the United States District Court of the Southern District of New York . . . the same court where I was prosecuted.

Judge Rakoff is also the judge who dismissed Sarah Palin's case against the *New York Times.* He's no stranger to tough cases, and an astute judge of our criminal justice system.

What he speaks of in his book, after years of working in the system, is what I experienced first-hand. Judge Rakoff has seen the problem of judicial abuse by prosecutors, and his book is a scathing report suggesting fixes to our broken system so that we may create a "more perfect union." The issues he outlines could be talking points for the corruption and abuse Donald Trump perpetrated during his tenure in the Oval Office. So, make no mistake, as Rakoff pointed out, the problems in the U.S. justice system are systemic, widespread, and have been ongoing for years.

Let me be clear—Donald Trump did not create the problems. He *exploited* them at a level never seen before in our country's history, with the possible exception of Richard Nixon. Donald Trump's one true gift is that he has mastered the art of exploitation and deceit.

Those inside the criminal justice system find themselves believing Rakoff's assessment more and more. One of those who works inside the DOJ spoke to us on the condition of background for this book. What he tells us, in specific terms, is that inside the Department it was believed I was the gatekeeper of all Trump's secrets—and that prosecuting me could lead to a plethora of information that, in actuality, I didn't have and never had. When it was found out that I wasn't the encyclopedia of Donald Trump and the raid the government conducted on my home, apartment, law office and safety deposit box came up with tens of thousands of pages of useless information—I was prosecuted anyway. It was inevitable for two reasons that led to the perfect storm: First, Donald Trump wanted it and, secondly, he used the Justice Department's inherent flaws to make it happen.

"This is how we do things," the DOJ official stated. "We thought (Trump) was a mob boss and that Cohen was his consigliere. But Cohen didn't know as much as we thought," or conversely the DOJ thought I was an expert at hiding shit. This does not minimize what I know or the information I provided to prosecutors. What the DOJ was specifically looking for were crimes by Trump relating to Russia. The DOJ was correct in stating I did not know as much as they suspected. In the end, the DOJ had to indict me on something. "We put a lot of effort into it and it was a high profile case," the agent stated.

"We're happy we got him on something—and we used a lot of pressure to get him to a plea deal. It's really questionable we would've been able to convict on some of those charges."

In explaining what "pressure" the DOJ used the agent confessed, "We pulled every record we could. We talked to everyone and tried to use anyone who we thought might have a connection to him [Cohen] to put pressure on him."

In the end it backfired. I was the only one prosecuted.

Ask any lawyer who has worked cases in the federal court, whether they're a prosecutor or a defense attorney, if they think my case is unique. Most will say, as did Mark Zaid, a nationally known attorney who deals with free speech constitutional claims and government accountability: "It is inconceivable to me that you would prosecute Michael Cohen for committing a crime and not prosecute the man who instructed him to do so." In 1998, Zaid founded the James Madison Project, an organization dedicated to reducing government secrecy. Zaid has sued both Republicans and Democrats and has spent a career holding elected officials accountable to the public.

"We have to change some of this," the DOJ source stated. "We're on the right side of history and the law. But sometimes we're arrogant. Our power makes us that way."

And all of this began because of the Steele Dossier: that pile of unsubstantiated bullshit fiction about me. The DOJ admitted it. So why did they continue to push? Why did they take the unprecedented step of raiding an attorney's office—and not just any attorney but the attorney to the *president of the United States*—a threshold seldom used and often derided?

In the end even the media reports questioned the significance of the raid on my home and the information that was seized. "It remains to be seen," wrote *The Hill*,

> whether any of the reconstructed documents are of use to federal prosecutors from the Southern District of New York in their ongoing probe into Cohen, whose home, office, and hotel room were raided by the FBI in April. They are among nearly 4 million individual paper records or electronic files discovered on more than a dozen cellphones, computers, and other devices. Some of the devices—including old cellphones, cameras, and laptops—belonged to Cohen's wife and children.[1]

It was all drama—kind of like when Michael Avenatti used a sketch artist to make a likeness of the individual who allegedly threatened Stormy Daniels in a parking garage—and the likeness was that of her ex-husband.

Incensed by the never-ending lies about me—specifically regarding Russia—by the end of June I had to respond. I had already told ABC, in an interview after the April raid, that the Steele Dossier's claims against me were false and I'd already shown my passport to prove I'd never been to Prague. On June 28, 2018 I tweeted: "My family & I are owed an apology. After 2 years, 15 hours of testimony before House & Senate under oath & producing more than 1000 documents, dossier misreports 15 allegations about me. My entire statement must be quoted—I had nothing to do with Russian collusion or meddling!"

What I didn't know is that the more I pushed, the more determined the government was to indict me. They had to. According to the DOJ source, I deserved "something." And I apologized for my mistakes. Yes. What I did was wrong. But, to try and enforce the law, the DOJ stretched it to the point of breaking. And as the DOJ official told me it all began "with that stupid dossier."

It took a long time before many in the media acknowledged the mistakes they made believing that report. During that time the Dossier was further manipulated and used by investigators inside the government. If the purpose was to hold Donald accountable they failed and failed miserably. From the very beginning the press cautioned us about believing reports based on "unvetted" information. That little fact sailed over most people's heads after the initial report—even among the government's investigators and the so called "elite" reporters who presented the misinformation to the public.

And it didn't stop the Department of Injustice.

As it turned out, they'd been investigating me since July of 2017. As a March 2019 story by the PBS News Hour reported, "The FBI was investigating President Donald Trump's former personal attorney and fixer for nearly a year before agents raided his home and office, documents released Tuesday show . . . far longer than had previously been known."[2]

There are those who told me I was under investigation for much longer. I know there are many who believe The Donald set me up from the get-go. Not actively. But passively; seeing me as nothing more than a card to be played in a hopefully inexhaustible supply of cards in a never-ending poker game.

I've thought about that often since I first became aware of the possibility that Donald Trump never saw me as anything more than a card to be played and disposed of. It makes sense. Absolutely. So, to that extent I have to admit the possibility that Trump always had me in play and may have reached out in some form or fashion to the Department of Justice at a time when we were still technically the "best of friends." As I said, Donald Trump is a master of manipulation. He uses people as human shields to protect himself from investigation and prosecution. As a result, to be in Donald Trump's orbit is to not only be in a spotlight of public attention, but also under the constant gaze of the criminal justice system.

As it turns out I *was* always under investigation from the time I took a job with Donald. I was under investigation by *Trump himself*. Any sign of weakness, anything that could be stored up and used later against me—he'd remember. That's how Trump operates. No one is safe from him and anyone who works for him will eventually get chewed up and spit out. But I didn't understand until I started working on this book how insidious Trump's efforts were when it came to using his closest confidants and allies. I do not know if Trump himself offered me up to the FBI, but he certainly did me no favors after the fact. The call to the DOJ to throw me under the bus could have come from a half a dozen people in his orbit. It could have been an off-hand comment. "Cohen is the logical choice," or "We always wondered about him." Remember what I said: Whoever has Trump's ear last, owns his brain.

If Trump had nothing to do with what happened to me, then he's the luckiest gambler on the planet—and no one is that lucky.

He hedged his bets by making sure that damaging information *was* available. The mainstream media wrote headlines that said Trump was worried because I was his fixer and I knew "where all the bodies are buried." The truth is, I was Trump's patsy. He's the fixer and only *he* knows where all the bodies are buried. The rest of us are expendable—pawns on the Donald Trump chess board.

To find out what really went on in the investigation against me, I had to file a Freedom of Information Act Request (FOIA). Then, when they didn't respond, I had to sue the DOJ to release that information to me. This should come as no surprise.

But how far those in government would go to corner me should turn everyone's head. Everyone and anyone is vulnerable. If they want you, then they'll get you. I found out after the fact that they even investigated my Facebook page. I received this message from Facebook in 2021 informing me of the FBI request for my information:

> This notice is to inform you that we received legal process from law enforcement seeking information about your account, and produced data as required by law. The legal process was accompanied by an order that prohibited us from disclosing information about the case until a specific time had expired and we were legally required to produce the records specified in the demand.
>
> If you would like additional information about the legal process, please let us know as soon as possible by responding to this email.

As it turns out, no stone was left unturned. And that's reassuring if you're going after international terrorists or serial killers. It's overkill when you're going after a guy who made a payoff to a former lover for his boss.

One DOJ investigator confided in us that I was "the Fall Guy" once Trump decided to run for office. "Cohen isn't family. He can go," this investigator told us. And I was purposely kept in the dark. "Don't tell Cohen too much," was Donald's mantra, according to this agent. Meanwhile those close to the president were privately pushing for the DOJ to investigate me. That's how things worked at the White House.

But the FBI and the Justice Department were not much better. At times they wouldn't even release information about me that I wanted released and that in no way would have compromised their investigations, their process, or their need for confidentiality. What's unusual in my case is that it's information about me that *I want released* to the public. I'm not arguing for a third party. I want *my* information to do what *I want* with it. Huge difference. But since we supposedly live in a free and fair democracy as a nation of laws, I put faith in the fact that we'd eventually get the information.

Judicial Watch in 2018 filed suit against the DOJ after they failed to respond to three FOIA requests. As one news report detailed:

> The first request was filed on April 12 of this year and sought "any and all records of correspondence and communications between the Office of Deputy Attorney General Rod Rosenstein and the Office of Special

Counsel Robert Mueller concerning, regarding, or relating to the April 9, 2018 raids on the office and hotel room of Michael Cohen."

The second request was filed on the same day and sought the search and seizure warrant executed by the FBI at Cohen's office and hotel room on April 9, 2018; the application for the search warrant; any affidavits submitted in support of the application; and all records about the recusal of U.S. Attorney Geoffrey Berman from the Michael Cohen investigation.[3]

The same report noted that the president of Judicial Watch, Tom Fitton, commented, "On its face, the raid on then-President Trump's lawyers seemed abusive and out of line. And so it is not surprising that the Mueller Special Counsel and the Justice Department would ignore FOIA law and refuse to respond to our basic request for information about this extraordinary raid."

At first it looked like the FBI was trying to "squeeze" me, as it was widely reported. Conventional wisdom would have you believe that the pressure applied to me was done so I'd spill everything I know about Donald Trump. But Donald Trump, drunk with his new-found power, believed what I knew could never kill the king. He was probably giddy as a kid at Christmas getting his own BB gun as he watched the DOJ go after me. Their success would be his exoneration.

So, who really benefited when I got arrested? Who benefitted the most by the raid, the investigation and the thousands of pages of useless information the raid provided that had to be read through, and which cost valuable manpower and hours to do? It certainly wasn't the Justice Department. They, as the DOJ source stated, were left scrambling trying to find something—anything they could hang their hat on to prosecute me. It was also about misdirection—the sleight of hand magicians use to distract your attention. One of the goals here was to make sure no one was looking at the Trump Organization's CFO Allen Weisselberg, and the financial crimes he and Trump allegedly committed on behalf of the company.

The answer is: Trump benefitted. He dodged a bullet and threw me to the wolves he saw hunting on his front lawn. To take that further, he used the FBI to make sure I was squeezed. Investigators firmly believed I knew more than I did. Where do you think that came from? Trump. He spread bread crumbs that sent the wolves hunting on my doorstep.

Look at another case of misdirection.

According to official FBI records on December 4, 2017, Assistant Special Counsel Andrew Goldstein spoke with Felix Ehrat, the general counsel of Novartis—a global healthcare company based in Switzerland.

The FBI was interested in a potential conflict of interest between Trump and Novartis—had he taken money from them to influence policy?—and, likewise, my relationship with Joseph Jimenez, the Novartis CEO who brought my name to Ehrat via email. Of course Ehrat knew who I was in 2016 when this all went down because, as he told the FBI he "read the papers and watched the news, specifically around the time of the 2016 United States Presidential election."[4]

I had exactly one meeting with Jimenez, on February 13, 2017. He wanted insight—as did many others—into the new administration, and it was logical to come to me. Novartis is a 51 billion dollar a year business. Insight into the new administration makes good business sense. And few people in Washington at the time knew anything about Trump, and certainly no one knew him as well as I did. Jimenez wanted to meet with me not as a lobbyist—which I wasn't—but simply to gain knowledge and understanding of the new government.

That meeting, according to the FBI, constituted a prior relationship. "Jimenez believed Cohen would help Novartis if the policy declarations being made by the Donald Trump administration became law or new regulations," the FBI's report said.[5]

At the time Novartis management was having serious conversations with the FDA about building a manufacturing plant—a plan with a potentially huge impact on their business. To come to me was natural. I was the president's personal attorney. I could provide valuable insight to them as a consultant outside of the government.

Let's not forget at the time that there were few people in the Washington lobbying groups and consulting firms at the time who knew Trump, because no one thought he was going to win the election. Thousands of people had joined K Street consulting firms, all with relationships to the Clintons. So after Clinton lost, people were scrambling to figure out Donald Trump and how to work with the incoming administration. How many people knew how Trump thinks? How many had insight into what Trump was intending to do? How many people knew what Trump liked or disliked? Few. Very Few. I was definitely one of them and, more importantly, I was not in government.

Still, the FBI noted the move was both "usual and unusual." The report blacks out what the FBI believed *was* unusual about it. But never mind that. The FBI was clearly trying to implicate me in something nefarious and illegal, but the time frame and the issues involved led the investigators to say "from that perspective it was not unusual."

That, of course didn't keep them from trying to make something out of nothing. "From Ehrat's conversation with Jimenez there was (*sic*) two reasons why Jimenez hired Cohen. Cohen knew the individuals in the Trump administration and how they thought. Additionally, Cohen could facilitate access to those individuals if necessary."

Ehrat was concerned about a "clear and proper" contractual relationship and said the risk was "no different than any other consultant." This is the blind alley the FBI went chasing after. Was it about bribery? Was I going to take a payoff or be involved in some kind of underhanded deal? Ehrat said I never mentioned my access to Trump or ability to influence him and wouldn't have taken a meeting with me if I had. Again, he and I both operated ethically. I edited the agreement that was sent to me. I inserted language that stated emphatically that my services would not include lobbying or government relations work. Ehrat had no problem with it and we executed a consulting agreement.

The FBI tried to make something out of the amount I was to be paid—$100,000 per month— but Ehrat noted that "Novartis paid hundreds of millions of dollars for outside legal advice." I was worth a little more than average, apparently, but there was nothing illegal or underhanded about the deal.

On March 1, 2017 I met with Ehrat. He was uncomfortable about an email I sent him and so we set up a meeting to discuss it. During the meeting Ehrat recalled that I took some phone calls which he described as "unprofessional." I don't recall my phone ringing, but usually the only thing that would interrupt such a meeting would be a phone call from my family. That's who I am. My family calls, and I answer. That's hardly a sin and I don't think it's unprofessional.

Ehrat claimed he was under the impression that I "did not really know" what I was talking about when we discussed Novartis's potential business expansion, when I suggested building a plant in Indiana. "Ehrat could not remember why Cohen suggested Indiana, but Ehrat assumed someone influential in the Trump administration was from Indiana."

Yeah. No shit. The vice president was from Indiana. How ignorant can you be not to know that? And his claims of me overstating my worth is laughable. My path crossed with Novartis on a day when we were both at the White House for different events. As I was leaving the White House briefing room, a half dozen reporters followed me as I passed a group of visitors on the macadam near the North Lawn. The Novartis team that was part of that group asked who I was.

By coincidence, Jimenez and I have a mutual friend and that's how the relationship began. Their interest was to understand Trump and to advance their business. At our initial meeting I suggested opening up a facility in Indiana to produce antibiotics. I also suggested Pennsylvania—which is a purple state—in hopes of turning the state red by producing jobs and needed antibiotics. Most people don't know this, but the majority of the antibiotics used in this country are produced in Mexico. And after Trump disparaged Mexico in numerous speeches, essentially calling the country a gang of low-life criminals, it became apparent we probably should be producing antibiotics domestically.

Anyway, the innocuous, humdrum FBI report rattled on for seven pages discussing how I did nothing wrong and Ehrat did nothing wrong. Novartis did nothing wrong. The FBI went on an extended fishing trip regarding my Novartis consulting agreement that amounted to a nothing burger. That's how jaded the investigation was.

But the shenanigans didn't end there.

One of the funniest and saddest parts of the DOJ investigation was when I was later asked if I had tried to get Trump in touch with Vladimir Putin during the campaign. I answered that of course I had. I'd made a phone call to the Kremlin.

Why? Well, I explained that Trump asked me to. These are two high profile, important men, why shouldn't they get together?

The truth is, it was merely a publicity stunt thought up by Trump himself. At that time, Trump had read in the newspaper that President Obama would not be meeting with Putin at the upcoming United Nation's General Assembly (UNGA). Trump saddled me with the task of inviting Putin to Trump Tower to have a Mar-A-Lago Burger together. Comically, it was the Kremlin that refused—claiming that to do so would not adhere to protocol.

The part of this no one could believe is how I ended up calling the Kremlin. Agents and members of Congress incessantly questioned me about how I had gotten the phone number. They believed that Donald or I must have had the number due to a perceived relationship.

A relationship that never existed. Several congressional members and agents fell off their seats when I stated that I simply Googled the phone number, found it, and placed the call.

Nothing ever happened—at least I never set up any playdate with Putin and Trump, but the FBI couldn't seem to fathom how things work in the real world. It's like they never heard of Google.

From the day the DOJ picked up my file, it was a bag job. The number of people involved may never be known. Most thought they were just doing their job. But others had less pure motives, and they're the ones who drove the investigation. From the FBI director Christopher Wray, to the exploitive and exploited prosecutors who took on this clown show, they were as guilty of subverting justice as many of those who were actually charged for doing so.

So, why would anyone, knowing they were innocent and fighting corruption plead guilty in the first place? Why did I?

First, consider a point made by Judge Rakoff in an article for the *New York Review of Books*:

"To the Founding Fathers, the critical element in the system was the jury trial, which served not only as a truth-seeking mechanism and a means of achieving fairness, but also as a shield against tyranny. As Thomas Jefferson famously said, "I consider [trial by jury] as the only anchor ever yet imagined by man, by which a government can be held to the principles of its constitution."[6]

Today's trial outcomes are mostly pre-determined by a prosecutor, subverting the Sixth Amendment's guarantee of a speedy public trial. Because of politics, and largely because of economics, the federal criminal justice system is an assembly line of plea bargaining[7] and negotiated deals. The public never sees the adjudication of the case and rarely learns what happened—that rare earth is reserved for officers of the court. There is also no major push to right this wrong. We've all just come to accept it.

Such a system is ripe for exploitation by someone like Donald Trump.

For example: my attorney Lanny Davis was always convinced there was something going on with my prosecution. What convinced him? At one point we approached the prosecution to volunteer information about who had obstructed justice and directed me to break the law. Davis called prosecutor Thomas McKay, but McKay said he wasn't interested.

"You're not interested?" Davis said. "Excuse me, did you just say you weren't interested?"

They absolutely weren't interested.

"The tax charge against Cohen was bogus," Davis later said. "Why isn't McKay under investigation?"

That's a great question and one I've tried to get an answer to. While I was being investigated, Lanny Davis and I continued to try for months to get McKay to sit down with me. He never would. In early 2022 I saw McKay in a Federal courtroom on an unrelated case—the prosecution of Michael Avenatti—and McKay sat down in front of me. I asked him if he'd agree to talk with me for this book. He got up and left. He has refused to return emails or phone calls. That speaks a lot about him, his arrogance and how he prosecuted my case.

I'm not the only one concerned about how the justice department works—not by a long stretch. The legal machinations "surrounding the materials seized in the FBI's raid of Trump Organization lawyer Michael Cohen are some of the juiciest tidbits of lawyer nerd gossip in years,"[8] Kathryn Rubino wrote online for "Above the Law." The reason is clear enough. If the Federal government can do what it did to me, it can do that and worse to others—all while being essentially unanswerable to the public.

The lack of concern on the part of Thomas McKay and Nicholas Roos (who took over prosecution of my case after McKay left for another high-profile case—the prosecution of New York state senator Dean Skelos for corruption) over who was behind the payment to Stormy Daniels was a bad move by the DOJ. It showed the Department already knew who was behind the payment and their subsequent lack of action against Donald Trump showed the heads of the DOJ didn't care. What they did care about, however, was doing well after they were done with me. Everyone involved has done exceptionally well for themselves after my prosecution—and so have members of my defense team.

It is worth noting again that this is *not* a new story. Years of propaganda from the government and television shows like Efrem Zimbalist Junior's "The FBI," aided and abetted by J. Edgar Hoover's image of the clean-cut "G-Men," led to decades of deception that the average American was unaware of—and most people couldn't even imagine.

In as much as the FBI is made of mortal men, it has always had troubles, even if its image was that of a government agency above reproach. Remember this is the same FBI that treated Bonnie and Clyde as a greater national problem than organized crime—and refused to admit organized crime even existed until Joseph Valachi, a foot soldier in the Genovese crime family, testified before Congress in 1963 and confirmed the existence of "La Cosa Nostra." That kind of thick-headedness permeates the halls of the DOJ even to this day.

In July 2021 the *New York Post* reported on an FBI investigation into a group of Michigan men plotting against Governor Gretchen Whitmer, saying, "The FBI knew these people had some beliefs and were egging them on and providing help and ammunition."[9] It's not the first time the FBI has been criticized for its use of informants. The notorious Boston mob boss Whitey Bulger was an even more glaring instance. In the end, it looks like the FBI's actions aid and abet criminals under the guise of trying to take them down. It's not necessarily their motives in question, but the tactical decisions made in pursuing criminals. Like many others the people of the FBI believe the ends justify the means.

That's *exactly* how Donald Trump operates.

Hoover's G-Men went so far as to spend countless man hours and taxpayer dollars investigating celebrities the FBI didn't like. It maintained files on numerous famous people, including Elvis Presley, Frank Sinatra, John Lennon, Jane Fonda, Groucho Marx, Lou Costello, Sonny Bono, Bob Dylan, Michael Jackson and Mickey Mantle.[10] Seriously. Groucho Marx? Lou Costello? The Mick? What the hell is going on here? The same still occurs today. The FBI takes out the steak knives and tries to carve up those in the spotlight while the real criminals are sometimes within their own ranks. Just as Costello asked, "Who's on First?"

One such notorious incident involving the FBI's own was agent Robert Hanssen. He was arrested in 2001 and is now serving 15 consecutive life sentences at a federal supermax prison near Florence, Colorado charged with spying for the Soviet Union and Russia from

1979 through 2001. FBI agents impersonated reporters from the Associated Press in 2007. In 2018 it failed to follow protocol in the Stoneman Douglas High School shooting case. And a DOJ watchdog report by DOJ Inspector General Michael Horowitz showed in 2018 that James Comey and the FBI's handling of Hillary Clinton emails "damaged the agencies' image of impartiality."[11]

In the latest round of questionable activites, *Politico* reported in December 2021 on the FBI pursuit of Representative Jeff Fortenberry of Nebraska, whom they had secretly recorded:

> The Justice Department's prosecution of a Republican lawmaker for allegedly lying to the FBI is raising thorny issues about the use of surreptitious tactics during investigations into members of Congress. . . . critics say the concerns—about the approval process and threshold to deploy arguably deceptive investigative tactics—are even more acute in Fortenberry's case.[12]

This is the predicate by which I assert that the FBI—particularly during the tenure of former President Donald Trump—was corrupt, vindictive, and intellectually lazy. In other words, if there were problems in the FBI before Trump—and there were—during Trump's tenure he exploited those weaknesses in furtherance of his own crooked agenda.

The facts are there. Career prosecutors and investigators have a long tradition of benefiting from investigating and prosecuting high-profile cases. My case was the highest profiled case that many of the investigators—including some of the young, brash 30-somethings who were involved—had ever had a chance to handle. In some respects there's nothing wrong with that. Being rewarded for a job well done is part of the fabric of the culture. But in this case, like everything related to Donald Trump, the reward was held out as a carrot on a very crooked stick, and no one bothered to question who was holding out the stick or the motives behind doing so. Everyone involved benefited from this approach, from Geoffrey Berman and Robert Khazami, to Nicholas Roos and Thomas McKay on down.

Here's what I know without a doubt: The case was accelerated and pursued—aided and abetted by Donald Trump. While those who handled it hands-on were most likely doing their job, and while it was treated as a righteous investigation and prosecution by them, those who pulled the strings knew what was up and why. Worse, they already had a predetermined outcome in mind.

It was underhanded. It was without precedent. Dealing with the Department of Justice or any part of the government while Trump was in office was like being thrown in a bag of poisonous snakes. You couldn't trust anyone—and you will definitely get bitten.

For example, take San Francisco-based IRS investigative analyst John Fry. It's well established how he and lawyer Michael Avenatti—may he rest in prison forever—schemed to put me in prison. How did this scheme work? Fry had access to the most coveted and important database this country keeps—the FINCEN system. FINCEN is a Fort Knox for financial information in this country that the government uses to safeguard the entire financial system. According to its government website, "FINCEN's mission is to safeguard the financial system from illicit use and combat money laundering and promote national security through the collection, analysis, and dissemination of financial intelligence and strategic use of financial authorities."[13] Its purpose is "to combat money laundering and terrorism financing."[14]

Yeah. That's right. *Terrorism.*

And yet, as a Treasury Department news release admitted, Fry, a longtime IRS employee, "logged on to the FINCEN database from his work computer and conducted additional searches related to Michael Cohen and Essential Consultants. He then called Michael Avenatti from his personal cell phone and verbally provided information contained in the searches. Fry admitted he had no official reason to disclose SAR records related to Cohen."

That's right, a government agent gave information about me from that system to Avenatti for no other reason than to harm me . . . and for Avenatti's insatiable need to remain relevant.

You have to be kidding me. The government cheated to help a scumbag like Avenatti while trying to prosecute me? On that day in January 2022 when I showed up in Federal Court and tried to talk to McKay, Avenatti approached me and asked me how I was enjoying those "Donald Trump knee pads." I told him they were unused but not to worry, I would send them to him because he was going to need them where he's going.

The hypocrisy of a member of the federal government cheating for Avenatti while trying to prosecute me is mind-blowing. As the *Courthouse News* website reported, "Fry was charged with one count of unauthorized disclosure of suspicious activity reports, two counts of misuse of a computer and one count of unauthorized use of a social security number." The possible repurcussions? "A maximum 20 years in prison and $1 million fine."[15] The U.S. attorney prosecuting him issued a stern statement: "Fry thought that his politics were more important than his obligation to follow the law, and in that he was mistaken."[16]

But in the end, the system definitely took care of its own. Fry got five years of probation and a five thousand dollar fine—nothing more—for disseminating sensitive information about a private individual that he had no right to divulge. Worse, he used a highly sensitive government database to do it. In the process, by the way, he not only released information about me, but about two other people, including a man from Israel and one from Toronto, Canada, who he mistook for me because they shared my name.

The DOJ cannot pretend to take the high road, cannot pretend to be for law and order when it takes the low road to try and go after me or anybody else while members of the DOJ break the law in the process. *This is one of the most underreported and least understood portions of the case against me.* The manipulation of the FINCEN system is nothing short of chilling. It should scare everybody in this country that a member of law enforcement can easily manipulate for their own ends a highly guarded, unique system that has sensitive financial information about potentially everyone on the planet.

And wait until you find out the reason *why* Fry decided to give Avenatti my information. Fry was an Avenatti fanboy. And Avenatti went on a media assault against me, because he desperately desired attention and fame. He was the modern-day Narcissus—the man who fell in love with his own reflection.

Here's how the two hooked up in the first place, according to the *New York Times*:

Amid the swirl of the scandal involving Stormy Daniels, Mr. Avenatti, her lawyer, took to Twitter one day in May 2018, and demanded that the Treasury Department release Mr. Cohen's records.

Mr. Fry, a longtime I.R.S. employee based in San Francisco, was one of the legions of followers of Mr. Avenatti's Twitter account, and had frequently liked his posts. Hours after Mr. Avenatti's tweet that day, Mr. Fry started searching for the documents on the government database, downloaded them, then immediately contacted Mr. Avenatti and later sent him Mr. Cohen's confidential records, according to court documents. "John: I cannot begin to tell you how much I appreciate this. Thank you," Mr. Avenatti wrote to Mr. Fry, according to the documents, then pressed him for more.[17]

Where is there justice in releasing private information from a secured government server and only receiving probation and a light fine? The U.S. government lowered the boom on me for a tax omission and paying off Donald Trump's lover.

Let's be clear, one of the government's own knowingly committed a felony by sharing sensitive financial information. To get that information he bypassed a warning on the home screen page that improper use is a crime punishable by imprisonment. Despite being the greatest intelligence gathering agency in the world, it took the FBI more than a year to bring that case forward even though they knew almost immediately who breached the system. Let's face it, a computer system *that* secure is constantly monitored. The FBI learned within seconds who was on the system. They knew which computer and who logged on—but refused to identify and indict their own— John Fry. "We could and should've found out within minutes, not months and we should've prosecuted it far more quickly," a former FBI official explained to me.

Why didn't they? Because they weren't interested in protecting me; they were only interested in *prosecuting* me.

More importantly they didn't want Fry's prosecution to be used as a part of my defense in the Southern District of New York. So, they waited a year to bring charges.

Meanwhile, in addition to Avenatti, Fry had also leaked the info to *New Yorker* journalist Ronan Farrow. As a Courthouse News report had noted, "Fry also searched for and attempted to retrieve other unauthorized reports in a separate criminal database, but because those reports were restricted, he could not access them." Farrow now pushed the narrative that those restricted records had "disappeared" and there was something nefarious going on at the Treasury Department on my behalf. As the *New York Times* later reported:

> It was a breathtaking story, written by the *New Yorker's* marquee reporter and published with an attention-grabbing headline: "Missing Files Motivated the Leak of Michael Cohen's Financial Records."
>
> In it, the reporter, Ronan Farrow, suggests something suspicious unfolding inside the Treasury Department: A civil servant had noticed that records about Mr. Cohen, the personal lawyer for President Trump,

mysteriously vanished from a government database in the spring of 2018. Mr. Farrow quotes the anonymous public servant as saying he was so concerned about the records' disappearance that he leaked other financial reports to the media to sound a public alarm about Mr. Cohen's financial activities.

The story set off a frenzied reaction . . .

Calling the reaction "frenzied" is an understatement. And I agree with the *New York Times* assessment of Farrow's reporting. But I'm not questioning Farrow's motives; I consider him an honorable man—but he should've known better.

At least Farrow was right about one thing—there was something suspicious unfolding inside the government. But it wasn't being done to *help* me. It was done to try and bury me.

The mistake I made, and most of America made—at least at the beginning of my fall from the Trump regime—was in assuming that I would also be protected.

As it turns out, the true story about how Avenatti and Fry hooked up is a case of a social media fanboy trying to get some attention for himself. It was the desire of someone saying *"Look at ME!"* that led to the information being released.

This is also key to Donald Trump—using people's personal greed and narcissism to fuel his own. Trump never had to say anything. He always counts on people being the worst version of themselves and he's seldom let down—because he encourages people to be the worst version of themselves—in essence, to be just like him. The truth is that there are those in our government who are conniving, smart, and corrupt, and those who are gullible, stupid, and corrupt. Fry, as it turns out, is the latter. As a *New York Times* story noted, "In Mr. Fry's defense, his lawyer said he had been watching 'hours and hours' of television, and described him as 'a victim of cable news.'"[18]

Yeah. Sure. "A victim of cable news." He was a victim of his infatuation with Avenatti.

John Fry's fall from grace was just an example of the "piling on" that occurred because of the Steele Dossier.

Fry and his attorney both refused to answer any questions I have for them despite repeated attempts to contact them.

In the beginning I went with a law firm I knew, the firm of McDermott, Will and Emery—which included Stephen Ryan, Joseph Evans, and Todd Harrison. My wife and I, on the recommendation of an acquaintance, later hired Guy Petrillo. One of the many reasons I hired him was because he was the former chief of the criminal division at the Southern District of New York, the office that was investigating me.

Now? Since the sentencing, I cannot get him on the phone, despite repeated attempts to do so. I can't get an email answered. He is just one of many who either represented me or testified before the government who won't even allow me to ask them questions today. I've even told all of them I plan to mention them in this book, but that hasn't moved anyone to come forward and be honest with me. It's a disappointing tell. And of all the disappointments wrapped up in this, Petrillo is one of the deepest.

He told Laura and me that because of the time he spent working in the government he knew all of the key players in the prosecution, including Geoffrey Berman, who occupied his old office, as well as Robert Khuzami—who handled the case after Geoffrey Berman recused himself for reasons unknown to this day. However, there was speculation that he recused himself because he was undergoing treatment for prostate cancer. There was also speculation that he recused himself because his brother had a relationship with David Pecker, the aforementioned president of the *National Enquirer*.

But back to Petrillo. Despite his knowledge, or maybe because of his knowledge of the prosecutors, we were having a difficult time getting them to talk with us as their investigation continued. I was so frustrated I even suggested to Petrillo that we purchase a bed and camp out in front of the US District Courthouse at 500 Pearl Street until Khuzami would meet with us.

For four months the government refused our calls and as far as I know never spoke with Petrillo. Finally, on August 18, 2018, I instructed Petrillo to put in writing a demand letter to Robert Khuzami seeking an audience to discuss the investigation. It was that letter that prompted a 5:30 p.m. phone call by Khuzami to Petrillo, whereby Petrillo was advised that we had until the following day Friday, August 19, to come in and discuss the investigation. Petrillo responded "Let me speak to my client and make sure he is available," to which, the SDNY responded, "No. You alone." Petrillo immediately called to advise me of the call, and I asked, "Is this normal? Why can't I go?"

Petrillo's response was that it was not at all normal, but that they did not want me there. He recommended I permit him to attend the proposed meeting without me, as he said it was beneficial to starting a dialogue with the government.

Twenty-four hours after Khuzami reached out, slightly after 5:30 p.m. on August 19, while Laura and I were at the home of a friend who'd just gone through surgery. I got a call from Petrillo on my cell phone, stating that he needed to see me and Laura in his office the following Saturday morning at 8 a.m.

Naturally, I asked what had transpired at the meeting, which clearly didn't last very long, and Petrillo said, "We'll discuss it tomorrow."

Can you imagine leaving someone twisting in the wind like that? How the hell could I leave it alone until the following morning. This was my life we were talking about. So, I said "I have to know what is going on."

That's when Petrillo dropped the hard facts on me; the Southern District of New York was demanding either I plead guilty to a series of crimes on Monday, or they would be filing an 85-page indictment that would include Laura. Why? Because our financial accounts were in both our names. What's more, they pointed out that if I didn't comply, we could both do the perp walk (known universally by reporters as the "Walk of Shame") out of our apartment.

Talk about a reality check.

"What are the charges?" I asked. I had no idea at this point what SDNY was looking at, or what they intended to charge. Petrillo abruptly replied, "Income tax evasion, misrepresentation to a bank, and campaign finance violations."

I began to shout, "What tax evasion? I've never in my life not paid taxes. I've never in my life been audited. I don't owe the IRS any money, nor have I ever lied to a bank for anything!"

Petrillo replied, "That's why we're meeting each other at eight in the morning. I'm not discussing this now."

I was dazed, as if sucker punched by Mike Tyson. If I hadn't been so stunned, I should've realized then that Petrillo was not on my side and didn't have my best interest at heart.

For four months I'd asked why the federal government didn't want to speak with me, if they were investigating me. Didn't they want some answers? I never once got a response to that question. You know, your natural curiosity as an investigator should've made you step forward and talk to me—especially if you were interested in pursuing a case against Donald Trump. Maybe I could help.

But, if you have no intention of investigating Donald Trump, then why speak to me at all? If you have me in the bag and aren't going to do anything else—it makes sense that the investigators wouldn't want to talk to me at all. And that's exactly what they did, and later it is exactly what Lanny Davis pointed out. The government had no intention of going after Trump. Getting me was all they cared about.

In any event, there was no chance I was going to let those bastards file anything against my wife. So, like a man in a hostage video, I agreed to the SDNY deal. And of course, right after sentencing, Petrillo then dumped me like trash. We haven't spoken to this day. They put a metaphoric gun to my wife's head and forced me to execute a plea deal while my former-federal-prosecutor attorney told me it was the best thing for me and Laura. Petrillo never took off the prosecutorial robe—ever. And I still have questions that remain unanswered. I gave Petrillo written permission to answer them for this book—but he didn't.

Here they are:

1. Have you ever seen a case like mine? In your entire practice has there ever been a case where the federal government wouldn't speak to the person they are investigating? Ideally isn't that part of the investigative process? Why wouldn't they take your call?

2. Why did Berman recuse himself from my case?

3. Did Khuzami work for you, as you said he did? I hired you based on your experience and the relationships you claimed with these people, as the former head of the criminal division of the SDNY. Your familiarity with how they might prosecute me was what I bought—because it's what you were selling. If anyone knew how they might proceed, and then how to counter it, it would be the person who previously wore the big boy pants.

4. Were there unique aspects of my case? What were they?

5. Have you ever worked a case while at the Justice Department or in private practice in which a defense attorney was told to arrive at a Justice Department meeting without their client? How often does this happen? Why?

6. *Business Insider* described you thusly: "He served as the chief of the criminal division in the US Attorney's Office for the Southern District of New York from 2008 through 2009, and was an assistant US attorney

in the office from 1990 through 1997." Assuming the accuracy of that statement (please correct if in error), and combined with your experience the same article said, either taking the case to trial or making a plea deal was well within "your wheelhouse." So, why did you recommend taking a deal instead of going to trial?

7. Why were you once described by Alan Dershowitz as being, "the kind of lawyer you would hire if you wanted to keep open the option of cooperation?"

That third question is key since he told my co-author, "He (Khuzami) was a deputy. He never worked for me." He also said, "I don't want to get into attorney/client discussions," though I told him it was okay to do so.

Again, remember that once I went to prison, everyone who touched this case somehow did well for themselves. Tatiana Martins, one of the former SDNY prosecutors, admitted she had little to do with the case, and merely reviewed some documents. My prosecution is cited in the first line of her biography at the white-shoe criminal defense firm Davis Polk, where she went on to work. Khuzami later did okay for himself, hiring out for top dollar to the private equity fund Guggenheim Partners. My defense team did okay too. Amy Lester, a fine young litigator with Petrillo, is now the lead attorney for McKesson Corporation—a pharmaceutical firm that employs 80,000 people.

As for me, though, soon enough I found myself in Federal Constructional Institution, Otisville.

During my time there many inmates elected to discuss their specific cases with me; despite the general rule never to do so. Most inmates assert their innocence despite the overwhelming evidence suggesting otherwise. Nevertheless there were approximately a dozen individuals who I met during my "vacation" at Otisville whose alleged crimes made no sense to me. They too stated that the prosecutors in their case were overzealous and abusive.

Judge Rakoff, in his book *Why the Innocent Plead Guilty and the Guilty Go Free*, makes an excellent point when he declares there needs to be judicial oversight on plea bargains. "To my mind, the best solution would be to involve another judge in the plea bargaining situation from very early on. That is currently prohibited. The results are that there are no neutral people taking a look at plea deals," Rakoff explained.

Just think about that! Plea bargaining is where some 97 percent of cases wind up, and the federal rule that says judges can't be involved means "judges aren't involved in 97 percent of the cases," as Rakoff explains.

> The argument is that if a judge is going to have to preside, he should be involved in plea bargaining. True. So, have a different judge handle the plea—not the trial judge. It's very simple to have a magistrate in charge of the plea—one who wouldn't report back to the trial judge.

Most prosecutors we spoke with and almost every defense attorney we spoke to for the purposes of this book agree with Judge Rakoff.

It's a huge problem in the system. And again, it wasn't created by Donald Trump, but his administration certainly took advantage of it, to his benefit and my detriment. Judge Rakoff, one of the people we interviewed, doesn't think there was any overt pressure placed on the prosecutors by the White House in my case. While I am not convinced he is right, it still doesn't mean Trump didn't take advantage of how the Southern District of New York operates. He certainly was well aware of its presence and how it operates after years of skirting disaster there regarding his business in New York. He knew many of the players there and how they would react.

The U.S. attorney's office there has a long, notorious history of being independent. In fact, SDNY has been said to stand for the "Sovereign District of New York" by many criminal defense attorneys. This, by the way, is not meant as a compliment, but rather an attack on the way they conduct themselves. They act in a manner that is completely independent from any judicial body, which is why Trump attempted to get Geoffrey Berman, the head of the criminal division there, to resign; which he refused. The question needing to be asked is, why would the president of the United States be so focused on this one facet of the Justice Department other than for the reason that it was the court prosecuting my case?

The answer is he wouldn't. Though Berman recused himself from my case that wasn't enough for Trump. Since Trump appointed Berman to this position, he believed Berman owed him loyalty, which included acquiescing to Trump's desire to silence me through incarceration. And the more I cooperated and provided damning information to the government about Trump, the greater Trump's need to silence me grew. Somehow he would find the weak link in the SDNY to do his bidding. This could not have occurred if the plea bargaining had included a second, independent, judge.

Judge Rakoff also noted something else which I found to be too true:

> The second problem often raised is that we have an adversarial system whereby judges don't play a role other than making sure the adversaries abide by the rules. And it's really something we shouldn't be doing in an adversarial system. That part is completely misplaced. Judges do this all the time in the European system.
>
> If anything, the American system may be too adversarial. The theory is each side has its own champion and fight it out or negotiate. In a criminal case, the prosecutor has far more power than the defense.

No kidding. In my case their power was absolute and it destroyed me. And as Rakoff noted, the irony is that in this country while we don't allow judicial involvement in criminal cases, we do allow it in settling civil cases—"And no one ever complains it's unfair there."

However, in criminal cases where defendants lose their liberty, their finances, their family, and their reputation, the system precludes independent judicial oversight. I don't know about anyone else, but for me personally, I would say had there been an independent judge involved in the plea deal, I am certain that I would not have been sentenced to live for 36 months on the government's dime while being separated from my family.

The day before I was to be in court, while sitting in Petrillo's office with Laura, Tom McKay forwarded to Petrillo an allocution—a formal statement made to the court by a defendant prior to sentencing—of what I was to say, and how I would respond, to Judge Pauley's questions from the bench. The script for my hostage video, basically. I don't suspect our founding fathers ever foresaw this kind of "justice."

On "plea day," I was fully prepared, as I was a well-rehearsed actor, knew my lines well, and had the script laid in front of me to insure full compliance to their demands. I was so angry that, while reading this letter of lies, I actually bit my inner cheek, causing blood to fill my mouth. As I stumbled through my reading, I was queasy—not from the blood, but from being helpless, and powerless, against a corrupt system.

Despite Judge Pauley's extensive legal background and knowledge of the process, he nevertheless ignored the facts completely. He just moved on.

The bottom line is I went to prison simply because I paid off Donald Trump's ex-lover. The irony here is I'm actually the one who got screwed.

CHAPTER THREE

TO OTISVILLE I GO!

ON THE DAY I LEFT my home to go to prison, I kissed my wife and children goodbye and was driven by myself to Otisville, in upstate New York. I elected to go alone because I couldn't take seeing my family crying any more after months of doing so. And so, I kissed them goodbye at the front door, went to the elevator, stepped in and rode down, staring at the reflective doors. It was a long ride, or so I felt. When I arrived downstairs I was met by a gaggle of reporters in front of the building, all looking for that Rocky Marciano, Jersey Joe Walcott broken-jaw moment.

A friend of mine had provided an Escalade and a driver who was, coincidentally, a former corrections officer. After I climbed into the SUV and we pulled away, I was shocked to see the reporters scrambling to follow us. A motorcade of paparazzi and mainstream reporters was suddenly following in their own vehicles. There were even helicopters following overhead, for the entirety of the approximately two-hour trip to Otisville.

When we arrived at the prison I was further stunned to see literally thousands of people lining the road. As the AP reported, the bureau of prisons had put up temporary concrete Jersey barricades to keep the throngs of people at bay. Most were fans, but there were also plenty of Trump supporters in attendance. Some were holding banners. "Stay Strong" was a popular one. Others were not so friendly or optimistic; "Hope you rot in hell," was another.

My driver handed his credentials to the prison officials when we arrived at the base entrance. They asked him if he was carrying a firearm. "Yes, I am," he replied.

"Sir, can you wait here, we can't permit a firearm on the premises," the official said. My entrance was further delayed. Meanwhile I could still see the throngs of people assembled outside the prison. I stared off at the "Hope you rot in hell" sign. It was held by a tall, blonde-haired guy. I thought it was Eric Trump.

Making the whole thing crazier, as if it wasn't chaotic enough, were the four helicopters flying overhead that had followed me all the way from Manhattan. Unbeknownst to me, the press helicopters created a big problem for the institution. I was later told that my arrival created a security risk because of the thousands of people lining the streets and the helicopters overhead. The institution contacted the FAA in an attempt to have them grounded but was unsuccessful. It turns out that the prison isn't classified as restricted airspace and the Bureau of Prisons couldn't do anything about it. Hey, it wasn't my fault. I was just the guy trying to check into prison.

But the institution took no chances. To ensure security, they actually did an "institutional lockdown," meaning no movement at all was allowed in the prison. What that means is that every inmate in the prison, whether they were in the medium security wing, or at the minimum security satellite camp, had to return to their cells or cubicles until such time that I was processed into the prison. Only then would the lockdown be lifted. Unfortunately, thanks in part to the circling helicopters, the lockdown lasted for approximately four hours. Let's just say I was instantly unpopular among the medium security inmates who lost their yard time and activity time because of me.

At the minimum security wing, which was a satellite camp, the inmates were less irritated and I was, surprisingly, warmly greeted upon my arrival. Almost every inmate made it their business to introduce themselves, each one asking whether there was anything that I needed. They had even filled my waiting empty locker with food, snacks, beverages, toiletries, clothing, and towels. One inmate even brought me a pair of Nike sneakers, while another brought me a radio, so that I could listen to various television audio feeds overnight. Who says inmates aren't good people?

Because my driver was carrying a weapon, he couldn't drive me into the main facility of my new government subsidized housing for processing. The prison had to bring out a vehicle of their own. As an AP report later detailed, I took off the blue blazer I wore on the ride up and left it with my driver.[1] I was then transferred into the institutional vehicle and brought up to the main facility for processing. A short time later I officially became inmate No. 86067-054.

At the main office I was greeted by several correctional officers who escorted me to the intake area, where I had the displeasure of meeting Executive Assistant Chris Entzel, who served as the camp administrator.

He didn't mince words. Standing about five foot six, he looked much like the colonel in *Inglourious Basterds* who got the swastika carved into his forehead. He started by telling me I was a nobody. He said I was no different from the other inmates and that I need to check my ego at the door.

Ego? I was in prison, for God's sake. I was like a zombie. I was there, but I wasn't there. I was physically there, but my head was somewhere else—I was in a fog. I had just ridden for two hours in some kind of slow-motion O.J. Simpson-like chase scene that had ended in a crowd of cheers and jeers. All I could think about was my family watching this madness on television, and wearing green for the next 30 months, and what my life at Otisville would be like. So far, Entzel wasn't painting a good picture of that.

After his perfunctory introduction designed to destroy any sense of self-esteem I had left, he asked about the red string around my wrist.

I explained it was a Kabbalah string. "A Kabba . . . what?" He asked.

"It's a Kabbalah string," I said evenly.

He said, "Take it off."

For the uninitiated, the Kabbalah string is blessed by a rabbi and worn as a bracelet. It's usually made from scarlet wool thread and is knotted seven times by someone saying the kabbalah bracelet prayer. It's a talisman you wear to ward off misfortune.

"I can't take it off," I replied. "It's a religious bracelet blessed by a rabbi in Israel. You wear it until it falls off. It's to protect you.'

"Take it off," he said again.

Still working to maintain an even tone, I replied. "Prison rules allow you to bring in one religious item."

Entzel should have known that much. It's in the BOP manual. But more to the point, as I later discovered, Entzel had been featured in a Catholic newspaper article in 2015 that mentions religion in prison.[2] Cardinal Timothy Dolan once showed up to give a Catholic service at Otisville, declaring that salvation was available to all prisoners. He even confirmed one of the inmates, Guy Lotz, saying, "Lotz fashioned his own confirmation stole from white cloth and decorated it with his patron saint's name and an image of the Holy Spirit as a dove."[3]

In other words, Lotz got to keep a religious item in prison. That is documented. I wasn't asking for any special treatment.

But Entzel wouldn't have it. (Several of the Jewish inmates I became friends with explained Entzel's behavior using just one word: "anti-Semite.")

"This isn't a religious item. It's a string. And it's color."

"Color?" I responded. "I don't understand." What the hell did the color of the item have to do with anything?

He said, "Color. It's red."

"I still don't know what that means," I replied.

"Red symbolizes a gang color."

"Are there gangs at the minimum security camp?"

"We don't permit gangs in the institution."

"Then why is this an issue?" I asked quietly.

He didn't answer.

Finally, I said, "Look, taking it off is bad luck. If you want it off, you'll have to cut it off."

He quickly produced a pair of scissors out of the top drawer of his desk and snipped off my Kabbalah string. It landed on his desk. He picked it up and dropped it in the waste basket.

"Now we have no issue," he said.

And with that, I was initiated into the gang hangout I would later learn was known as Camp Cupcake, where the only gang battles I would witness were between the Orthodox rabbis and the Chabadniks over who received the biggest piece of babka.

During my fifth month behind bars in the splendor of the federal prison in Otisville, my wife advised me on a phone call (which was always monitored and recorded for someone's protection—definitely not mine) that Lanny Davis, one of my attorneys, wanted to speak with me.

Lanny had been my lawyer for a while. In fact, he was involved almost from the beginning of my case after the DOJ raid, concurrent with Petrillo but handling different aspects of the case. He was prominently visible when I was called to testify to the House Oversight Committee. He could be seen on television right over my right shoulder, which for some reason raised the ire of several GOP congress members. Maybe they got angry because Lanny is well known and is politically connected. For several years Lanny was the liberal spokesman that G. Gordon Liddy would bring on to his national radio show to argue for Bill Clinton's administration.

After my wife told me he wanted to speak, I immediately called Lanny, who expressed concern about the monitoring and recording of the call. This was natural as the topic to be discussed was about the DOJ. However, Lanny felt our conversation was so important that he actually drove four hours from D.C. to visit me at Otisville so we could speak privately. Lanny has little regard for the DOJ and that stems not only from his long political and legal experience, but because of his direct knowledge of their distasteful treatment of me.

"The prosecution against Michael Cohen was unique and there's no doubt in my mind that he wasn't given a fair shake, and that the justice department had treated him unfairly," Lanny has said publicly on more than one occasion.

I gladly welcomed the opportunity to talk to Lanny not only because of his gravitas and the fact that he was a friend, but of course, at that point in time, I would've talked to anyone who might give me a glimmer of hope of leaving Otisville early. Lanny's visit was also a welcome intrusion into my daily routine of welding, fire hydrant repair and rebuilding bathrooms. Prison life can often be nothing more than dull routine. What Lanny had to tell me was my first glimpse of hope: the Manhattan District Attorney's office wanted to talk to me about an investigation they were conducting looking into the Trump Organization. Maybe, I thought, I could put federal prison behind me soon. I certainly knew enough about the Trump Organization to help, having been its executive vice president.

The Federal Correctional Institution in Otisville is a medium security prison for male inmates. The facility also includes a satellite prison camp for *minimum security* male offenders, like me. I actually requested to be sent to Otisville at my sentencing because it is also known for its relatively high number of Jewish inmates.[4]

What isn't widely known is that the medium security housing unit holds up to 800 inmates in a series of massive concrete structures behind three rows of barbed wire fence, on grounds patrolled by hundreds of correctional officers. Life there was a real gritty movie-like existence replete with fights and occasional riots by inmates with too much time on their hands. Some of the more infamous alumni of Otisville includes mobsters and murderers like

Sicilian banker Michele Sindona. He was extradited September 25, 1984 to face murder charges in Italy—and was originally sentenced to 25 years. Another is Deryl Dedmon who is currently serving a 50-year sentence for a hate crime in which he stabbed to death an African American. There's also former NFL star Darren Sharper who is currently serving 20 years at Otisville after pleading guilty to multiple rape and drug-related charges. He's also a resident of the main housing unit.

Okay. I didn't serve time in that part of the prison—except for 51 days due to COVID and an unconstitutional remand that we will talk about later.

That's not where I was. I was in the satellite camp, the minimum security prison, with the lowest classified offenders, generally white-collar criminals. That place is known as a country club, referred to, as I mentioned, as Camp Cupcake, by staff, inmates, and casual observers. In the satellite camp there are up to 120 inmates who are overseen by about half a dozen correctional officers.

Here's another fun fact about Camp Cupcake. It had no gates. If you wanted to break out, you merely needed to call an Uber—well, until I got there. More on that in a moment.

There was little fear of violence or fights in our section of the prison. In fact, every Sunday, weather permitting, we played softball and had aluminum bats at our disposal. We played tennis, paddleball, and basketball . . . we even had a bocce court. We were not the type to try to escape or start fights. Even the kosher tuna came in metal cans with round sharp lids that peeled off. Unlike what would occur on the other end of the property, we didn't use the lids as shivs to cut our fellow inmates. Rather, we used them to cut vegetables that we snuck out of the kitchen. Our little satellite camp was filled with doctors, lawyers, accountants, and businessmen. If you twisted your ankle you went to cubicle 16, 24 or 31. You could also make some good future business connections.

Among those housed there was Dean Skelos, the New York state senator sentenced to prison for bribery. By coincidence, Tom McKay also prosecuted him and in fact stepped aside from his lead chair in my prosecution when he took on the Skelos case.

During the time we spent together at Otisville, I got to know and spent considerable time with Skelos—whose only crime I could see was in trying to get his troublesome son a job. I mean seriously—51 months for that? The state called it bribery. I called it overzealous parenting, but also overzealous prosecution and disproportionate sentencing.

Disproportionate sentencing, in fact, is something Lanny Davis and I often spoke about. It was a common theme in federal prosecution. For example, another high profile Otisville roommate was Michael "The Situation" Sorrentino, a star of the Bravo reality television show Jersey Shore.

He entered Otisville in early 2019, sentenced to eight months for tax evasion. *People* Magazine gave a rundown of our treatment as I joined this motley crew:

> According to the official handbook, Otisville prisoners are woken up at 6 a.m. on weekdays, have breakfast at 6:15 and report to work at 7:30. The work involves providing services for the prison, such as laundry or landscaping.

Prisoners eat lunch between 10:45 a.m. and 12:30
p.m., and dinner from 4:30 p.m. to 6 p.m. Lights are
turned off by 11:30 p.m.

Upon arrival, prisoners are given a set of clothing
along with a standard bed roll consisting of two sheets,
one pillowcase, two towels and two wash cloths.

Inmates can't bring much with them, but they are
allowed to keep medical or orthopedic devices, legal
documents, prescription eye glasses and religious items,
as long as they do not pose a security threat.[5]

"The Sitch," as he was also known, fit right in, and was a great guy. Of
all the miserable time I spent in Otisville, spending time with "The
Sitch" was among some of the best. I love the time I smashed the
softball over his head to win the ballgame. We had a lot in common,
especially when it came to our reasons for being in prison.

Sorrentino and his brother Marc were indicted in September 2014
for tax offenses and conspiring to defraud the United States after allegedly failing to properly pay taxes on $8.9 million in income from
2010 to 2012. In April 2017 both men were indicted on additional
charges including tax evasion and structuring and falsifying records.[6]

"The Sitch" pled guilty to just one count of tax evasion. Three
different years of tax returns for him yielded one charge. I had five
different years that led to five charges. He didn't pay taxes on $8.9
million in income. He didn't even file tax returns. I filed, and on
time, and paid what I was told by my accountant was due on my
income. I just *underpaid* by $1.39 million.

He received an eight-month sentence. I received thirty-six.

Seriously though—how can that be justice? On what scale does this seem like proportional sentencing? It wasn't. That's the Donald Trump touch.

But it isn't just The Donald's influence on the Department of Justice. Disproportionate sentencing is endemic. Often there seems to be no inherent logic in the sentencing of criminals—regardless of sentencing guidelines.

For example, in another case, actor Stoney Westmoreland, the star of Disney's *Andi Mack*, also seen in *Star Trek Voyager*, was sentenced to just two years in federal prison for a sex crime involving a minor. He also had to register as a sex offender.

Still think I'm wrong? Then take a look at Matthew Greene. He is the head of the Proud Boys and a participant in the January 6 insurrection. He faces the same amount of time, or less, behind bars for his accused actions of trying to overthrow the government as Skelos, whose basic crime was helping his kid.

There is no way a man who is being tried for attempting a coup on his government should face less time in prison than a man who was trying to help his son get a paying job.

That's not justice.

The DOJ would do well to remember that disproportionate sentencing *might* encourage other seditious activities if traitors aren't treated more harshly than a septuagenarian who tries to help out his child.

Still having problems seeing it?

Let me walk you through Skelos's case.

Skelos is the former Senate majority leader of New York State and

Ronald Reagan was among his early mentors. An affable man, Skelos gained a reputation for working across the aisle with his Democratic colleagues. In fact on January 14, 2013 he suspended Senate rules to push through the NY SAFE Act (New York Secure Ammunition and Firearms Enforcement Act) of 2013. He led eight other Republicans to work with the state Democratic party and the gun control measure passed 43 to 18. Democratic Governor Andrew Cuomo signed the legislation shortly thereafter.

As good as Skelos was at getting gun control legislation passed, he apparently was horrible at managing his private life—at least when it came to his son Adam.[7] Skelos got 51 months in prison and his son got four years for bribes taken to keep Adam employed. "Skelos was accused of taking official actions to benefit a small Arizona environmental company, AbTech Industries, and a large New York developer, Glenwood Management, that had financial ties to AbTech. According to the complaint, Senator Skelos agreed to do so as long as the companies paid his son,"[8] the *New York Times* reported.

Skelos never personally benefitted from the crime, but what he did was a felony and, unfortunately for the senator, his (and his son's) arrest came when prosecutors were trying to clean up corruption in the New York State legislature. Skelos fit the bill. He went down hard.

Did he screw up? Sure. But he's hardly the first parent who went to extreme lengths to help their child. Again, In NO way does that compare to trying to overthrow the federal government in a failed coup that resulted in death and injury to police officers, Capitol staff as well as the destruction of public property—in this case the U.S. Capitol Building, for God's sake.

You want to really put it in perspective? *Time* Magazine reported

January 6, 2022 on the outcome of those already tried for their part
in the insurrection a year earlier:

> According to the U.S. Attorney's Office for the Dis-
> trict of Columbia, 31 defendants were sentenced to
> periods of incarceration, with longer prison terms for
> those who engaged in violence or threats. So far, the
> median prison sentence for the Jan. 6 rioters is 45 days.
> An additional 18 rioters have been sentenced to periods
> of home detention, while most sentences have included
> fines, community service and probation for low-level
> offenses like illegally parading or demonstrating in the
> Capitol, which is a misdemeanor. [9]

Forty-five days for taking part in a failed violent coup attempt that
cost police officers their lives, versus 51 months for bribing a company
to hire your son and get him off your personal payroll?

This is disproportionate sentencing.

I have no doubt Donald Trump enjoyed the light sentencing of
those found guilty in the insurrection. I'm sure he felt justified and
emboldened by the lack of accountability of his followers who were
found guilty of breaking the law. And I'm as sure of that as I am certain Donald could not relate to making any sacrifices for his children.

Upon my entry into Camp Cupcake, I was immediately assigned to
work at the HVAC Pipe Shop. I worked under the mentorship of correctional officer Mr. Diamond, a very cool guy who shares my love

for racing motorcycles. I enjoy working with my hands and I learned to weld and work on various construction jobs. We rebuilt bathrooms and hung dry wall. Need plumbing? No problem. In one of my first jobs, Mr. Diamond taught me to bend metal which was later used to help build and install my own prison gates.

Prior to my arrival at Otisville, there had never been gates at the entrance of Camp Cupcake. Three months after my arrival, the institution notified me that there had been a hit placed on me. I got called into the lieutenant's office and was told, "We have a significant number of death threats against you, which includes a potential hit on you."

I was surprised, but not shocked. After witnessing the level of insanity—and actions—that Trump could inspire in his followers, it would have been par for the course. In any case, the administration was more concerned about it than I was.

What they feared was that in the middle of the night, with no gates and only one correctional officer in the facility—who was usually sleeping—someone could easily slip inside and kill me; an easy target. Concerned, they offered me the opportunity to be placed in a third section of the facility, the "J" Unit, which is somewhat similar to the satellite camp, but located in a far remote corner of the property. The "J" Unit housed those in the witness protection program. Despite the building being of better construction than where I was housed, and though each inmate got his own room and television, I elected to pass because many of those housed in that facility are gang members and violent criminals. Additionally, you lose access to the outdoors and I wasn't in the mood to stay indoors 24/7 for an untold number of months.

Let me explain. We didn't have a traditional prison yard. We had our building. Then there was the outside. It was just a large piece of property and we often traveled on campus to a variety of locations— sometimes we just walked the grounds for exercise. I even had the opportunity to drive a truck and took my fellow inmates to remote locations on the campus as we did a variety of chores for the prison. Hell, sometimes we got to just drive around the property listening to the radio while enjoying the truck's air conditioning. There was essentially no one guarding us. We were *technically* on our own.

But, after the death threats came, the prison got a little more serious about security—especially when I turned down the offer to relocate to "J" unit. So, the construction team installed the gate. Using the metal I had bent.

Yeah. Figure that one out. I was part of a construction group required to install a gate at Otisville to protect me from potentially violent criminals who weren't residents of the prison but came from *outside* the facility.

Still, I truly enjoyed spending time with some of the other inmates as we worked on various projects—guys like Big Sprinkles, Isaac, and Scream, whose voice was enough to make you want to go deaf. We laughed a lot, worked hard, and used our jobs as a way of forgetting where we truly were.

Did I mention I also did a lot of painting? I painted the whole place during my time there—or close to it. With buckets of white and battleship gray paint, the required colors of BOP facilities. I had the urge one day to sign my work (in gray on white—very tasteful) behind my locker; to leave something for someone to find and remember me by once I left. I was told by my friend Steve, a very-well regarded and admired trustee, to immediately paint over it as it was bad luck. He stated to me that you don't want your name or initials anywhere in this hellhole. You don't want to remember it and you don't want it to remember you. You want to leave, never come back and forget you were ever there.

No truer or more prophetic words were ever said.

So for 13 months I worked, and read 97 books, such as Viktor Frankl's *Man's Search for Meaning* (very therapeutic), *The Splendid and the Vile,* by Erik Larson (historical masterpiece), *The Immortal Life of Henrietta Lacks,* by Rebecca Skloot (incredible book), and *Educated* by Tara Westover (inspiring). I even found the strength to read political books, including John Bolton's *The Room Where It Happened* (horrible book), *Unhinged* by my friend Omarosa Manigault Newman (entertaining), and even *Full Disclosure,* by Stormy Daniels (an eye-opener).

I minded my own business. G. Gordon Liddy, the chief operative in Nixon's Watergate scandal spent time in a D.C. institution. He regularly wrote and spoke about a guy who worked at the pipe shop who constructed a "fighting ring" for him. Those rings are designed with very razored edges and used to create an advantage in prison fights. Those rings usually cost a sizable amount of cigarettes, mackerel, and stamps—common currency in the prison system. Liddy talked about getting his nose deeply cut and broken in his first prison fight, which left him with a lifetime scar.

Camp Cupcake didn't have fighting rings and I witnessed very few altercations. In that respect, I didn't get the Liddy prison experience and I never had to worry about making or selling fighting rings—let alone use one. Disagreements at Camp Cupcake were mostly verbal. On rare occasions they produced a shove here, and maybe a fist thrown there. In fact, during my time in Otisville, I recall only three or four fights which usually had something to do with a gambling debt.

There was also no need for Liddy-style fighting rings because we all had *power* tools at our disposal. Hammers, power drills, and screwdrivers were always available. To check out an item all we had to do was present our prisoner ID card to the correctional officer on duty. Perhaps it was the fear of not getting your ID card back that prevented violent assaults.

After eight months I elected to leave the pipe shop and requested a transfer to the Waste Disposal facility, which was monitored by Mr. Stryker, another absolutely great guy and former Marine. Semper fi! The Waste Disposal facility was also offhandedly referred to as the "Shit House." In essence, I went from the White House to the Shit House—something my fellow inmates reminded me of regularly. It was so clever and so true, I considered it for the original title of my first book.

Do not misunderstand me.

Despite my characterization of Otisville as just a really shitty YMCA Summer camp, the place was hell. I was away from my wife, children, family and friends, and truly hated every second of every minute of every hour of every day of every month I was there. Every inmate felt the same way. Most of us tried to help each other through our shared ordeal.

I kept my nose clean, worked hard, and stayed out of trouble for a very good reason: To pass the time, yes, but also to increase my chances of getting out of prison early. At my sentencing, Judge Pauley stated that I had not cooperated fully with the government during my prosecution and he could not therefore provide me with any credit that would reduce my prison sentence.

One day when my friend and attorney David Schwartz came to visit me, he reminded me of Judge Pauley's public monologue at the end of my sentencing. In it, Pauley stated that while I hadn't cooperated with the government up to that point, he said that should I cooperate in the future, then I could have my counsel request a "Rule 35 motion for reduction consideration."

That's when David suggested I retain Roger Adler, a seasoned New York criminal defense attorney, to pursue the Rule 35 motion. I explained to David that Lanny Davis had visited me several days prior and informed me that he'd been contacted by the Manhattan District Attorney's office, requesting a meeting with me in Otisville and seeking my assistance. I had already provided the Mueller team and nine different Congressional committees in the House and Senate with more than 300 hours of testimony, none of which was acknowledged by Judge Pauley in his scolding of me. He even ignored the historic Mueller Report, and my participation in that investigation. I was cited in the Mueller Report more than anyone else except White House General Counsel Don McGahn. That's why I say Judge Pauley simply ignored the facts—why I wholeheartedly believe he was a willing participant in what I can only call the Department of Injustice.

In any event, getting out of Otisville even one day earlier than my scheduled release date was my goal. So when Lanny visited me at Otisville and presented the option to help the Manhattan District attorney, I took it. By cooperating it would give more ammunition to Roger Adler to insure a favorable outcome in my Rule 35 motion.

Meanwhile, though, don't anyone misunderstand: I was *still* an inmate doing time at Federal Correctional Institution Otisville. And why was I there? I was there because I became the *scapegoat* for Trump's crimes. While Trump was stuffing his face with Mar-a-*Lardo* Burgers and ice cream, I was eating expired food that you wouldn't feed to your dog. While he was occupying the White House, I took up residence in a pre-fab Butler Building consisting of a metal frame covered by aluminum siding. The building, of course, had no insulation—which made weather conditions very severe. You either roasted or froze depending on the weather. During the winter months, my cubicle was generally at 40 degrees, abetted by the fact that the doors had no weather stripping. Over the years, the building had warped leaving one to two inch gaps at the bottom of the doors, through which the weather and vermin found easy ingress and egress. We, the proud residents of Camp Cupcake, lived in a dilapidated tin-can shack. Plain and simple.

Being outside wasn't much better. Spring and summer were easier to cope with and many of us passed the time playing bocce, tennis, and softball. And while that doesn't sound too bad for prison, I assure you it definitely *wasn't* a vacation spot. In fact, many of the inmates would describe their stay in Otisville as mental torture. So let's drop the pretense that incarceration in this country is about anything other than punishment, both physical and mental. The notion of rehabilitation is pure bullshit propaganda created and disseminated by the DOJ to validate incarceration. It is merely human warehousing of individuals so that the Department of Justice can claim that the rest of the country is safe from criminals.

Rest assured that even in a minimum, low security satellite camp like Otisville, the government's goal is to break your spirit and crush your soul. One of the more draconian and barbaric ways they do this is by restricting all outside communication. For example, you are only allowed to purchase 300 telephone minutes a month to speak with family and friends. That's not even 10 minutes a day, and the minutes aren't free—the government adds insult to injury by charging you 25 cents a minute. According to the manual, you are limited to no more than 15 minutes of phone use a day.[10] If you use the maximum number of minutes every day then at the end of 20 days you're done. You can't use the phone again for nearly a week and a half. I went through that experience early on as my daughter was experiencing some minor complications post-hip surgery (you may remember the photographs of her at my sentencing when she was using crutches).

Imagine calling your child who needs fatherly advice to solve a problem—and we all know every child experiences issues daily. Unfortunately you just can't do it—there's just not enough time afforded. Your calls are basically reduced to perfunctory communications. I will acknowledge that some conversation is better than nothing, but at the same time it was a torturous tease. It was just enough to make you understand exactly what you were missing by being behind bars.

Lanny's visit, then, was the thing that gave me hope. He told me that he had personally spoken with Manhattan District Attorney Cyrus Vance, who wanted my permission to send his top brass to speak with me in Otisville.

That was how I came to assist the Manhattan District Attorney at the beginning of the Cyrus Vance criminal investigation into Donald Trump. I hoped it would end with indictments being hand delivered to Trump and other members of the Trump Organization, including

CFO Allen Weisselberg. If pursued to its logical conclusion, then the investigations would result in indictments and expose the corrupt and improper actions of Trump and his organization. It was what Donald feared the most—an independent investigation into him, his company and activities. But, as this book shows, Donald Trump never had to fear a system as corrupt as he—he merely had to figure out how to game it.

And game it he did. He demonstrably showed how a person of power and standing can destroy the chances for the rest of us to be treated fairly and equitably. If you get nothing else from what I'm writing here, understand it plain and clear: Justice in the United States is an *illusion* unavailable to most of us.

At the time, however, I was still hoping justice might show up, blind or otherwise. Remember I had been living five months in a tin can so I thought, well, what the hell do I have to lose. And so I agreed to talk to the prosecutors.

While I walked the track outside, somberly thinking about the proposition, I remained guarded because of how I had been treated and improperly incarcerated in the first place. So it wasn't an easy thing to agree to cooperate. In fact, my close colleagues in prison chimed in asking how was I going to end up better by assisting the Manhattan district attorney? Another raised the question why would I assist any additional investigation into Trump or anyone else after being railroaded by the system in the first place?

These questions all went through my head as I took a day of sober reflection to weigh the pros and cons, but in the end, I accepted the meeting request, because I wanted to honor my promise to my family and my country, as well as to continue to tell the true story about this case. Even though I was in prison green, cut off from the outside world, I believed that the information I could provide would help hold Trump accountable for his actions and stop his engineered destruction of our democracy. The Manhattan DA, it seemed, believed it as well.

It quickly became apparent within minutes of our first meeting, that the prosecutors wanted to get hold of Trump's tax returns. It was there I could provide some solid assistance and did. The prosecutors believed the tax returns would corroborate the answers I'd given to their questions. That meeting required me to be escorted to the medium facility building, a place that every camper wanted to avoid. At the time I was under nearly constant surveillance, so even when I met for more than five hours with prosecutors, at least one member of the Otisville staff had to be present.

When the prosecutors arrived they were very pleasant. I was less so—hard to believe, I know.

"Explain to me the benefit of me assisting you in anything since I find the Department of Justice to be the most corrupt group of individuals I've ever met?" I asked them. "You lied about me. You prosecuted me off of lies. You got people to lie about me."

I mean, there I was sitting in my prison greens and they were sitting there in suits.

The simple answer they gave me was, "Our office didn't prosecute you, Mr. Cohen. So, give us a shot."

I sat still for a moment. "You know what?" I replied. "You're right."

They were with the Manhattan district attorney's office, not the federal government, and for a lot of reasons I felt more trust was due to the local guys trying to serve justice—they actually weren't part of the Department of Injustice. So I said yes.

They came with three-ring notebooks, documents, and a lot of questions—and I talked with them. We got to know each other and discussed everything—how the Trump company worked, how money moved and how documents were prepared. I gave them the floor plan for the company. I could tell that this was not going to be the last request to visit or to speak with me, and it wasn't. The sad part was at a time when I couldn't speak with my family for more than five hours a month, again, I was spending more than that in a given day speaking to the assistant DAs who came to visit. I could talk to prosecutors all day long about Donald Trump—but talking to my family for such a length of time about important family concerns? Not a chance. There is no such thing as a level playing field. Period.

Vance's people returned to Otisville two more times; each time drilling down more on the information they needed.

I want to be very clear about my next statement; I don't want Donald Trump or any of the members of his family and inner circle to go to prison out of revenge. I don't want them to be prosecuted and convicted because I despise him or fundamentally disagree with most everything that comes out of his mouth. I want him to stand before a judge in a court of law for crimes we all know he has committed. I want him to face an indictment and I want him prosecuted *based on those crimes*. If that doesn't happen, then we further disintegrate faith in the justice department—and prove the Republicans correct. Some people are above the law. After I was sent to prison, Trump's press secretary Sarah Huckabee Sanders stood in the Brady Briefing Room of the White House and told reporters that no one is above the law. Donald Trump continues to put that to the test.

While I worked with the Manhattan DA's office, Roger Adler was drafting the Rule 35 motion which sought my release. Not only had I previously provided more than 300 hours of cooperation to nine different agencies, but now I was assisting the Manhattan DA as well. If I don't deserve a Get Out of Jail Free card, shouldn't I at least get a Get Out of Jail *EARLY* card?

Judge Pauley didn't trust me, but you know who did?

Robert Mueller trusted me. His investigation went on for months and he specifically commented on my testimony before the Mueller Committee as being "truthful and accurate and relevant" to his investigation. The Senate Select Committee, the House Committee on Intelligence, the attorney general and the Senate Judiciary Committee all acknowledged that the information I provided them was truthful, accurate, and corroborated by documentary evidence, as well as by corroborating witness statements.

On December 11, 2019 Roger Adler filed the Rule 35 motion asking for a reduction of my three-year prison term to one year and one day. The motion outlined my case, how I pled guilty and the salient background facts of the case. What's more, it noted:

> Upon information and belief, Defendant Cohen has fully paid the resulting tax obligation encompassed in the five tax counts, received no money (nor caused the lender to experience any loss) on the "line of credit," and acted as the conduit for payments to "Stormy Dan-

iels" to secure "confidentiality agreements" on behalf of Donald J. Trump to silence salacious intimate encounters allegedly involving women with whom President Trump was involved.[ll]

It also addressed the "campaign finance" counts against me:

> COHEN is, Your Affirmant notes, not alleged to have been a Trump Campaign official, or employee charged with the legal responsibility to report not a monetary donation, but what Acting United States Attorney Robert Kuzami viewed to be an "in kind contribution," whose Trump Campaign Treasurer omission of them was perceived to be willfully violative of the federal election law.
>
> The Government hewed to this View even as President Trump's decision, to make monetary amends with porn star "Stormy Daniels," was focused as much (if not more) on preserving his marriage from a potentially devastating charge of serial philandering/ Penal Law adultery (Penal Law Section 255.17) than targeted campaign strategizing.
>
> Notwithstanding Defendant Cohen's plea, the Government's ardor to fully clean the proverbial Trump Organization "Augean stables," and, in turn, hold the "Trump Campaign" Treasurer Donald McGahn, Ms. Hope Hicks (whom Trump consulted concerning the "Stormy Daniels" payments), a Trump Campaign me-

dia leader, or the "Trump Organization" (which effectively funded the subject settlement. Upon information
and belief, Donald McGahn, Esq. (who later became
White House counsel) was the Trump Campaign's
designated campaign Treasurer. He was not, however,
criminally charged with filing inaccurate campaign reports with the REG.[12]

I made 90 different points in the pleading. I recounted prosecutor
Tom McKay's reticence in searching for the truth and how his un-
willingness to pursue a case against Donald Trump was an injustice
done to everyone in this country. I called out Bill Barr for acting as
the president's new consigliere and I called out the president too in
the very last point made in the pleading:

> Like the character "Mayhem" in the auto insurance ad,
> the President has a combustible governing style, and a
> fondness for litigation unparalleled in U.S. history. The
> refusal to support a Rule 35 is a Trumpian response
> which should be seen for what it is. Like Orwell's "Ani-
> mal Farm," some are more equal than others, and any-
> one who cooperates is a "rat."

In the last point in the filing, I asked for a public hearing. That's
because I knew that in an open hearing there would be transparency
about my efforts to assist the government.

But the government just didn't care. Judge Pauley didn't want to listen. Remember what he had said upon my sentencing, "You made the plea for leniency for the anticipated cooperation you were going to continue to give. I cannot give you credit for something you have not done, but if you do, your lawyer is fully aware of a Rule 35 motion that would be taken into consideration."

Now, he said that the prosecutor had to make the request to the court, not my attorney. That's not the way most people, including my attorneys, read the statute. And, as some rightly pointed out in the media, the court's ruling against me "is truly indicative of how little bargaining power a cooperating defendant has against DOJ. It's not a fair fight."[13]

But this was hardly news. I had faced an uphill battle since the FBI raided my offices and home. I was a public pariah. As CNN noted,

> Before reporting to prison in May, Cohen asked top Democrats on three congressional committees to write letters to federal prosecutors outlining his cooperation in private and public testimony in hopes of reducing his sentence and delaying the start date. Cohen's lawyers said he needed additional time to review newly discovered files. None of the lawmakers responded to his request.[14]

One of the biggest questions I've faced, and it's a fair one, is: Would I still be in the Donald Trump cult if I hadn't paid for my experience with time in prison? On the one hand, it isn't hard extricating yourself from the cult of Donald Trump. All you have to do is tell the truth and piss him off. But otherwise, it is extremely difficult, as demonstrated by the actions of so many of his GOP sycophants. Had I not been thrown under the bus, I cannot, with any honesty, say that I would be out of the cult of Trump. But what I can emphatically state is that I would not be touting the bulk of the statements Donald Trump has spewed. I wouldn't be touting his agenda of racist, sexist, misogynistic, xenophobic, homophobic, Islamophobic and anti-Semitic crap that has further divided this country.

This I am certain of and I hope that's explanation enough.

Whatever the extent of my deprogramming, though, seemed immaterial to the Court. Those who knew Judge Pauley said he thought I was a common criminal and a danger to my country. So be it. But if that's the case, then justice wasn't on his mind. It was revenge.

Still, while the government didn't feel a pressing need to help me, they continued to seek my assistance—which I freely gave. I continued to help out the Manhattan district attorney's office.

There were some in the DOJ who were shocked that I said yes initially, and then were shocked again after I continued to help following my poor treatment by the SDNY and Judge Pauley. After all, there was no benefit in it for me. "I was surprised. I wouldn't have done it," a member of the DOJ later explained. But in the end, some at the Department of Justice got it. "A guy accused of being a scumbag lawyer for Trump showed more respect for the law than most . . ." a member of the DOJ explained to us on background. "Maybe it was revenge, but he did the right thing even when it didn't directly benefit him to do so."[15] The cynics among us might say I did so to curry favor. But when none came and I continued to help out the prosecution, then you really can't make that argument.

My time with the prosecutors was productive, I thought. So did they. In fact the only reason why they didn't visit me in prison more often was that the Covid pandemic broke out and no one was allowed in the facility.

The BOP decided to combat the spread of Covid in the prison by placing us in solitary confinement. We were put in a building that wasn't even supposed to be open—a building known as E-A, which was actually closed and slated to undergo full renovation. But it got pressed into service for the denizens of Camp Cupcake during Covid.

I was there for a grand total of 51 days on two different occasions—36 straight days the first time, and 15 the second. Let me tell you, if you want to break someone, if you want to humiliate them, if you want to torture them, then solitary confinement is an excellent way to arrange it. It's misery.

I was in an 8 by 10 concrete slab room that contained a toilet, a sink, a small locker for my personal toiletries, a desk, a plastic chair and a bed. The toilet was broken and didn't flush. The sink was in no better shape than the toilet. The floors and everything else were filthy when I got there. What made my 15-day stay there the most difficult was the fact that the window was also broken—it couldn't be opened or closed and a piece of glass was missing. The window was located directly above the bed.

Because Otisville is at the top of a mountain in upstate New York, the weather is extreme. The room I was in reached temperatures of 100 degrees. There was no air conditioning, and no ventilation—unless you count the broken window. Whenever it rained I got a free shower because of the missing glass in the window. Also, flies? I shared my room with hundreds.

All my requests for a piece of plastic and a piece of tape were ignored.

The flies and the weather were my most frequent visitors, but every third day you were at least permitted to make a 15-minute phone call. In the 51 days I spent in solitary confinement, I was only allowed to change clothes once. You only showered Monday, Wednesdays and Fridays, despite the fact the temperature was over 100 degrees and inside my hot box there was no real ventilation—just the aforementioned very friendly flies. They were the type that flew in voluminous clouds together and while they were social among themselves, they never got along with me. I was denied the request to place plastic over the window to keep my new flying roommates from taking over the place.

Eventually, it occurred to me to use a T-shirt to stuff the hole in the window to keep them out. Fortunately, it worked.

What got me out of prison early was not Judge Pauley seeing the error of his ways, but the pandemic, combined with some ongoing health issues I had. As it turns out, the Department of Justice had one soft spot—they didn't want me to actually die in prison because of Covid. (Although it would've made Trump happy.) I don't think it was because they cared about me at all. I think it was because Covid was a snowballing political as well as health care problem for them and they were avoiding lawsuits. As a March 7, 2022 NPR report put it, the BOP had a problem because prisons were "a petri dish for COVID-19," and "health experts said the most effective way to deal with that problem was to make the prison population much smaller—and quickly."[16]

Of course, the Bureau of Prisons initially lied about the Covid threat inside the nation's prisons. The same NPR story reported that the BOP initially downplayed the danger to its staff and inmates, with one correctional officer saying, "I don't trust anything the Bureau of Prisons says. We've had places catch on fire with COVID."[17]

I had Roger Adler petition the court to grant me home confinement. Our letter got some attention:

> MANHATTAN (CN) – Skewering the U.S. response to the coronavirus pandemic, the president's convicted former lawyer Michael Cohen asked a federal judge Tuesday to give him home confinement.
>
> "In absence of presidential leadership, judges should act thoughtfully and decisively," attorney Roger Bennet Adler said in a brief letter on Cohen's behalf. "President Trump apparently does not subscribe to President Harry Truman's observation 'The buck stops here.'"
>
> Just this past Friday, Trump washed his hands of any fault for widespread lack of testing for the COVID-19 pandemic or weeks of minimizing its threat.
>
> "I don't take responsibility at all," Trump told reporters at the Rose Garden.
>
> Cohen, however, pointed a finger at the man for whom he was once a trusted attorney and fixer.

"This letter seeks to focus my pending application on a sentence modification as a consequence of the Bureau of Prisons being demonstrably incapable of safeguarding and treating B.O.P. inmates who are obligated to live in close quarters and are at enhanced risk of catching coronavirus," Adler wrote.[18]

Adler, of course, was his usual colorful self. He closed with this:

We request the Court to seek appropriate input from the Federal Bureau of Prisons documenting the absence of hand sanitizer and the actual living arrangements which Otisville Camp inmates are required to reside in. The six-foot distancing directed by Dr. Fauci and others is simply not being followed. Mr. Cohen has had two hospitalizations, and a pre-existing condition of pulmonary issues. I reiterate my belief that the coronavirus provides a basis for an appropriate modification of the venue in which his previously imposed sentence will be served, and that the sentence of 36 months should not end up being a capital crime depriving my client of his life.[19]

Meanwhile, my health concerns in such an environment were real. I have long-standing respiratory issues as a direct result of a Deep Vein Thrombosis (DVT) which caused a series of pulmonary embolisms that nearly ended my life when I was 39 years old.

After arriving at Camp Cupcake I developed high blood pressure because of the absolutely insane levels of salt in the food at Otisville. Donald Trump never gave me high blood pressure. He drove me nuts. He pissed me off. But it was being sentenced to Otisville that did me in on that count. In fact I was hospitalized twice out of fear from the nursing staff that I would stroke out because of my blood pressure.

My hospitalization was a scary but sobering experience. In the end, I guess you could say the pandemic helped save my life; that and Doctor Linley and Nurse Anne Stewart. Without those two I would have either finished out my imprisonment in the hospital or died there.

Nurse Stewart was my personal guardian angel. She really kept me alive—from regulating my blood pressure multiple times a day to keeping me from jumping off a fucking roof. And she advocated for my release, out of fear that I would contract Covid inside the prison. The BOP and I were lucky to have her and everyone under her care is lucky to have her still.

Still, I almost didn't make the cut. The prison gathered us together to place us in solitary confinement for 14 days of isolation, and then to be released pursuant to the CARES act. My name was the last one called—along with a snide remark from the prison official who said my name. "He shouldn't be getting this, but he's going home too," he said in front of a group of inmates.

I had reported to Otisville May 6, 2019. I was released a year later on May 21, 2020, to serve the rest of my sentence under house arrest.

The big news on the day that I was released was about Covid, as it had been for months. My story was lumped in with Paul Manafort's early release as proof that I was given preferential treatment. "Michael Cohen is just the latest well-connected federal prisoner to be sent home early because of the coronavirus, even though he has served only a third of his sentence," said the Marshall Project, which reports about the justice system."[20] What a joke.

I had been out of prison for about two months and was working hard to get re-acclimated to civilian life, not wearing prison greens and eating salt licks which passed for food. I thought I could relax and start to reclaim my life. I was working on my book *Disloyal*, and thought the worst was behind me.

I was wrong—again.

Toward the end of June 2020, I received a call from a Mr. Patrick Gill at GEO Reentry Services, a third party contractor for the Bureau of Prisons that helps administer paroles. He told me to go to an office in the Bronx where I would go through a process, sign a few documents, and then the people from the probation department would visit my home, check things out and fit me with an ankle monitor.

The day before this was to happen my probation officer, Adam Pakula, called me and told me I was to report to 500 Pearl Street in Manhattan—the Federal Courthouse—instead of the first address I was given.

Right away, I knew something was amiss.

I had actually been looking forward to getting the ankle monitor because I knew there would be little chance of me returning to prison as long as I followed the in-home incarceration rules. I would be in the probation system for real.

I explained to Pakula that someone from GEO had already instructed me to report to the Bronx. Pakula insisted that I had to go downtown to the Pearl Street office.

Well, I naturally called the first guy, Mr. Gill, who said he'd never heard of anything like this in the 30 years he's been doing his job at Geo. I gave him Pakula's phone number; he called Pakula, then called me back.

"I can't do anything about it," he said. I had to go to Pearl Street.

I immediately called Jeffrey Levine, an attorney who'd been my friend since we were in our teens. When I told him what was going on, he became as concerned as I was. So he called Pakula himself, and after their conversation Jeff was even more concerned than I was. The government wasn't following established protocol. As Jeff explained later in a court declaration, "I asked Probation Officer Pakula why the USPO (the US Probation Office), rather than GEO, would be monitoring Mr. Cohen. . . . Probation Officer Pakula stated that he could not give me any additional insight into why this occurred and that he would not comment."

The government had called an audible, changed the location of my meeting, wouldn't meet me in my home and also wouldn't provide an advanced copy of the standard form agreement they expected me to sign—a Federal Location Monitoring (FLM) Agreement. All of these actions violated normal protocol. I knew it, Mr. Gill knew it, and the DOJ knew it.

As Jeff said in his declaration, "Minutes after my call with Probation Officer Pakula, he sent me an email to advise that he was not authorized to release the paperwork prior to the meeting. I did not view this with any concern because I fully expected Mr. Cohen to be provided the opportunity to review, discuss, and ultimately execute the FLM Agreement as the next step in finalizing his home confinement."

Jeffrey also said, "I didn't understand why we couldn't just meet at Michael's apartment and get everything done there," he later explained.

That's a good question, especially since standard protocol dictated that's exactly how nearly every other case was handled—in the home.

We found out what the DOJ was secretly up to when we arrived at Pearl Street the following morning, Thursday, July 9, 2020.

Things weren't right from the very beginning. There were already reporters hanging around outside the place. Friends of mine in the media later confirmed some of them had been given a heads-up that I would be appearing that morning. I don't know if any of them knew what was in store that day. I sure didn't. Jeffrey Levine didn't. We just had our suspicions that something was wrong and it turned out we were right.

As Jeff later recalled:

> I didn't trust the government. So we went down that morning. There was press at the front. I don't know how they knew we were there. It was the morning when Trump had an adverse ruling in the Supreme Court. The press said "what do you think of the Trump ruling?" Michael said, "We'll talk about that when we get out."

We waited and one of the probation officers came out in a mask and took us back to Enid Febus [Supervisory Probation Officer of the United States Probation and Pretrial Services, and Adam Pakula's immediate supervisor]—who wore no mask in a closed window office. Adam Pakula sits down and takes off his mask. They know who he [Cohen] is and his risk profile. So both of them are sitting in a room with no masks, and we looked at each other and didn't take our masks off. They were setting the stage. They were in control and it went downhill from there.

They didn't waste any time. Pakula—a young guy in a cheap suit who looked like a climber, now involved in the most significant case he'll ever touch—handed me the FLM agreement to sign before they would fit me with the ankle monitor. Febus looked more concerned than Pakula, for some reason. Despite her look, she was strangely adamant in telling me that the document and procedure being implemented was "absolutely routine."

It was a two page document with eight provisions. And as I read it I knew: This wasn't routine. It wasn't normal. In fact, the document didn't even have the required federal reference number all such documents are required to include.

Right off the bat, for example, the first paragraph: "No engagement of any kind with the media, including print, TV, film, books, or any form of media/news. Prohibition from all social media platforms. No posting on social media and a requirement that you communicate with friends and family to exercise discretion in not posting on your behalf or posting any information about you." And elsewhere, in case I missed the point: "Mr. Cohen must comply with bureau policies, including requirements that he consent to electronic monitoring and obtain approval for any media interviews."[21]

I had to ask for approval to talk to reporters? That's a textbook example of prior restraint. It's a violation of the First Amendment. This clause even issued prior restraint against my "friends and family"!

What's more, it censored me from publishing the book I'd just written, *Disloyal*. I had recently tweeted out that I was anticipating its publication in the fall, and I'd informed Pakula about it, too, just a few days before. And, by the way, the tweet and the response it got (I had over 600,000 followers at the time) shows without a doubt that people in the executive branch—specifically the president—knew I was writing a book.

This was revenge, plain and simple.

I was in shock at the extremity of it all, but I managed to point out that this was a violation of my First Amendment rights before Jeff intervened and tried to reason with them, asking if we could discuss some modifications. But they said those were the conditions. I tried to be polite—I said I knew they were just doing their job—but I couldn't help asking if the provision censoring me had been drafted specifically for me?

They both denied that, saying it was a standard form.

I knew a Trump move when I saw one. That's when I said that I felt like I was being treated differently, and that provision seemed crafted specifically for me. "And it was probably drafted in Washington," I added. "The next time you speak to Attorney General Bill Barr, tell him I say hello." That's also when Febus lied and said I was wrong—that there was nothing special about the form. Maybe she later had a guilty conscience. Who knows? I do know she retired and left public service a very short time later.

To be clear, I *didn't* refuse to sign the agreement at that time—as Jeff would later testify—but I did try to negotiate it with them. I explained that if I signed it then I'd be in immediate violation of the order, as I already had written the book and spoken with the media. They said, they could put that aside for the time being and we could go over the other paragraphs. I could nitpick the remaining eight points, and I have to admit I was concerned about not being able to go shopping at my local grocery store, but Jeffrey convinced me to let those things go and I agreed in principle to sign the agreement—if we could make a few changes to only the first paragraph so that it didn't violate my First Amendment rights.

"Give us some time so that we can go back to our superiors and see if we can alter some of this language to make it acceptable," Febus said. Pakula agreed. I thanked them. So did Jeffrey and they told us it would be about an hour. Mind you, my son had driven us downtown and was downstairs in the car waiting to drive me home to get the monitor attached. After waiting about 45 minutes I asked if I could use their phone, because you're not allowed to bring your phone in the building and I wanted to call my son and let him know we were delayed. They granted me one call and I told my son this was looking like it would take a while. He should go get some lunch.

They wouldn't even let us leave to go get a bottle of water.

I didn't know what would happen next. After an hour, Jeffrey went up to the door and knocked on it and asked if we could get an update. At that time there were only two of us in this heavily secure waiting room, and we were stuck watching NY1 news. I think Al Sharpton was on, protesting something. I wished I could've been there with him.

Jeffrey asked Pakula what was going on. Pakula had said he had not heard back from his people yet about any changes in the agreement. "We're waiting the same as you. Just sit tight," he told us.

According to the statement he made later before the court, Pakula was actually reaching out to pass the buck. He told his superiors, "Given Cohen's intransigence, Supervisory Probation Officer Febus and I decided to contact the BOP to find out how it wished to proceed."

A few minutes later three marshals arrived wearing bullet proof vests and carrying handcuffs and shackles. At first glance they looked like a tactical squad ready to breach the perimeter. However, there were only two of us in the waiting room and we certainly offered no threat of violence. But Jeffrey sensed something about their presence and so did I. "I hope they're not for you," Jeffrey said. "Knowing what's going on I wouldn't be surprised," I replied.

Sure enough, they were there for me.

They told me to stand up and face the wall.

"What for?" I asked.

"Stand up and face the wall," they said again.

"Why?" I asked quietly.

"You're being remanded. Give your coat, your wallet, your belt and watch to your attorney. You're being remanded." I was told.

At that point Pakula and Febus came out of their office with the remand order. They hadn't been waiting to hear from their superiors.

They'd been putting together documents to remand me back to prison based on my questioning their conditions of in-home incarceration. "We haven't refused," Jeffrey said. "We're negotiating right now."

"Sorry, we're just doing our jobs," the lead marshal said. I couldn't believe what was happening. Jeff started yelling, "Give us the papers we'll sign them."

But they refused.

"It's too late," Pakula told us with a grin. The SOB actually grinned. "It's out of our hands. We're not involved anymore."

They took my jacket, wallet and belt and set them aside, then handcuffed and shackled me. Jeff protested.

"I told them there was no reason for this," he said later. "We were in a closed environment. There was no need to treat him that way. I was trying to be reasonable. We were on the fifth floor of a secured building."

But reason wasn't in the offing for me that day. It was about the press seeing me in shackles. It was about belittling me, humbling me, embarrassing me and ultimately breaking me. They accomplished that last task. They broke me. I was in total shock.

Luckily, Jeff kept his wits about him and sprang into action. He grabbed my personal belongings and raced out of the building to call the head counsel for the Bureau of Prisons. "I just starting working my way up the ladder," he explained. "One guy didn't call me back for five months. Everyone denied knowledge of what was going on, so with time running out I went to the press." He told the assembled reporters—many of whom had been called by the government—that, "They've got him." Meaning me.

Jeff then ran off to the Metropolitan Detention Center in

Brooklyn, where he'd been told I was going to be taken first. When he didn't find me there, he returned to Manhattan, apparently followed by a press caravan. In Manhattan the gatekeeper at the prison told Jeff no one was there. No one could help him.

As he later recalled, Jeff was beyond frustrated:

> In the back of my mind I knew Trump was behind all of this. What other conclusion could I draw than that Trump had his hand in this? Take a look at the evidence. Manafort got out. He had far more than 18 months left on his sentence. Manafort was in Trump's pocket, and he got out. My client is against Trump and he's the higher health risk. And they throw him back in.

Meanwhile, nobody—not Jeff, not Lanny Davis, or Laura and the kids—knew where I was.

They told me I was going to the Metropolitan Detention Center in Brooklyn, marched me to the basement parking lot, and placed me in a car. Then they left me handcuffed and shackled in the back seat of the parked car for about twenty minutes. Then they removed me from the car, still in handcuffs and shackles. I was dazed and confused. They paraded me from one location to another, telling me to face the wall or stand for a photograph, more fingerprinting . . . I felt like a blindfoldeded kid being spun around in a pin-the-tail-on-the-donkey game from hell. I believe this was all in the subterranean depths of Pearl Street, but I couldn't tell you where. Eventually I found myself back in the detention facility.

They made me put on a paper-thin jump suit and stuck me in a holding cell that was like a refrigerator—I'm guessing it was around 40 degrees—and left me there for hours. No food. No water. I was so cold. The air conditioning left the top of my head frozen, and my teeth chattering so uncontrollably I thought they were going to fall out of my mouth. Everything hurt. Finally after several hours they brought me a frozen peanut butter sandwich.

Eventually they took me out of the refrigerated cell and brought me outside the holding area into the hallway. It was warmer there and I was so thankful for that. I was dazed and confused from the chain of events as well as from the air conditioning. Then I see these two guys, correctional officers, who looked familiar. I thought I was hallucinating until one of them said, "Michael, come over here."

I looked at them.

"Cohen, come here, we're taking you back to Otisville."

That's where I knew them from.

We reached the prison at 10:45 p.m. that night—45 minutes after the evening head count, so I had to be held in the "SHU"—a segregated housing unit.

The next day they put me back in solitary confinement.

I share this story with you not to make you feel sorry for me, but to illustrate the depths the DOJ can be manipulated into sinking to in an authoritarian presidency.

Needless to say, I did not take this lightly. I didn't accept it at all. But . . . like I had a choice?

My wife Laura found the perfect attorney to attack the remand. Danya Perry is a marathon runner and runs a high-powered law firm on the side. For 11 years she worked as an assistant United States attorney for the Southern District of New York. Few lawyers know their way around the system like Danya. (By coincidence, a year later she would also be Michael Avenatti's attorney in his first criminal trial—the Nike extortion trial.)

For her part, Danya was struck by my conditions when she heard about my situation at Otisville.

"I remember his description so clearly," she recalled later. "It was 100 degrees. Michael was in horrific shape. He wasn't allowed out of his cell and he had significant underlying health problems. Laura was legitimately concerned for his life."

Then there was the case against me.

"Very quickly I saw that the government had over-reached," Danya told us for this book. "A first year law student could see it." And Danya also saw the taint and stench of Donald Trump in the case. "At the end of the day I'm certain it went to the highest levels and given the open borders between the DOJ and the White House—Donald Trump went out of his way to threaten and ridicule Michael Cohen. It would surprise me if he *weren't* aware of this."

(By the way, she was right—I would later hear from reporters and others that members of Trump's inner circle bragged about putting me back in prison.)

She filed a writ of habeas corpus and an emergency restraining order.

After filing, Danya offered a written response to the government's disingenuous reasons for remanding me to Otisville, noting in particular that the government was throwing up a smokescreen because they couldn't defend the First Amendment violation: "Unable to defend their position on the constitutional issue that is at the fore-front, Respondents instead raise several factual issues as distraction," she wrote.[22]

She was right on target. She got it. "Distraction." In Trumpland we called it "deflection." That's all the government had. Lies and mis-direction. And you're trying to tell me Donald Trump had nothing to do with my remand? That's his fingerprint. Bullshit. Lies. Distortion. Deflection. The moves the government made are more than a vindi-cation for me, they're an indictment of and prima facia evidence of a Department of Justice that has been commandeered by the president of the United States to be used as his own personal billy club.

In a declaration Danya made in support of my release, she told the court that on July 12—two days after we'd hired her—she had reached out via email to Thomas McKay and Nicolas Roos, who had been responsible for the prosecution of my criminal case. She also spoke to them by phone. As she said, "My purpose in reach-ing out . . . was to share with them my conviction that the Bureau of Prisons had violated Mr. Cohen's First Amendment rights by re-manding him to the Federal Correctional Institution, Otisville, after he had questioned a condition of his home confinement that would have operated as a blanket gag order."

The next day she wrote a letter following up with McKay. "I was invested with a great sense of urgency," she said, "because Mr. Cohen was unlawfully in solitary confinement and was suffering badly . . . due to his significant medical issues and his horrific conditions of confinement."

She also pointed out how the Department of Justice was bullshit-ting everyone by claiming they had no idea I was writing a book:

While he was at Otisville, and consistent with BOP regulations, Mr. Cohen was permitted to work on his book. *See* BOP Program Statement on Inmate Manuscripts § 551.81 (permitting inmates to prepare manuscripts for publication while in custody without staff approval). Indeed, there was significant publicity around the fact that Mr. Cohen was working on his book while at Otisville. [23]

The DOJ had also included, in its list of reasons to send me back to prison, that my wife and I had gone out to dinner at a restaurant— we had, to a restaurant on my block where we dined on the sidewalk with another couple who were some of our closest friends. And so what? There was no rule saying I couldn't leave the apartment.

But nothing I did would look good in the eyes of Donald and the corrupt DOJ. They didn't want me on social media. They didn't want me to work. They didn't want me to write a book. And they didn't want to see me anywhere in public. Donald Trump wanted me gone.

So Danya spelled it out for McKay:

Mr. Cohen was in prison for 13 months, of which he served the last 35 days in solitary confinement, desperately alone. On a human level, he was understandably eager to visit with, on a very limited basis and close to his apartment, a select few close and trusted friends, once it was safe to do so. He was responsibly following federal, state and local guidelines, all of which point to the safety of such outdoor meetings, particularly with trusted companions who may form a so-called "isolation pod." Indeed, the Cohens and their friends decided to dine at an outdoor restaurant rather than in their apartment precisely because it is safer to do so. The vanishingly low risk of this activity cannot seriously be compared to the grave, known risk he faces once again in the viral vector that is our prison system. [24]

Despite Danya's concerns, McKay had none for my health and said the BOP lawyer who could decide to reverse the decision remanding me to Otisville, "did not have a timeline for when such a decision would be made."

Danya had enough and on July 18 informed McKay, "We intend to seek judicial intervention on Monday if we are not able to resolve the outstanding issues."[25]

She filed a writ of habeas corpus and an emergency restraining order.

Shortly thereafter, the ACLU filed an amicus brief in support. Vera Eidelman, Arianna Demas, and Brian Haus filed a memorandum of law that pointed out how I was released because of my health concerns and how, after I announced I planned to publish a book, (including posting a tweet with the hashtag #WillSpeakSoon, on June 26) I was "remanded into custody for questioning a surprise gag order."

"Honestly, it didn't take a legal scholar to figure this one out," a spokesperson for the ACLU explained to us on background for this book. "This was in-your-face fuckery."

Speaking of which, Audrey Strauss, the acting U.S. Attorney for the Southern District of New York had also filed a brief, saying,

Petitioner's contention that he was not placed on home confinement on July 9, 2020, in retaliation for a book that he is planning to publish that is critical of the President of the United States is not supported by the evidence . . . the evidence instead shows that Petitioner, who had been released from prison on furlough, was remanded into custody on July 9, 2020, because he was antagonistic during a meeting with probation officers at which he was supposed to sign the agreement that would have allowed him to complete the remaining portion of his criminal sentence in-home confinement.

Ten days after Danya filed, on July 23, 2020, we got a zoom hearing before the Honorable Alvin K. Hellerstein, Senior U.S. District Judge of the SDNY.

I wasn't there, obviously—I was shvitzing in solitary confinement—but what follows is from the court transcript. According to Assistant U.S. Attorney Allison Rovner, I *was not* sent back to jail because I was writing a book. She said I was tossed back because I *refused* to sign a gag order—I don't know if she was saying what she was told to say, but that was a lie. She also said I was rude and belligerent—another lie, as Jeff, who was a witness, testified. Rovner's also denied that anyone from the executive branch, "let alone a high-level official with any motive to prevent the release" of my book, made the decision to send me back to prison.[26]

Rovner made a particular point of underscoring how hostile the government found my behavior during this entire process. She said Pakula called me "combative" and she referred to "the totality of

Mr. Cohen being combative . . ." What's more, to hear the prosecutor tell it, no one in the government had any idea that I was writing a book—despite the amazing coincidence that they wanted me to sign a gag order preventing me from doing so.

Judge Hellerstein questioned the portrayal of either Jeff Levine or me as "combative" with government employees the day they illegally remanded me. It was a negotiation. "Why couldn't something like that be a subject of negotiation with an attorney? What's an attorney for if he's not going to negotiate an agreement with his client?" he asked.

Which only made sense. But it was a lie that had the stench of Donald Trump all over it. I worked for him. I know how it's done.

I mean, really? I was "antagonistic" to a probation officer? Look, I know I can be combative. I have not been called a pit bull of a lawyer for nothing. I have also admitted my regret over some instances of my bullying in this book and in *Disloyal*. But I wasn't like that in my meeting with Pakula and Febus. It was a serious meeting, I was in the middle of the most humbling experience of my life, and the stakes were high. I kept my wits about me, as Jeff Levine said I did, and I had every right to ask the questions that I did over such a blatant violation of my First Amendment rights.

Hell, I even agreed to sign the order—no matter what! But, as Jeff testified, "They wouldn't hear of it. It was predetermined that Michael was going back to prison the moment he walked into the office on Pearl Street."

They had no plans to turn me loose once I walked through the door that day. They had lured me there for arrest.

So, who pulled Pakula's and Febus' strings? They were low on the totem pole. They couldn't have made the decision themselves.

We know they reached out to Patrick McFarland, their immediate supervisor, because he signed the remand order. But how did he come to make that decision? You think a career mid-level public servant makes that kind of decision? At the time I was the highest profile prisoner in the system. I was the former personal attorney for the president of the United States. One unapproved move by McFarland would be his last. Follow the bread crumbs.

Jon Gustin, the administrator for the Federal Bureau of Prison's Residential Reentry Management Branch (RRMB), works out of the BOP in Washington D.C.—a stone's throw from the White House. He declared that he didn't review the unique agreement Febus and Pakula tried to get me to sign. He said McFarland did, and that he concurred with its terms.

In his testimony, Gustin stuck with the lie that I was antagonistic, and that I had refused to sign the FLM. He also implied that I lied about my health problems and COVID concerns because I "was reportedly seen dining out at Manhattan restaurants on more than one occasion, including on or about July 2, 2020."[27]

And even though he said he hadn't read the FLM, Gustin *owned* the decision to remand me to prison for not signing it. He said he'd contacted Hugh Hurwitz, the assistant director of the Reentry Division, and Gene Beasley, the deputy director of the BOP, and they concurred with him. Even though I said I would sign the agreement, he said, "it likely would not have changed my decision to remand him, given his behavior prior to the appearances of USMS (U.S. Marshals)."

Gustin denied that remanding me had anything to do with my First Amendment rights, and that while everyone knew I was writing a book "Cohen's intent to publish a book thus played no role whatsoever in my decision to remand him." According to him I could work on the book in prison—I just couldn't talk to anybody in the press.

So, who benefitted from me being remanded? Who didn't want me talking to the press? It sure wasn't Gustin or anyone else. Again, follow the bread crumbs.

Judge Hellerstein did exactly that. And he didn't buy anything the government was selling.

"It seems to me that what Mr. Pakula is saying is combative is an attorney's effort to negotiate an agreement, which is very common," he told Rovner. "That doesn't mean that the person won't sign. It means that the attorney is trying to get the best deal possible for his client. And Mr. Cohen was never given a chance to say, 'If this is it, I will sign.'"

As for the FLM they were trying to force upon me to sign, the judge didn't miss a thing. "This document is not vetted in the normal way in the probation office," Hellerstein noted. "It's not part of the forms typically used by the probation office." He especially wasn't buying the infamous first clause, prohibiting me speaking to the press and publishing a book: "I've never seen such a clause. In 21 years of being a judge and sentencing people and looking at the terms and conditions of supervised release, I have never seen such a clause." He asked, "Why would Pakula ask for something like this unless there was a purpose to it, unless there was a retaliatory purpose? How can I take any other inference but that it was retaliatory?"

At that point one of my least favorite tormentors, Tom McKay, tried to jump in. It was obvious the judge wasn't buying the government's bullshit and McKay couldn't keep his mouth shut. "Can I just jump in with a factual point on the timeline?" McKay asked the judge.

"Mr. McKay, is Ms. Rovner not capable of answering my questions?" Hellerstein asked.

"She certainly is, your honor," McKay answered.

"You will keep quiet and if Ms. Rovner wants to consult you, she may. One person speaks on a side."

I would hear later that some of the members of the SDNY cheered the judge's comment.

With scenes like that, Danya Perry hadn't had to do much.

"I'd pulled an all-nighter," she remembered. "I had my notes, I was ready for a robust discussion. Then, you know what? I kept my mouth shut for the most part because it was obvious from the beginning that the judge got it. He grilled the DOJ and they dug their own grave. That hearing went very fast."

On Thursday, July 23, 2020, I had no idea where my life was headed. I was curled up in a hotbox at Otisville, sweating in a room that would be perfect in an Orwellian nightmare. I was trying to remain hopeful, but I really didn't know what was going on. The prison as an institution didn't feel a need to keep me in the loop, so my only connection to the outside world was a sorry excuse for a radio like something from *Gilligan's Island.* The radio worked well enough that even as I sweat out my fate—figuratively and literally—I could listen to NPR occasionally. That was it.

That day, through the static, heat and mind numbing dullness I heard a voice saying, "Michael Cohen had to be released within 24 hours." At first I thought I was hallucinating.

Then they said it again, confirming what I heard the first time: Judge Hellerstein had granted the Perry Motion, ordering that I serve the remainder of my term in home confinement. He'd ordered my immediate release.

I stood up wearing only my boxers, as it was hot as hell, and began to scream.

"YES! YES!" I shouted, thinking I'd get out of there right then. But that's not what happened.

I had to take a Covid test and test negative for it.

I didn't care. How the hell was I going to get Covid in solitary? From one of the gnats and flies in my cell? Not even the QAnon cult believes that to be the case.

My son, who was 20 at the time, drove for the second time up to Otisville to pick up his old man.

That same day, after leaving Otisville, I was required to present myself in the Bronx to get an ankle monitor—as I had originally been ordered to do more than two weeks previously. As I finally arrived home—to find a horde of reporters waiting for me, much as when I had arrived at the prison, except this time calling out prurient and salacious questions about my ordeal—I couldn't help thinking that the last two weeks of my life had been meaningless torture.

But I was finally free. Sure, I was chained to an ugly ankle monitor, but at least I was back home with my wife and children . . .

Seeing my family *was* uplifting, but I still felt violated. Over the next weeks and months I sat in a corner of my apartment lost in thought for more hours than I can remember. I just sat on the floor with every single emotion hitting me all at the same time. Confusion. Anger. Depression. Happiness. Name an emotion, I had it.

For the longest time I couldn't develop a daily routine. Nothing was going on. I just sat at home, or I took walks like a zombie in

Central Park. During those walks, flashes of what happened in the last few months replayed in my head, and snippets of what happened to me stuck firmly in my mind. Try walking around with memories like that. I kept thinking of what the goons who remanded me kept saying: "We're just following orders." That's real Nazi-like shit.

It took me almost a year to process it. In July 2021, I had recovered enough to start taking action.

A CNBC report from July 2, 2021 covered step one: "Former Trump lawyer Michael Cohen moves to sue U.S. for $20 million on claim of prison retaliation for book." [28]

> Michael Cohen, the former personal lawyer and fixer for ex-President Donald Trump, has moved to sue the U.S. government for $20 million on a claim that he was illegally returned to prison last year in retaliation for planning to write a book about Trump.
>
> Cohen, in a notice of claim filed against the U.S. Bureau of Prisons, accuses the government of false arrest, false imprisonment and wrongful confinement.
>
> Cohen, 54, says he suffered "emotional pain and suffering, mental anguish and loss of freedom" from being sent back to a federal prison in July 2020 just weeks after being furloughed early due to concerns over his risk from Covid-19.
>
> Cohen's lawyers are preparing a second claim alleging that then-Attorney General William Barr and BOP Director Michael Carvajal violated his First Amendment right to free speech by returning him to prison. [29]

It was almost exactly a year since Judge Hellerstein had ordered my release, ruling that the purpose of Bill Barr remanding me back to prison "was retaliatory in response to Cohen intending to exercise his First Amendment rights to publish a book critical of the President and to discuss the book on social media."[30]

Thank God he said that in open court.

I got some good and fair coverage for this—most of it, in fact—but I was also getting some unfavorable coverage for my attempt to stand up for the free speech rights of everyone—including, of course, members of the press. It's always interesting to see when those who depend upon free speech to do their job fail to understand when free speech is being lost. It's even more curious when reporters who should know better jump on that bandwagon—never realizing they could and often are the next in line to be steamrolled.

But one thing that Hellerstein had granted me was the ability to speak to the press. So another thing I decided to do was to create a podcast—to keep my brain active, to be productive, and, maybe most importantly, to get the word out about the nonsense going on. I called it "Mea Culpa" in an acknowledgement of my wrongdoing. My first podcast was with Rosie O'Donnell. I also interviewed Anthony Scaramucci, Malcolm Nance, Ben Stiller, Ellie Hoenig, Harry Littman, John Dean, and by the time of the writing of this book I've now interviewed some 200 others. It's also my initials so I figured it had the right meaning.

It took off right away.

But it wasn't enough. Things were still gnawing at me.

"Michael Cohen was a political prisoner in the United States," Danya Perry told us for this book. "And I was moved and concerned for him. 'This is actually going to kill me,' he told me at one point. 'They won't stop until I'm dead.' This wasn't fantastical talk. This wasn't delusional. Michael had a legitimate concern and the government had none for his well-being."

I kept thinking of Judge Hellerstein's observation that the clause keeping me from writing was unique to my case—and yet another example of the Department of Injustice. "I've never seen such a clause in 21 years in being a judge and sentencing people," he'd said.

Think about that for just a second.

Using fictional material to get me investigated; then using an accountant's error to get me to plead guilty; then stuffing me in solitary confinement to break me, the U.S. government had subverted *every single precept of justice.* Trump used his corruption of the government to further his own corruption, and to get me to take the fall for his own misdeed—and to keep me from telling everyone in the country about the injustice that could befall us all.

It was frustrating. It was infuriating. It was illegal. It was unconstitutional.

It was then I determined that such treatment at the hands of the Justice Department meant the DOJ had to be investigated, had to be exposed, and had to be held accountable.

CHAPTER FOUR

HOW MANY ACCOUNTANTS DOES IT TAKE TO SCREW IN A LIGHTBULB?

FOR THOSE WHO HOLD THE KEYS to power it is a game. As George Carlin noted in one of his last standup performances, "They don't care." Those in charge only care about one thing—themselves. They game the system to enhance their lives and use the rest of us as pawns in the game.

So, I pushed back with a series of court actions and inquiries including, but not limited to, Freedom of Information requests about my prosecution, incarceration, and unconstitutional remand. I also sued the U.S. government, the Department of Justice, former President Trump, former Attorney General Bill Barr and others regarding the unconstitutional remand.

I did this to hold them accountable for what they did to me, but also to ensure that these type of actions never happen again.

As one of my attorneys, Andrew Laufer, noted about my lawsuit against Trump, Barr, and federal prison officials,

The complaint outlines a history of retaliation during Trump's presidency, including a June 2020 lawsuit against former national security adviser John Bolton to stop him from publishing a memoir. This is just part and parcel to what the Trump administration represented. They stomped on people's rights, they retaliated against those who fell out of favor, and they just ignored the Constitution and the law. And we intend on having them answer for that.[1]

Laufer also pointed out specific constitutional violations that occurred when the government remanded me, such as the First Amendment violation, but also a Fourth Amendment violation—an unlawful seizure:

They put him in wrist and ankle shackles and put him into custody. They brought him back to Otisville and put him in Solitary. He's got health issues—for which they released him from prison—and now they're bringing him back to prison and they knew it risked his health and could lead to serious illness and death. They were indifferent to his needs.

As I've said, beyond Trump, the Justice Department—Bill Barr in particular—wanted to break me.

So, when Laufer confirmed that he had personally delivered the court papers for my suit to Bill Barr, I was not silent. "Happy New Year Asshole," I tweeted.

The government made a motion to stay discovery until their

motion to dismiss the complaint was heard. And that's where it stands as of the writing of this book.

And this is typical of the government. They simply refuse to comply on any fact-finding informational requests.

While in this case this refusal to provide documentation is specific to me, there are attorneys who make their living trying to pry information from the government. And here's the thing: The government has statutes that cover this. The Freedom of Information Act (FOIA) requires the government to reply in a timely fashion and provide public information at anyone's request. Most of the time it is already determined what is and is not on the public record. There are some topics of contention of course, but by and large the government already knows whether or not the information a citizen requests falls under the Freedom of Information Act—and sometimes the government nonetheless still refuses to provide that information.

In the spring of 2019, soon after getting out of prison, I filed a request for information from the Office of the Inspector General regarding the U.S. Department of Justice's handling of my case.

That first FOIA request we filed asked the Inspector General some very pointed questions:

> The news of Mr. Cohen's remand to Otisville and subsequent release by Judge Hellerstein was widely reported in the media and to that end I am inquiring whether or not an investigation into the facts and circumstances surrounding my client's remand was instigated. If so I am requesting to learn whatever you can share under FOIA. If, on the other hand, no

investigation was undertaken then it is respectfully requested that this be accepted as Mr. Cohen's complaint and request to open an investigation without delay.

To this day, I have yet to receive any materials from this request.

Let's not miss the point: Every person in the country is entitled to whatever information the government has on them. I wasn't asking for a third party—I was asking about myself!

Thankfully, however, I was not alone in this wrestling match.

With the help of the James Madison Project and attorney Mark Zaid, I also filed a Freedom of Information request to pursue information from the DOJ in the preparation of this book. I got delays and denials on that request, too.

And, on July 24, 2020 congressmen Ted Lieu and Hakeem Jeffries wrote the Department of Justice's Office of Inspector General to request the OIG to "investigate the potentially unlawful actions of [Attorney General William] Barr and officials at the Federal Bureau of Prisons in depriving Michael Cohen of his freedom in order to silence him."[2]

This is no small thing.

More importantly it was a major issue taken up by members of *Congress*. You'd think the Department of Justice would respond to the letter from Congressmen as soon as possible.

But that's not what happened.

Michael E. Horowitz, the inspector general, was indeed obliged to answer promptly. But representatives Lieu and Jeffries waited more than a week, then more than a month, then more than a year for Horowitz to respond. That's right. Horowitz waited *18 months* before responding to the government for which he works! When he finally did respond, he didn't address my case specifically, but said the OIG had initiated a "systemic review of the BOP's use of home confinement as a response to the COVID 19 pandemic."[3]

That wasn't the question and that wasn't an answer. Imagine if your boss asked you as a department head if the allegations of beating someone up were real and you responded, "I'll conduct a system-wide investigation to see if we've had any problems since the pandemic started."

You'd be fired. And your boss would be justified in doing it.

Horowitz thumbed his nose at Congress, then added insult to injury in the letter by thanking Congress for its "continued support for my Office."

Horowitz and his office refused several attempts to speak with me for this book.

Doesn't matter. His actions speak for themselves. They need no further explanation.

The system is corrupt.

Part of the reason for this pushback is obvious: the Department of Justice will expose its own guilt by releasing this information. And God knows what else may be in the hundreds of thousands of pages they now admit they have on me.

It's not just my First and Fourth Amendment rights that got trampled. The DOJ doesn't want the world to know exactly how inhumanely and cruelly I and others at Otisville and throughout the penal system are treated. That's also a clear Eighth Amendment violation.

"It was cruel and inhuman," Laufer explained.

> They wanted him to get sick and seriously ill. They didn't have enough space to properly house him. They

took advantage of the situation. Cohen was a prob-
lem. Cohen was an issue because of what he knew of
Trump's activities. He's a political enemy of Donald
Trump. And so, they made him a political prisoner.

So, what did Trump do? He did what most mob bosses do: "He does
whatever he can to make these people as uncomfortable and threatened as possible. He's a mobster. This is how they operate," Laufer said.

My pressure campaign against Trump and his minions didn't end
with that lawsuit or my FOIA requests. In March of 2019 I had also
sued the Trump Organization for my legal fees.

I had an agreement with Trump that he, and the organization,
would cover expenses for my legal fees after I became a focus of federal
prosecutors in New York, and after I was called to testify before the
Mueller investigation. In total, I incurred more than $3 million in legal
fees with Trump paying approximately $1.7 million of those expenses.
However, in June 2018 Trump abruptly stopped paying those expenses
when the information I divulged and my actions no longer served his
interest and benefit. I stopped lying for him, so he turned off the spigot.

But I figured, well, a deal's a deal. These were certainly work-
related expenses.

In November 2021, though, New York Judge Joel M. Cohen (not
a chance we're related) ruled against me and took Trump's family
company off the hook for my legal fees, saying, "Mr. Cohen's legal
fees arise out of his (sometimes unlawful) service to Mr. Trump personally, to Mr. Trump's campaign, and to the Trump Foundation,
but not out of his service to the business of the Trump Organization,
which is the only defendant in this case."[4]

The Trump Organization issued a statement calling the ruling an "incredible victory" and threatened a countersuit over my "despicable conduct."[5]

Let's take a good look to see what was despicable here. First of all, this decision is now on appeal in the Second Federal Circuit. Secondly, the judge erred in his ruling that my service was done solely for Donald Trump personally and not the Trump Organization. Here's the reason why that ruling is incorrect; Donald Trump *is* the Trump Organization. The actions I pleaded guilty to were not done for the benefit of the Trump Organization? What kind of legally convoluted, hair-splitting logic is that? Sure, I worked for the Trump Organization. But, it isn't a publicly traded company; it is a privately held company owned by one person. Remember my title—Executive Vice-President and special counsel to Donald J. Trump. If he directed me to do something then rest assured I did it. And be assured it was seen as being for the benefit of his company—because it benefits him. You can't separate Trump from the Trump Organization. And yet Judge Cohen ignores the case law we provided and, after denying two previous summary judgement attempts, granted the defendant's motion on their third attempt.

Just so you understand, The Trump Organization is a mom and pop company that is predominantly run by about 14 people (I was one of them), all of whom have pledged their loyalty to him. Well, all of them other than me pledged their loyalty, because they're indebted to him by money. He owns them. Obviously, he didn't own me. And that never sat well with him.

Three of those employees, by the way, have the last name of Trump.

My road from Trump perdition back to the reality the rest of us inhabit not only included pressing Trump in court, but also testifying before Congress and taking questions from the House Oversight Committee. In February 2019, I started with an apology for what I'd done and for lying to Congress, then told them everything I knew about Trump. And I also issued a blunt warning to the Republican members who were still Trump loyalists—people like Mark Meadows and Jim Jordan—not to make the same mistakes I did: "I did the same thing that you're doing now for 10 years. I protected Mr. Trump for 10 years," I told them. "I can only warn people. The more people that follow Mr. Trump—as I did blindly—are going to suffer the same consequences that I'm suffering." Had they listened to what I said, it is doubtful we'd have to deal with the insurrection on January 6, 2021. But they didn't and we do.

As the *Los Angeles Times* noted, I'd been there before:

> In 2017, President Trump's former personal attorney was on Capitol Hill to defend his boss, in testimony he now admits contained lies. Since then, in the wake of what Cohen called 'the daily destruction of our civility to one another,' the former fixer flipped on the president and pleaded guilty to lying to Congress, tax evasion and other criminal activity.[6]

USA Today described the

> testimony from Michael Cohen, President Trump's former fixer, detailing what he described as bank

fraud, hush money payments, racist chatter, perjury and more by his one-time boss. His explosive 30-minute opening statement was followed by hours of sometimes-combative exchanges over Trump's conduct and Cohen's credibility.[1]

CNN listed 29 different lines they thought were most memorable in my testimony. "I'm ashamed because I know what Mr. Trump is. He is a racist. He is a conman. He is a cheat," was one of them.

I outlined the fact that Roger Stone was talking with Julian Assange about a WikiLeaks drop of Democratic National Committee emails. I showed a copy of the check Trump wrote from his personal bank account to reimburse me for paying off Stormy Daniels. ("Cohen has the receipts—literally," CNN noted.)[8] I also testified that there were a half a dozen times between the Iowa Caucus and the end of June when Trump asked me, "How's it going in Russia?" — referring to the Moscow Tower project.

I recounted the time he asked me if I could name a country run by a black person that wasn't a "shithole"—at a time when Barack Obama was our president. How he told me black people would never vote for him because they were too stupid. And I noted that I was talking about a man who declares himself brilliant but directed me to threaten his high school, his colleges and the College Board to never release his grades or SAT scores.

And finally, in my closing statement, I warned everyone about the potential calamity that the 2020 election held for our country and our democracy. "I fear that if he loses the presidential election in 2020, there will never be a peaceful transition of power."

I'm not a prognosticator. I can't foretell the future. But I know Donald Trump.

At the time of my testimony Trump was in Hanoi, Vietnam trying to negotiate a deal with North Korea that no one ever thought would happen—and of course it didn't. I heard from Trump insiders that he was beyond furious that the House Oversight Committee called me to testify while he was overseas, leading him to blow off a lunch with Kim Jong-un (two guys who don't like to miss a meal), end the "peace talks," and return stateside. The thing that irked him the most, apparently, was when I stared right into the camera and said how ironic it was that Trump was in Vietnam discussing peace when it was a place he had avoided going to as a young man—by lying about having bone spurs in his foot—when his country called him to serve in the Vietnam War.

Journalists covering Trump at the time also reported that my testimony rattled him, and after he returned with no deal, still reeling from my testimony, he took his stand-up routine to a C-PAC convention, where he spoke for two hours in a speech that included him embracing an American flag on stage in a gesture that looked both comical and pornographic.

Noting that it was "one of the longest speeches in presidential history," *Playboy* Magazine observed astutely,

> Anyone who viewed the president's sweaty long-winded standup act at C-PAC as anything more than blowing off steam and entertaining his best buddies like a poor lounge comic from the 1950s doesn't understand Donald Trump. Every bit of him is an act. He has no idea where reality begins or ends.

The performance, the report added, "did nothing to convince people his 10-year veteran attorney didn't lay a finger on the big D in a WWF *Smackdown* match before Congress."[9] *Playboy* also noted, "Pundits have already described Cohen's testimony as a 'Valachi Papers' moment, referring to Joseph Valachi, who was the first to testify before Congress about the inner workings of the Italian mob." Democratic Maryland Congressman Jamie Raskin observed something similar. "One of the things that surprised me was the Mob-like references to the Trump family," he said.[10]

But those who knew him always knew this was how Trump operated. He was drawn to the machismo of the mafia don and acquired the talent of deflection many mobsters use. He became a deflection master. He thought he was brilliant, but he sounded like a petulant child on the playground shouting, "I'm rubber. You are glue. Whatever you say about me sticks to you."

That childish playground taunt essentially became Trump's professional mantra, and for a long time it has worked—as delusional and juvenile as it is.

He clearly used it in my case. For example, in the past he publicly stated only stupid people pay taxes. When he became president he clearly knew that could be a potential Achilles' heel for him. He also knew I had knowledge of some of the questionable things he had done regarding taxes. So, if my taxes became a significant issue in my prosecution, how then how could I, according to Trump's playground reasoning, provide credible testimony about his personal financial statements and potential tax problems emanating from them?

How did it work? How did Trump get the DOJ and the IRS to get me on taxes?

First, the DOJ made sure I couldn't mount much of a defense by giving me only 48 hours to plead guilty—or have my wife indicted—from the time they first raised the issue of income tax evasion. Over that time, through my counsel, I continuously tried to explain to the SDNY prosecutors that there was no tax evasion scheme and that none of the elements of tax evasion existed.

That didn't matter. It was obvious why they wanted a guaranteed conviction. The benefits were threefold:

1. The first is that it would destroy my credibility—especially as I had already provided evidence of Trump's potential income tax evasion.
2. The accusation of the crime occurred outside of actions taken for Trump, meaning that Donald had a great talking point against me that had nothing to do with him, and he could begin to effectively distance himself from me.
3. Income tax evasion would justify a sentence of several years and ruin my credibility for life while, bottom line, serving as a warning shot across the bow of anyone else in the Trump circle who dared to cross him.

Proving a tax evasion case, though, is a difficult proposition. It requires that the prosecutor can prove intent—they have to make people believe that you purposely tried to avoid paying the tax and didn't do it accidentally. When you hire an accountant to prepare your taxes, it becomes easier to prove intent if the accountant will step up and offer that testimony to the prosecutor. In my case the SDNY would need information from my accountant, Jeffrey Getzel, in front of a grand jury. If Getzel steps in and says any omission was simply an oversight, then chances are there would be no charges filed against me. It would be a civil matter. An IRS agent would be assigned to the case and we would have met to negotiate a settlement. The fact that I was charged with income tax evasion, however, tells us that the government, in its current atmosphere of not prosecuting anything they don't have a slam dunk win on, had spoken to my accountant.

And that's the reason I sued Jeffrey Getzel.

But that's also why the case never got to the discovery stage. The government did not want to expose how it co-opted Getzel, or any of its other dirty secrets in the way it prosecuted me. The judge threw out my suit because he said since I had pleaded guilty to income tax evasion it negated any responsibility my accountant may or may not have had.

Why? Because, again, the government doesn't want me to gain information about what went on between Getzel and the prosecutors. It would clearly show the improper actions taken against me to get a conviction. And who benefits? Donald Trump.

Again, the master of deflection seems to have won, as my attorney in that case, Daniel Wolf, explained:

> That's just not how it works. There are various degrees of responsibility (in the Cohen tax evasion case), and just because Michael Cohen bears some responsibility, doesn't negate the responsibility of those who prepared his income tax returns. Getzel failed to report income on taxi medallions and that amounted to about $4 million in taxes, late fees,

penalties and interest.

We never even got to depose anyone in that case. We never got to go on a fact-finding mission. But in the paper work filed for the case the DOJ names "cooperating witness #1," it's pretty obvious they're talking about Getzel. So, he screwed up, and when the Fed knocked on his door, Getzel simply threw [Cohen] him under the bus. That part is exceedingly clear.

Wolf also argued, and of course I agree, that the judge in this case didn't even take a good look at case law:

> In New York state law there can be multiple faults for things—our position is just that there is more than one person responsible. Just because Michael pled guilty to income tax invasion, doesn't mean he's solely responsible for the returns he filed.

Want to look at it another way? I took action on behalf of Trump when I paid off Stormy Daniels. I went to prison. He didn't even get charged. In my income tax case Getzel took action on my behalf, he didn't get charged at all—but I did. How is this justice?

Getzel, of course, had his own point of view about me and told reporters, "[Cohen] wants the world to believe he is an innocent soul that fell upon troubled times only because his accountants failed and betrayed him. The assertion is absurd."[11]

What's actually absurd is how and why the case got dismissed.

The case got to the point where Getzel was required to provide discovery that included all communications with the Southern District of New York—all information from the prosecutors, and any government employee in regard to the criminal case brought against me in the United States vs. Michael Cohen. That's when it got dismissed.

Why is all of this important? I believe in supplying the communications, the statements, there would be irrefutable evidence that the SDNY prosecutors acted in an illegal or improper manner when they demanded that I plead guilty in 48 hours over a weekend, or have my wife join me in an indictment.

But that's not all the government did in my tax case. They didn't stop with Getzel. To bolster their case against me, they relied on Gene Friedman, the biggest tax cheat in the city and state of New York—the infamous "Taxi King."

Over the course of several years, Friedman was charged with theft of more than $35 million from the city. Understand, each time you enter a cab in NYC, the initial charge to the rider includes two types of taxes being levied. The first is a tax that goes to the Metropolitan Transit Authority, and the second is a Taxi Improvement Fund (TIF). Gene was the head of a medallion management company, which handled medallions owned by people like me. As such, he became the custodian of that tax money—no different from any store that collects sales tax. The difference is Gene liked keeping the tax money he collected without sharing it with its rightful owners—the city and the state.

Yeah. He managed my medallions. But more importantly the government got him to testify before the grand jury—apparently about me and the taxi medallions he mismanaged for me. He was reportedly "high as a kite" Rudy Giuliani-style when he did so, his own lawyer told me.

My point is *this* is who the SDNY presented to a grand jury to indict me. This is a guy who bounced $700K worth of checks to me in a year and a half. He screwed over every single medallion owner he had under management whether they were 40 or 90. More people went bankrupt because of Gene than anyone else in the industry. For example, there was an elderly man who only owned one medallion—which he had owned and operated himself since the 1970s. The guy lived off of Social Security, supplemented by the lease payment he'd receive monthly on that medallion. By the time Gene got caught the medallion was encumbered by so much tax liability that it was completely worthless—rendering the old man penniless.

Gene was forced to pay millions in restitution, was known throughout the tri-state area as a scumbag, faced prison time in Chicago for his actions, and this is the guy they used to come after me.

This is how the government moves. This is how they go after you when they want you.

And more importantly it shows the lengths the government would go to in pursuing me. And that begs the question, why didn't they use this much energy to go after Donald Trump?

Ask yourself why not? Why wouldn't they want it? If you follow the bread crumbs, the logic and the evidence, you cannot deny the fix was in.

Donald Trump made sure of that.

So how does it work, this "fix"?

Norm Eisen is a scholar, author, lawyer, former U.S. ambassador, and one of the most highly regarded ethical scholars in the United States. He's the board chair of Citizens for Responsibility and Ethics in Washington (CREW). He was the co-counsel for the House Judiciary Committee during the first impeachment and trial of The Donald in 2020. You remember that one—the time he got impeached for trying to blackmail Ukraine? Not the time he got impeached for trying to overthrow the U.S. government.

Norm has worked with the presidential transition teams of both Democrats and Republicans. He quit work on the Trump transition team when Trump violated the emolument clause and refused to sell off his private business after assuming the presidency. The fact that he owned a hotel blocks away from the White House that could and did book foreign dignitaries is all the evidence a reasonably sane person would need to understand that Donald Trump was making money off of his presidency. The Donald didn't care about established protocols. He didn't care about the law. He didn't care about the history of the presidency. He only cared about himself.

"Everyone else had complied with the law," Eisen reminded us when we spoke with him.

Eisen and I are friends now, and though I always respected him, as Donald Trump's personal lawyer at the time of the transition, I wouldn't say we were natural allies. But he wasn't wrong about The Donald then or now.

He also wasn't wrong when he said he knew from the moment I was remanded back to Otisville that Donald Trump was behind it all. "The Michael Cohen case," Eisen explained on a recent political podcast, "is, as it turns out, a perfect case that exposed corruption at several levels in the department of justice.[12]

He wasn't just talking about the corruption at the top of the food chain. Mid-level and senior career prosecutors were corrupted by their arrogance, and their need to close cases to get to larger firms. Some, by their very personal desire to make Donald Trump pay. And in my case, since Donald Trump never pays, *I* had to pay.

As Eisen and others have pointed out, the pressure can come from both ends of the spectrum. Some people at the Department of Justice, for all the reasons Eisen pointed out, wanted me to pay because they thought hurting me would hurt Donald Trump—although they should've learned *that* wasn't true at the same time I did: The moment Trump referred to me, after my home and business were raided, as "one of his lawyers." I knew I was fucked when I heard that. The Don had dismissed me like Paulie dismissed Henry Hill in *Goodfellas*. Some in the DOJ thought he was bluffing, some didn't care for a variety of reasons—but all of them wanted to see me fry, and the Don loved it. He took advantage of everyone's self-interest to serve his own.

His success, in part, lies in his ability to take advantage of people's inherent weaknesses, their vulnerabilities and their faults. To those ends, he had a fertile ground in the Justice Department.

As a long-time investigator at the DOJ, who had experience in several key offices there, explained to us for this book; "The DOJ has its own protocols and methodology that Trump used in quick fashion to twist the Department of Justice to his own ends." Think about it— if the DOJ *didn't* already have problems, Trump would never have been able to corrupt it so easily. But Jeff Sessions, Donald Trump's first attorney general, was a lackey who helped Trump manipulate the instution, and his second AG, Bill Barr, even more so.

This is not exactly new. Though the DOJ likes to pretend to be independent of the presidency, it has been compromised for years. There are no more John J. Crittendens, or even Robert Kennedys. We are left with fixers like John Mitchell and Jeff Sessions and Bill Barr. Trust me, I know fixers when I see them. I was one. And these guys don't care about the rule of law. They care about protecting the presidents they serve.

According to our long-time DOJ investigator, who is now retired, it is very easy to corrupt the department. "It's about closures. It's about never having to try a case," it was explained to me. "The single greatest problem with the Department of Justice is that when a new, young attorney comes in, they are immediately corrupted by the power the department wields—and forget they wield it for the American people, and not themselves or their superiors."

A new attorney at the DOJ is taught to close cases. A new investigator is taught to approach each case with a wrecking ball and use whatever means possible to intimidate witnesses and defendants in order to achieve the results desired by middle and upper management. This all becomes heightened when these new prosecutors and investigators are assigned to a high-profile case. Add in the narcotic of reporters calling several times a day seeking comment and you have a recipe for disaster. Losing a case is not an option for them, and they will dive deep into the dumpster to succeed.

Don't take my word for it—take the word of people who know far better than I do.

"They appeal to your sense of country, your sense of duty," said our source.

You may work long hours. You'll receive an "attaboy" and other more tangible perks by closing cases fast. You're made to believe you're doing these things in the interest of justice. Most of the lawyers and investigators who remain as career employees soon stop questioning why things are done the way they are—they just assume they're being done right and for the benefit of the country.

There's an increasing temptation to take short cuts, an increasing temptation to cut corners. It's all done under the name of "justice" but it's all about personal gain. A better office. More pay. A good track record meant you could eventually get out of the DOJ and make tons of money in private practice. Very few come out of this without being tainted. The worst of them know what they're doing—and don't care.

Now, introduce someone as corrupt as Donald Trump into the mix and see where playing to the self-serving interests of some in middle management take you. As we prepared this book, at least a half dozen people said something along the lines of, "Had I heard what Michael Cohen is accusing the DOJ of even five years ago I would have thought him crazy. Today, I'm not so sure."

I am sure.

I am sure all of the evidence we've provided in this book shows exactly how corrupt the DOJ is and how it works to sustain itself and reward its prosecutors and investigators at the cost of losing the ability to fairly administer justice in this country.

There are investigators inside the government who spoke with us for this book who believe the same thing. These investigators—who work in New York and Washington either for the State of New York or the U.S. Department of justice—all told me the exact same thing: (1) Donald Trump manipulated the system to go after me, and (2) he wouldn't have had the success he had unless there was a pre-existing problem inside the Department of Justice.

Casual observers of the system have long decried the treatment of immigrants, women, minorities and those in the LGBTQ community. Famed singer and activist John Legend spoke out in May of 2022 about just those things.[13] According to Legend, part of the problem is that for far too long prosecutors have progressed through the system with one statement: "We're tough on crime. We're going to lock more people up."

Legend and others believe that the poor, the disenfranchised, and the marginalized in society are the easiest to prosecute, and thus when prosecutors claim they are going to get tough on crime, they aren't talking about putting rich white people behind bars, they are talking about everyone else. That's a pernicious brand of corruption.

He's not wrong, and yet he doesn't go far enough. My case shows that the corruption is more pervasive; the Department of Justice will put anyone and *everyone* away who gets in the way of what those in power want. Look at it another way: If you have a cancer in every major organ of your body, you're not technically wrong to say you have lung cancer. You just haven't gone far enough.

So yes, the DOJ—the system—is racist, as Legend pointed out. But, it's even more pervasive than that. Wiser men than me have said that the loss of rights for one means the loss of rights for us all.

My case certainly helps reiterate that point. Power protects power. The rest (pretending there is "justice for all") is just window dressing designed to help you forget you're being screwed.

But there have been many who are slow to understand this—particularly in Congress.

For those who wonder how it is so corrupt, I refer to the investigators I spoke with who would talk with me on background. They paint a picture of corruption born from slogans, greed and unenlightened self-interest.

To begin with, John Legend touched on a very important problem. For years we've promoted, supported, hired and elected prosecutors based on the concept of "Getting Tough on Crime." It seems simple doesn't it? Just punish criminals. But the idea is extremely simple-*minded*. It is a slogan that doesn't stand up to scrutiny, and more importantly, it encourages corruption. How? Well, as the investigators told me, once you accept that slogan as a way of doing business, you don't work on the root causes of crime. You concentrate on closing cases quickly—to prove you are "tough on crime."

Soon, you're hiring like-minded individuals who believe that justice amounts to locking up as many people as possible to make that point. Prosecutors want to close cases. Hell, they have to close cases, they don't want to litigate. They don't even think about it, and the sad truth is many of them are very poor litigants.

So, as a result, both prosecutors and judges encourage plea deals. Overworked judges who sometimes face backlogs of several years seldom look deeply into cases when the prosecution and defense present them with an agreed-upon plea deal. This allows the judge to hold a single hearing to settle a case that—had it gone to trial—could take weeks or months. Instead, it's one hearing that usually lasts less than an hour. The system would crumble if every defendant sought a trial. Some defense attorneys have stated that's why judges often hand down harsher sentences to those who plead not guilty versus those who adhere to prosecutor's demands. Prosecutors get the win while judges get a more manageable calendar and everyone goes home happy but the defendant.

As I say, prosecutors who close the most cases are often rewarded. They get raises. They get promotions. When law firms who have to deal with the criminal justice system are looking for attorneys, those who've been promoted, given raises, and closed cases are the rock stars the large white-shoe law firms want to hire.

And this, according to one of our DOJ sources, is what led to my downfall. "Michael Cohen was a victim of this insidious corruption," they explained. "No one will speak on the record about this. No one wants to admit it. Cohen got screwed. But so do many others. What was different in Cohen's case is that his was a case of political corruption. Michael was a political prisoner."

According to our sources at the DOJ Trump was preparing to toss me under the bus months before my office and home were raided, and I was culled from the Trump herd in order to spare the corrupt leader.

"Trump could use the very things that we preach to go after Cohen," it was explained to me. "The bosses at the top could preach the sermon 'Tough on Crime' and it would take very little encouragement for McKay or any other prosecutor to feel like they were righteous in their prosecution."

But, remember the sinister corruption I've pointed out inside the

Department of Justice—if I'm right, you should see smart and driven career prosecutors jumping from high-profile case to high-profile case just to boost their careers; maybe even leaving one high-profile case to prosecute another while the first was still going on.

No. That would be too much. No one would be that blatant.

Oh. Yeah. Wait. As I stated in Chapter Three, that's what Thomas McKay did in my case.

He left my case to prosecute New York state senator Dean Skelos and grab more headlines for himself. On July 11, 2018, the "firebrand prosecutor" referred to in various news reports as a rising federal star gave his closing argument in the bribery case against Skelos. According to the *New York Times*: "Dean Skelos tried to blame his son," a prosecutor, Thomas McKay, said in his closing arguments in Federal District Court . . . testimony that Mr. McKay called "shameless," which prompted the defense attorney to say it was McKay's "argument that was shameless—and 'frankly, I say, disgusting.'"[14] A *Wall Street Journal* report noted that McKay accused Skelos of having "flat-out lied" to the jury, and asked the judge for a longer sentence. [15]

The DOJ's curious laissez-faire attitude toward its own prosecutors, such as McKay, would be acceptable if everyone in Justice acted like an adult. Sadly, our civil society is undeniably uncivil in many subtle and devious ways. And many in the DOJ act like anything other than adults.

Now, who does that remind you of?

With all the government did to me, many people have asked me why I would continue to help by speaking with, or testifying for, various government investigations. The only answer I can give is that I am trying to do the right thing. Yes, at one point I hoped it would get my sentence reduced. But I'm out of prison now. And yes, I would like to be seen as, well, reformed, making up for my sins. But mostly, I'm just trying to do the right thing.

And I've tried to right a few wrongs—in my own life and for others. Part of that was offering 400 hours of testimony before seven different congressional committees, talking to the Manhattan District Attorney, the AG and the Department of Justice. I cooperated with them all.

As for the substance of cooperation, I want to make clear exactly what I gave to the government concerning Donald Trump. I gave them a road map. I gave them everything I knew about Donald Trump. I provided the government with the basic understanding of how the Trump Organization operates with Donald at the helm. I explained the various roles of other executives, and countless acts of illegal activities. These crimes mostly centered around finances. I provided, among other things, Trump's personal financial statements for various years, copies of checks and other assorted documents.

I talked about every action I took on his behalf. I answered every question posed. Even if my response was "I have no knowledge about that matter," I steered my interrogators toward people I thought who would have the information. For the matters I had first-hand knowledge of, I gave them times, dates, motives—insider knowledge that could lead them where they needed to go to expose Trump's corruption.

It's everyone's obligation, prosecutors will argue, to provide the government with relevant facts in criminal investigations. The court is entitled to everyone's testimony. Moreover, when it came to my testimony before Congress, I was subpoenaed to be there. Obeying a subpoena is a legal obligation Donald Trump has never fulfilled, nor have many of his highest ranking political sycophants. That, too, is one reason why I broke from Donald Trump—he doesn't believe in the law. He doesn't care. I did and still do.

And what does the country have to show for Trump's lack of respect for the law or anyone other than himself? As of this writing, in the summer of 2022, a year and a half after Donald Trump fled town with his angry mob, he still remains free. I tried to help people. I will keep trying.

One of the ways I had been trying was in my cooperation with the Manhattan DA, Cyrus Vance. After I got out of prison and back home, I continued to cooperate with Vance's investigative efforts into Donald Trump and the Trump Organization. I had high hopes that Vance would corner Trump and personally serve him with a subpoena. But his term as DA expired at the end of 2021 and the new DA, Alvin Bragg, took over. Bragg let the grand jury Vance had seated for the purposes of hearing evidence on Trump, expire without charges being filed.

Bragg tried to tell everyone that it didn't mean the investigation was over, but in March, two of the case's top investigators, Mark Pomerantz and Carey Dunne resigned in anger at the decision. Norm Eisen, members of Congress, and members of the Democratic party denounced the virtual end of the investigation. Bragg was accused of being afraid to indict Trump because—typical of any prosecutor—the Donald wasn't a "slam dunk" on prosecution. "Because Bragg was afraid of the politics he did not act," Norm Eisen told us. "It is obvious there was more than enough information and testimony to charge Donald Trump." Eisen also indicated that a jury "without a doubt" would find Trump guilty. (He also very kindly nodded to how many hours I'd spent speaking with the investigators, saying, "Cohen and all the witness against Donald Trump have been terribly dishonored by Bragg.")

Pomerantz was scathing in his letter of resignation. He called Bragg's decision not to pursue the case "misguided and completely contrary to the public interest," continuing:

> In my view, the public interest warrants the criminal prosecution of Mr. Trump, and such a prosecution should be brought without any further delay. Because of the complexity of the facts, the refusal of Mr. Trump and the Trump Organization to cooperate with our investigation, and their affirmative steps to frustrate our ability to follow the facts, this investigation has already consumed a great deal of time. As to Mr. Trump, the great bulk of the evidence relates to his management of the Trump Organization before he became President of the United States. These facts are already dated, and our ability to establish what happened may erode with the further passage of time. Many of the salient facts have been made public in proceedings brought by the Office of the Attorney General, and the public has rightly inquired about the pace of our investigation. Most importantly, the further passage of time will raise additional questions about the failure to hold Mr. Trump accountable for his criminal conduct.

> I fear that your decision means that Mr. Trump
> will not be held fully accountable for his crimes. I have
> worked too hard as a lawyer, and for too long, now to
> become a passive participant in what I believe to be a
> grave failure of justice. I therefore resign from my posi-
> tion as a Special Assistant District Attorney, effective
> immediately.[16]

I love this guy. Every point he raised is a point I have made. But I never thought any prosecutor could see it as logically as Pomerantz did.

Let me explain the depth of my frustration. I knew who Trump was, but I never expected that when he became president he'd debase the office as much as he did. You can call me naïve. Maybe I was. But the shit Trump pulled before he was president was typical for the New York real estate business. He wasn't much different than any other developer in that world. I had hopes that he'd actually elevate himself to meet the demands of the office. I wasn't alone. I know reporters, people who really didn't even like Trump, say that they hoped the presidency would thrust him into a different realm and he could be the president we needed. And I believed then, and I believe now, that we certainly need new blood in Washington, D.C. The Geritol crowd needs to go. But Trump never grew into his role. He debased the office of the presidency as no one had before. He turned it into a dumpster fire. Like millions of others in this country, I was hoping someone, anyone, would hold Trump accountable.

And, I admit, some of my disappointment was personal: I'd worked hard with the Manhattan district attorney, and as I previously said, gave them a basic road map to the Trump Organization.

But after Bragg gave up, he joined the chorus of people who blamed me—joining the chorus who said I was a liar and nothing I said could ever be trusted—despite Mueller, Pomerantz, Dunne, and dozens of others who all stated the opposite. In the end, it was just a lame excuse. As Norm Eisen said, "He didn't want to risk losing political capital."

Pomerantz addressed the lack of courage of the DA in his resignation letter and conceded the case against Trump would be a challenge and there were "risks" of bringing it to court, but he argued it was in the public interest to prosecute Trump, "even if a conviction is not certain."[17]

As I say, somewhere along the line, too many prosecutors—like Alvin Bragg—have forgotten exactly what Pomerantz was talking about: that their role in the process is to prosecute crimes and not to worry about the conviction—that's the job of the judge and jury.

Bragg's decision was some kind of setback for me, mentally and spiritually.

I was tired. I was exhausted. I'd spent hundreds of hours being interviewed and trying to help the investigation. I'd provided them with box after box of documents. Hell, I'd worked so closely with them, as a *Daily Beast* report noted, the DA's investigators named the case after me: it was known internally as "The Fixer."[18] And now, there would be nothing to show for it. I was despondent.

Everyone knew it was the end of the Trump investigation, despite Bragg denying it.

But it was.

By April, I'd become so exasperated I'd had enough. When Bragg issued a statement in response to the intense criticism he'd gotten and insisted that the investigation was ongoing—he said he had new evidence—I decided to call his bluff.

On a *Law & Crime* podcast, I told host Adam Kalsfeld, "I call bullshit on that. I know the evidence that they had. I was responsible for providing them with a lot of it. . . . There is no new evidence that we did not discuss."[19] And I told the *Daily Beast* that while Bragg was saying the investigation was ongoing, he was going to let the grand jury's term expire—which he did, just a few days later—and that if he did that, I was out. I wasn't going to start all over again with Bragg if he sat a new grand jury, which I knew he wouldn't anyway. [20]

I obviously felt the same way as Pomerantz and Dunne, who had also elected to walk away from Bragg. A few days later, the media was seeing things more clearly. Alvin Bragg gave up. He let the grand jury's term expire, without a word about seating a new one.

Trump once again avoided the noose.

"What is it about Donald Trump that scares every prosecutor who crosses his path?" asked the headline of an article in *Esquire* by journalist Charles P. Pierce shortly thereafter. Pierce continued:

> I've seen prosecutors who would chew off their own foot rather than give up on a $20 hand-to-hand drug deal. I've seen U.S. Attorneys who would start with the damn part-time janitor in the building where corrupt business was being conducted and work their way mercilessly up the food chain from there. What is it about this ambulatory lump of triglycerides that scares the daylights out of every prosecutor who crosses his path?

I mean, the guy isn't even as rich as he says he is.[21]

To make matters worse, after he gave up, Bragg magically found a scapegoat: me. Bragg started circulating stories about me—or rather I should say "people familiar with Bragg's thinking" began circulating stories, such as that that I would lose him the case because a jury would never believe me. "Michael Cohen Overstated Role in Manhattan DA's Trump investigation: Prosecutors," ran the headline of a *New York Daily News* story.[22]

So why did all the brilliant investigators like Pomerantz, Dunne and Cy Vance himself spend so much time talking to me? If it truly was my credibility that was the roadblock to proceeding against Trump, then there are clearly others who could have corroborated what I said and verified the documentation I provided.

It was easy to point the finger at me and blame me for everything. But there's no denying the fact that over the last two years all new information has verified my statements and disqualified the many spurious lies told about me. The simple truth? As Norm Eisen said in an interview for this book, "It's obvious that the district attorney simply didn't want to take a chance. It had nothing to do with Michael. They had more than enough evidence to proceed."

People are getting tired of bullshit finger-pointing. It's old. The general public isn't buying it any more.

But it still seems to be my lot in life.

I was also accused of lying and being a vindictive witness by the Trump Organization's CFO, Allen Weisselberg, in a motion that he filed to dismiss the New York district attorney's indictment against him in the same case. (Cy Vance had been leveraging him hard.)

As the longest serving employee at the Trump Organization with more than forty years on the clock, Allen was included in every-thing—not for his legal mind or his strategic abilities, but because he controlled all of the money. In every financial transaction, legitimate or otherwise, Weisellberg was somehow involved. My role? I was dis-patched to clean up messes created by others in the company. Allen's role? Make the numbers look good.

Weisselberg's lawyers allege that all of the information the Manhattan prosecutors were using to break their client was based on lies he accused me of telling federal investigators. But Bragg's office said that none of the prosecutors had ever seen or been briefed on the contents of Weisselberg's testimony against me to the feds.[23]

Let me tell you exactly who the real liar is here. Allen Weisselberg lied to SDNY prosecutors about the hush money payment to Stormy Daniels and they then used that testimony to charge me and granted him immunity.

Don't take my word for it—a CNN story reported that the Feds had indeed given Weisselberg immunity, but "came to suspect he had lied to them" about how the company reimbursed me.[24]

Like the old Ginsu knife commercial would say—but wait there's more.

I had no idea I was so powerful. After all, it was the *Trump Organization*; a small boutique family company with too much clout and not enough common sense run by one man—Donald Trump—not Michael Cohen or anyone else who worked there. Everything, and I mean everything, was the responsibility of, and all actions were conducted at the direction of Donald Trump for his benefit. You cannot separate the man from the company any more than you can split yourself in half. That's the essence of what I told Congress and many prosecutors. Now, if you think that in some way I overstated my importance, then you are welcome to your opinion. But give me this: 1) It is a fact that Donald Trump rarely, if ever, does anything for anyone but himself. 2) Donald Trump will do anything to protect his own ass so he can continue following rule number one.

Then just follow the evidence after that. Donald Trump is a very simple man.

The Donald's success is in sweet-talking you, engaging you, as he uses you and then ultimately discards you. Afterwards, if you don't like it, he'll threaten you for good measure. Enter the old Michael Cohen. I was the guy who took care of the threats, payoffs, and lawsuits. That's how it worked, and Trump's CFO Allen Weisselburg *knows* it because he was an integral part of Trump's boutique. His inside knowledge also made him aware—before it even happened—that from the time I got out of jail, I'd still be a favorite Trump target. Hell, I'm the example he could trot out to warn any of his minions that the same thing could happen to them that happened to me.

Omerta, baby. It's a real thing.

So, after being involved with the criminal justice system as intimately as I have for the last few years, I've learned there is one immutable truth: There is simply no way to fix what's wrong with this country without addressing the huge discrepancies in the administering of justice in the United States.

As we witnessed the blatant and obvious violations of law by Trump and his associates on a daily basis, Democrats continued their battle cry that no one is above the law. Reporters even asked members of the Trump administration including, but not limited to, Sarah Sanders, Sean Spicer, Bill Shine, Bill Barr, and Jeff Sessions if they thought the president was above the law. Everyone always said no.

Wait? Did they really say "No"?

Clearly part of the job requires them to be oblivious to Donald Trump's actions. But as someone who knows Donald better than anyone else, permit me to make this observation: In Donald Trump's mind he is and was always above the law.

As president, he believed he could do anything and that the president was like a king (an actual Donald Trump statement). Any pushback to his agenda would be handled by his new personal attorneys, Bill Barr and the staff of the Department of Justice. As a New York real estate mogul, Trump appreciated that the DOJ had been corrupted for years; a victim of its own abuse of power, the avarice and greed of its managers and the environment they created. So, he took advantage of it, and manipulated it, in an attempt to destroy me.

In this process Trump has shown us all why the Justice Department desperately needs to be reformed.

CHAPTER FIVE

DEMOCRACY IN PERIL

I AM NOT THE FIRST PERSON to call out the actions of the Department of Justice for being antithetical to the ideals of this country, nor will I be the last.

Nor am I the first to be horrified by the way those who yield power—granted by the president—treat those who try to do the right thing. As I sat and watched the January 6 hearings, my heart went out to Wandrea "Shaye" Moss and her mother "Lady Ruby" Freeman as they described the horror that their lives became after Rudy Giuliani—working as the president's personal attorney—accused them of rigging the outcome of the presidential race in Fulton County, Georgia.[1]

As it was reported in the *Washington Post*,

> Giuliani claimed that Moss and Freeman had plotted to kick out observers at the State Farm Arena, where the county had set up a ballot counting operation. They had brought in suitcases filled with fraudulent ballots

for Biden and scanned them through the tabulating
teams multiple times, he said. He described surveillance video from the arena that he claimed showed the
two exchanging USB memory sticks, presumably containing fraudulent vote counts, "as if they're vials of
cocaine."[2]

Giuliani said their homes should be searched, and that they were
a menace to the democratic process. He said a lot of other horrible
things about these honorable people, and it was all lies. Giuliani eagerly spewed this venomous garbage in order to advance Trump's
ridiculous claims of voter fraud that didn't exist. As veteran former
federal prosecutor Renato Mariotti, who worked white-collar crime
in Chicago for more than ten years said, "Giuliani is the guy you
hand a glass of wine to and he'll say anything. In the end, he made
up a lot of stuff and left his ass hanging out in the breeze."

I know what it's like to have Giuliani tell lies about you to advance Trump's potentially criminal agenda. After I testified before
Congress in February of 2018, trying to warn people exactly what
Trump was capable of, Giuliani called me pathetic and a "serial
liar" to any reporter who would listen. I know for a fact that he
called some reporters, eager to denigrate me. He volunteered to go
on national television to do the same. He also blamed me for most
of Donald Trump's troubles, while ignoring Trump's own criminal
behavior.[3]

And as it turns out the lies Giuliani told about me were as trans-
parently pathetic as the lies he told about Moss and her mother. It
wasn't my credibility that was in question—it was Giuliani's. And

it wasn't Moss and her mother's credibility in question either. They weren't seen on videotape passing a thumb drive filled with false election data as Rudy claimed; they were passing a ginger mint between them. Sadly, too many people believed the lies Giuliani spewed about them and me.

You can draw a direct line from what happened to me at the beginning of the Trump administration to what happened at the end of his term. He showed us early on in his presidency the lengths he would go to in order to save himself. At the beginning it only affected me and few people cared. I was the scapegoat. In the end, the entire country was sacrificed to satisfy Trump's narcissism, rage, and criminal-like attempt to hold on to power in a failed coup. And in both cases, the Department of Justice was complicit in his plans.

But in the beginning, I was alone in this journey—literally. Not only did few believe me when I spoke about Trump, but the system worked hard to make sure no one ever did. So did the Trump Organization, whose members painted *me* as the menace and not the president.

In an essay published by Trump loyalist and former Trump Organization assistant general counsel George Sorial the Sunday before I went to prison, he said that I was "a bluffing, boasting New Yorker who overstated his role at the company and that he only had himself to blame for going to prison."[4] Of course, he had to try and stick the knife in deep, painting me as "going rogue," as Trump himself had claimed, by writing in the *Wall Street Journal* that "Cohen had no real decision-making authority and was rather "a lone wolf constantly seeking the boss's approval and fearing others would take his credit."[5]

Both Sorial and Trump knew that not to be the case. That, of course, would never stop either of them from being disingenuous with the truth.

I cannot adequately describe how lonely that felt. I realized: I'm really on my own now.

I was also saddened by George's comments, in that I had considered him more than just a colleague, but a friend. I had spent countless hours listening to his complaining how Trump, Weisselberg, the kids, how everyone at the Trump Organization had done him wrong at one time or another. I expected more from him, but then again, after spending more than a decade at the organization, all your values get flushed down the toilet. Anything for a paycheck.

Meanwhile, Trump and his acolytes kept impressing upon the DOJ the importance of making my prison stay as uncomfortable as possible. As early as January 18, 2019 Trump even tweeted "Don't forget Michael Cohen has already been convicted of perjury and fraud, and as recently as this week, the *Wall Street Journal* has suggested that he may have stolen tens of thousands of dollars . . . Lying to reduce his jail time! Watch father-in-law."[6]

You think Donald Trump had no say in how I was treated in prison? Think again.

For Trump to execute this type of action, it would merely take a phone call, probably not made by him, to make his desire a reality. From the second Trump was inaugurated he abused the power of the presidency. Through his abuse, Trump placed our democracy in peril. It was his misguided belief that he wielded enough power over the three branches of government to overthrow our democracy and obliterate our Constitution.

If you have any doubt about the veracity of that, just take a quick look at the recent decision by the Supreme Court to overturn Roe v. Wade, no thanks to three Federalist judges Trump appointed to the bench.

Because of the actions of Neil Gorsuch, Brett Kavanaugh, and Amy Coney Barrett, our nation is staring into an abyss that could very well lead this country back to the days of Jim Crow, racism, and misogyny, where anyone who isn't a white Christian heterosexual will have to fear for their freedom, if not their lives. We have Donald Trump to thank for this.

If you think that sentiment has no merit, then let's revisit Shaye Moss and Lady Ruby Freeman. "I won't even introduce myself by my name anymore," Lady Ruby testified to the January 6 committee.

> I get nervous when I bump into someone I know in the grocery store who says my name. I'm worried about who is listening. I get nervous when I have to give my name for food orders. I'm always concerned of who is around me. I've lost my name, and I've lost my reputation. I've lost my sense of security.[1]

I have been there and know exactly how she feels. In fact, the straightforward testimony of Lady Ruby that offered what could stand as an eloquent explanation of my personal dealings with Trump after leaving the cult. "There is nowhere I feel safe. Nowhere," she said.

> Do you know how it feels to have the president of the United States target you? The president of the United

States is supposed to represent every American, not to target one. But he targeted me, Lady Ruby, a small-business owner, a mother, a proud American citizen who stood up to help Fulton County run an election in the middle of a pandemic.[8]

I bring up the January 6 hearings for a very vital reason. Those hearings put on display the hell Donald Trump and his minions have put this country through, and what I had warned people about in my Congressional testimony. In fact, many of the side players in my case played similar roles in the insurrection. Matt Gaetz, the feckless frat boy of Congress, was sanctioned for a threatening tweet he directed at me the day before I was scheduled to testify about Trump to the House Oversight Committee:

> Hey @MichaelCohen212—Do your wife & father-in-law know about your girlfriends? Maybe tonight would be a good time for that chat. I wonder if she'll remain faithful when you're in prison. She's about to learn a lot . . .[9]

My wife knew it was bullshit from the moment he made the accusation, and Gaetz—recently under Federal investigation for charges of sex trafficking and having sex with a minor[10]—was quickly admonished by the House.[11]

More importantly, as *Roll Call* reported, "At that hearing, Cohen referred to Trump as a 'racist' and 'con man' and said he came forward because he was concerned Trump would not accept the result of the 2020 election."[12]

Believe me now?

Of course, I was right. Trump didn't accept the results of the election, and Gaetz, after actively supporting Trump's Big Lie (he calls the people who stormed the Capitol "patriotic Americans")[13] found himself shopping for a pardon—even before the January 6 insurrection. Former Trump White House aide Cassidy Hutchinson, an aide to former White House chief of staff Mark Meadows, testified in fact that "Gaetz was personally pushing for a pardon, and he was doing so since early December. I'm not sure why. He reached out to me to ask if he could have a meeting with Mr. Meadows about receiving a presidential pardon."[14]

Eric Herschmann, a Trump White House lawyer, testified that Gaetz had sought a wide-reaching pardon from the president that would conceivably "go back to the beginning of time."

Gaetz felt that "We may get prosecuted because we were defensive of the president's positions on these things," Herschmann said. "The pardon that he was discussing, requesting, was as broad as you could describe, from the beginning of time up until today, for any and all things. He mentioned Nixon and I said Nixon's pardon was never nearly that broad."[15]

Jim Jordan was another player in both my case and in the insurrection. During my Congressional testimony, he accused me of being remorseless. "His remorse is nonexistent," Jordan said. "He just debated a member of Congress, saying, 'I really didn't do anything wrong with the false bank things that I'm guilty of and going to prison for.'"

"Mr. Jordan, that's not what I said," I responded. "And you know that that's not what I said. I pled guilty and I take responsibility for my actions. Shame on you, Mr. Jordan. That's not what I said." [16]

After the insurrection, Jordan—who voted against certification of the vote and had "multiple" mysterious phone calls with Trump on January 6[17]—apparently never directly asked for a pardon, but asked for updates on whether or not pardons *would be available* to members of Congress who supported Trump in the insurrection.[18]

But wait, there's more. Let's take a look at Louie Gohmert, the feeble-minded and inept congressman who said I "needed a colonoscopy from lawmakers," as he tried to spread the story that I had gone to Prague when I never did.[19] He followed Trump into the insurrection dumpster fire and crawled out smelling like shit, begging for a pardon as well. Maybe *he* is the one in need of a colonoscopy from lawmakers.

These three Congressmen who defended Trump and disparaged me are also three of the six Republicans who were interested in getting a pardon from Trump after they defended him, disparaged the election, tried to sell the Big Lie, and helped try to explain away the insurrection for Donald Trump.

By the way, if anyone in Congress had listened to me, they would've been well aware that Trump would not willingly give up the power of the presidency. I desperately tried to warn everyone what was about to happen when I went to Congress in 2019, testified and faced off with Jordan.

Let me be clear, I am not Nostradamus and I have no great superpower of prognostication. But I do know Donald Trump very well. In a September 2020 *Rolling Stone* interview, I foretold exactly what Trump would do:

"Donald Trump will do anything and everything within which to win. And I believe that includes manipulating the ballots," Cohen said. "I believe that he would even go so far as to start a war in order to prevent himself from being removed from office. My biggest fear is that there will not be a peaceful transition of power in 2020." [20]

Just two short weeks later, in the Brady Briefing room of the White House, the president of the United States, Donald Trump, made history by being the *first* president to ever admit publicly that he wouldn't necessarily accept a peaceful transfer of power. "We'll have to see," he infamously said after being asked. "If you stop counting the votes there won't be a transition," he added.

One of the key players in what was eventually ruled my unlawful and unconstitutional remand into Otisville, and in the January 6 insurrection, was the man sitting at the top of the Justice Department: former Attorney General Bill Barr. I am talking about the same Bill Barr who later told congressional investigators that Donald Trump was delusional if he believed the claims of voter fraud. He told them that Trump had no interest in facts. In his testimony to the January 6 committee, he claimed he told Trump that the Department of Justice wasn't his personal attorney. But that's exactly how Barr acted for Trump in my case—as Trump's personal attorney, with the Department of Justice acting as his personal law firm. The redoubtable Bill Barr we see now is not the Bill Barr we've seen in public for the last several years.

Several weeks before the election, Barr told Congress that "an election with a lot of mail-in votes would not be secure, a conclusion he said was backed by "common sense."

After the votes were cast, Barr never let the public know that he felt Trump was doing what he said in his deposition was a "disservice" to the country.

Since he stepped down as attorney general in December 2020, and during the time he was apparently testifying negatively about Trump to the January 6 Committee, Barr has publicly lauded the former president. During his 2022 book tour he said that if Trump were again the Republican candidate for president that he would vote for him.[21] (Too bad Trump doesn't hold Barr in the same esteem. In June 2022, he simply said that Barr sucked.[22])

This is the same Bill Barr who defended Trump during the Mueller investigation. You'd think they were as thick as thieves, but as soon as Barr accused Trump of being "delusional" and full of "bullshit," Trump went after him. Neil Cavuto on his Fox News show asked Barr what he thought of that. After chuckling for a few seconds, Barr said, "Well, I considered the source."

Barr may have dismissed Trump after the insurrection, but it is also believed that Barr played a significant role in remanding me to Otisville—in addition to helping shield Trump after the election. As former federal prosecutor Mariotti said, "Bill Barr knew exactly what to do without Trump telling him. He didn't have to talk to him. Cohen said the same thing when he worked for Trump. Cohen just knew. Barr knew."

That's exactly right.

Barr was Trump's ready-made accomplice and assisted Trump

both in my case and after the insurrection—that is until the point that Barr would personally be on the line for his actions. There was no congressional investigation that would subpoena Barr in my case. But when he was hauled in front of investigators about the insurrection, Barr did not hesitate to do to Trump what Trump did to me and anyone else who displeased him—he threw him under the bus.

"Barr wasn't stupid enough to leave his ass hanging out in the breeze," Mariotti said. "Jeffrey Clark, John Eastman, and Rudy Giuliani are a different matter. They were. They shielded Trump and Trump's mistake is that he thought they were his 'Get out of Jail Free' card."

It remains to be seen if Trump will survive the current investigations into his actions as president, but the playbook used in the insurrection was the same playbook he used to come after me. More importantly, it included many of the same players.

I have testified, before Congress, about the danger Donald Trump represents. It was ignored. I am again sounding the warning alarm, this time about the Department of Justice.

I beg you to listen while there is still time to save our democracy.

The Department of Justice is in desperate need of being overhauled. It shoulders a fair amount of blame for the problems we are facing today. I've outlined them repeatedly and there are others with far more information about the department than I have who agree with this statement. If we do not clean up the problems within the Department of Justice, there will be no justice left for anyone but the elite few who can afford to avoid charges, prosecution and/or prison.

Let me wrap it up in a pretty bow, or as Sean Spicer used to say, "unicorns and rainbows." Below are some changes that if instituted would certainly be a start. Some are suggested by Judge Rakoff, and some of them were suggested privately to me by DOJ staff who know of my experience in the system.

A short summary of these possible changes is listed in the chart below. After reading them, we will examine them individually:

Changes to the Department of Justice

Back up the independence of the department by making it a criminal act for any member of the executive branch to directly intercede in a case for personal reasons.

Allow an independent judge – not associated with a particular case – the ability to oversee plea deals.

Allow more direct congressional oversight of actions in the justice department.

Institute more judicial oversight on plea bargaining. 97 percent of the cases end up there.

Appoint a congressional committee to investigate and recommend changes to the ongoing DOJ culture that emphasizes closure rates and stiff sentences.

Re-examine the maxim "Tough on Crime" to address real life issues – including mandatory sentencing guidelines.

> Institute guidelines to reduce the adversarial nature of
> the American justice system and make the defense and
> the prosecution more equal under law.

Some of these changes are impossible; not because it can't be done, but because Congress will never do it. The remaining suggestions are so simple to implement it boggles the mind that they haven't already been done. According to former federal prosecutor Michael Zeldin, a person in the executive branch can already be prosecuted for interfering in an investigation. "Probably," he explained, but it would have to be "pretty fact-specific."

There are many who want to make it easier to do so, and more importantly there are many in the DOJ who admit the department needs to be more transparent in how it operates—especially in how it interacts with the executive branch of government.

In addition, there are prosecutors and investigators who want the culture upended at the DOJ so prosecutors don't make their careers on high-profile cases. "That's a problem," Mariotti explained.

> That's part of the culture. Look, I tried and won some
> big cases. No one really cares about the numbers you
> put up, but the prosecutors have an incentive to win
> high profile cases because they do help you build your
> career—and that's a fair assessment and criticism. The
> question is, what do we do about it?

I have an idea: End it.

Part of the problem is that the DOJ uses high-profile cases as a deterrent. "How many people are really prosecuted for tax evasion? Not that many," Mariotti explained. "But prosecute a Wesley Snipes or a Michael Cohen for it, and the DOJ believes that deters others from evading taxes."

Here's the reality: Very few taxpayers go to jail for tax evasion. In 2015, the IRS indicted only 1,330 taxpayers out of 150 million for legal-source tax evasion (as opposed to illegal activity or narcotics).

The IRS mainly targets people who understate what they owe. As H&R Block warns its customers, tax evasion cases mostly start with taxpayers who misreport income, credits, and/or deductions on tax returns, or who don't file a required tax return. The IRS doesn't pursue many tax evasion cases for people who can't pay their taxes. [23]

In other words, the agency saves criminal prosecution for exceptional cases.

There may be some logic in that, but when that is combined with a president and attorney general with an axe to grind, it cuts both ways. Trump could easily use my case to deter others in his camp from cooperating with the government about allegations against him.

"That's an interesting point," Mariotti told us.

> Look, there's no doubt that Cohen was "aggressively" prosecuted. But the SDNY has a history of that. Donald Trump is a master of using the system to his advantage. He knows more about the court system than most give him credit for, so yes, I can see him using the playbook against Cohen or anyone else that crosses him.

It is well documented that Trump often meddled in the activities of the Justice Department, blurring the separation of powers sought in our Constitution. Look at Roger Stone, for example. Kim Wehle, a University of Baltimore Law School professor who previously served as an assistant U.S. attorney in Washington, D.C., noted that in Stone's case there was direct evidence that Trump tried to get involved in his sentencing. "Particularly after Watergate, there's a norm, sort of, of independence between the Justice Department and the president," she told us. "The idea being that, not only for fairness for individual defendants, but also for the legitimacy of the department itself, to avoid the appearance of a conflict of interest, the president has stayed, at least in the public eye, out of decisions relating to individual prosecutions."[24]

Wehle said that line prosecutors from DOJ made a sentencing recommendation for Stone, who was convicted of making false statements to the House Intelligence Committee, among other crimes. The president tweeted that he disagreed with the recommendation, "and then lo and behold, there was an intervention by the upper echelons of the Justice Department, through Attorney General Barr, to change that," Wehle said.[25] John Yoo, the co-author of this study, later responded that he believes there is no evidence that the president ordered that the recommendations be changed and, rather, Barr may have intervened in the sentencing before the president tweeted about it.

In any event, Wehle said Barr's intervention was unusual.

"It suggests that the president's unhappiness with [the sentencing recommendation] was what made the attorney general make the change."[26]

The Stone case, and what Barr and Trump did in my case, show beyond a reasonable doubt that there must be consequences for members of the executive branch subverting justice. As of today, there have been none.

As for the other changes in our list that were suggested to us, Judge Jed Rakoff favors suggestions two and four and wrote about them extensively in his book, *Why the Innocent Plead Guilty and the Guilty Go Free*. And he knows a lot about plea deals. As I've already discussed in Chapter Two, his suggestion to add an independent judge to the process makes sense. "The argument is that if the judge is going to have to preside, he/she shouldn't be involved in the plea bargain. True, so have a different judge handle the plea—not the trial judge. It's very simple to have a magistrate in charge—who wouldn't report back to the trial judge," Rakoff explained.

Some of this may seem like it's getting in the weeds for casual readers, but we need to make ourselves aware of the problems inside the criminal justice system. Donald Trump is the worst-case scenario in this cluttered and corrupt culture. As Mariotti explained, Trump knows what he's doing. We have to make sure he and anyone else who would act as the former president did are no longer able to do so.

Rakoff, Mariotti, and many others who spoke to us on the condition of anonymity who still toil inside the Department of Justice have a growing concern about the ability of the system to actually mete out justice. "If anything, the American system may be too adversarial," Rakoff said.

Mariotti agreed. "But, what are you going to do?" he said.

> The government has a lot more resources at its disposal
> than even the richest client. I don't see Congress toss-
> ing any money at the system for defense counsel. But
> some of these cases are extremely costly to defend and
> take a great deal of time to prepare for. The government
> has a great advantage in that department.

At the end of the day, there has to be something done, and that's why some in the DOJ believe there needs to be a congressional committee or a think tank that studies the problem and comes up with reasonable and cogent solutions. I'd volunteer to testify before such an entity—and I'd bring this book with me to illustrate the point.

But let's bring these suggestions back home.

No man is above the law. At least that's how the adage goes.

Yet, those of wealth, privilege, and power get one brand of justice while the rest of us get another. Some of us get nothing but pain. Did Shaye Moss and Ruby Freedman get justice? Did any of the people killed defending the Capitol on the day Donald Trump sent insurrectionists there get justice?

And there's no better case to point out the problems inherent in our system than the criminal case that landed me in federal prison.

As Renato Mariotti said to us, "There is no doubt that Michael Cohen was 'aggressively' prosecuted."

But it's not just that I was "aggressively" prosecuted. As Mariotti noted, the Department of Justice is "risk-averse" in prosecuting cases.

The Federal government has a great track record for convictions because it can turn down cases it doesn't want to take—and push them back down to the state level. It keeps the high-profile cases that can lead to headlines and television appearances because that's what suits the department—not necessarily justice.

There's another problem. The federal government, as previously noted, has massive resources it can throw at a case. It can intimidate you whether it's in the form of the FBI showing up and politely going through your office, apartment, or even your daughter's underwear drawer. As a result of that power, there is an inherent bias in the system—as Mariotti points out. "Jurors assume someone is guilty if charged. It's a problem. But it's a reality. Judges are also going to give more weight to government assertions because the government lawyers are before them all the time. They know each other," he said. In fact, their offices are generally in the same building and only a few floors below.

Those who still work in the system and would speak to us on background admit the DOJ can even have a "dark agenda," and it isn't unknown for prosecutors to be "overly aggressive" to those they believe are a threat or are a "high profile" defendant. In my case? "His high profile contributed to his aggressive prosecution," Mariotti said. "I do think Michael is right. The DOJ gets a lot of press prosecuting high profiled individuals like Michael Cohen."

The DOJ is then both cautious in the cases it takes and overly aggressive in high-profile cases to make their point. And the DOJ loves to make deals because it doesn't want contentious trials that take up time and money which would crash the system.

It's not only that they want to win—they need to win. In order to make this a reality, these unscrupulous prosecutors will threaten you and your family with increased jail time or even the indictment of a family member to get you to play ball with them. But it's not a level playing field. They wield all the power. It's like a high school basketball team playing the U.S. Olympic team. You know who the winner is going to be before the tipoff.

So, what's the best way to defend yourself against federal prosecution when it is corrupted by money and power? Never get on their radar. That's the best way.

"It certainly is the case that the best defense is not to be on their radar screen," Mariotti said. "If you are, they will act in ways that are unfair—once they come after you. Michael Cohen got the book thrown at him harder than other people. Absolutely."

There it is, in plain English from a former federal prosecutor who knows how it works.

And now, hopefully the people of the United States, after watching the January 6 hearing, understand. The Department of Justice, because of its nature—already passively corrupt—became violently so under Donald Trump. Luckily, there were some in the Department of Justice who wouldn't do his bidding and told him to his face—the only thing that saved our country.

They were in the right place at the right time, but what if it had been Jeffrey Clark?

We cannot always count on the right people to be in the right place.

It should be noted that there were just 17 days left in the Trump administration when Rosen, Engel, and Donoghue told him "No." Where were they when Trump was running roughshod over American democracy? Where were they when my case was being discussed? Silent!

Somebody who wasn't silent was Matt Gaetz—then under investigation for alleged improper sexual relations with underaged girls. Jim Jordan? A guy who allegedly turned a blind eye to college wrestlers being sexually abused by their coach. Also not the right guy. What do these two morons have in common? They both fit the mold for Trump.

You know who is the right person?

When I testified before the House Oversight Committee, I found a truly decent human being.

That man, may he rest in peace, was the honorable Elijah Cummings. In private, he told me that what I was doing was saving our democracy. "You're owning your mistakes. That's the first part of redemption," he said. He never attacked me publicly and never tried to make up shit about me. He told me to be the best version of myself.

He called me the night after my testimony, not as a member of Congress, but as a caring, loving father, son, brother, human being. He cried and we wept together. We bonded over country, family and fate. He saw the pain in my soul; the pain that stemmed from the knowledge that I would be separated from my wife and children for three long years. The pain he saw that I experienced as hundreds of photographers documented my every move. He felt my anguish like no other. He showed the empathy that a man I thought was my friend, a man I pledged my loyalty to, a man I said I would have taken a bullet for never showed me.

But it was his closing comments at the hearing before the House Oversight Committee moved not only me but the country, and he was right about everything he said, including my mistakes, my honesty, and my commitment to make amends. I could paraphrase it. I could cut a few quotes from it, but to understand my personal journey and to understand why I still am trying to get things changed—why I am writing this book—you have to read the entire Cummings closing statement. This was probably the most significant statement anyone made to me up to this point, and it was one of the main reasons why I elected to meet with the district attorney while I was in Otisville. I made a promise to a very decent man.

I offer his comments here in the hope they inspire you, as they inspired me, to be better:

> You know I've sat here, and I've listened to all this, and it's very painful. It's very painful. You made a lot of mistakes, Mr. Cohen—and you've admitted that. And, you know, one of the saddest parts of this whole thing is that some very innocent people are hurting too. And you acknowledged that. And, um, that's your family.
>
> And, so you come here today, you . . . deep in my heart . . . when I practiced law I represented a lot of lawyers who got in trouble. And, you come saying I have made my mistakes, but now I want to change my life. And you know, if we . . . as a nation did not give people an opportunity after they've made mistakes to change their lives, a whole lot of people would not do very well.
>
> I don't know where you go from here. As I sat here and I listened to both sides, I just felt as if . . . and you

know . . . people are now using my words, that they took from me, that didn't give me any credit. We are better than this. . . . We really are. As a country, we are so much better than this.

And, you know, I told you, and for some reason, Mr. Cohen, I tell my children, I say 'When bad things happen to you, do not ask the question "Why did it happen to me?" Ask the question, "Why did it happen for me?" I don't know why this is happening for you. But it's my hope that a small part of it is for our country to be better. If I hear you correctly, it sounds like you're crying out for a new normal—for us getting back to normal. It sounds to me like you want to make sure that our democracy stays intact.

The one meeting I had with President Trump, I said to him "The greatest gift that you and I, Mr. President, can give to our children, is making sure we give them a democracy that is intact. A . . . democracy better than the one we came upon." And I'm hoping that, the things you said today will help us again to get back there.

You know, I mean come on now. I mean, when you got, according to the *Washington Post*, our president has made at least 8,718 . . . false or misleading statements. That's stunning. That's not what we teach our children. I don't teach mine that. And, for whatever reason, it sounds like you got caught up in it. You got caught up in it. You got caught up in it.

And, some kind of way, I hope that you will, I know

that it's painful going to prison. I know it's got to be painful being called a rat. And let me explain, a lot of people don't know the significance of that, but I live in the inner city of Baltimore, all right? And when you call somebody a rat, that's one of the worst things you can call them because when they go to prison, that means a snitch. I'm just saying. And so, the president called you a rat. We're better than that! We really are. And I'm hoping that all of us can get back to this democracy that we want, and that we should be passing on to our children so they can do better than what we did.

So you wonder whether people believe you—I don't know. I don't know whether they believe you. But the fact is, that you've come, you have your head down, and this has got to be one of the hardest things that you could do.

Let me tell you the picture that really, really pained me. You were leaving the prison, you were leaving the courthouse, and, I guess it's your daughter, had braces or something on. Man that thing, man that thing hurt me. As a father of two daughters, it hurt me. And I can imagine how it must feel for you. But I'm just saying to you—I want to first of all thank you. I know that this has been hard. I know that you've faced a lot. I know that you are worried about your family. But this is a part of your destiny. And hopefully this portion of your destiny will lead to a better, a better, a better Michael Cohen, a better Donald Trump, a better United States of America, and a better world. And I mean that from the depths of my heart.

When we're dancing with the angels, the question we'll be asked: In 2019, what did we do to make sure we kept our democracy intact? Did we stand on the sidelines and say nothing?

And I'm tired of statements saying . . . people come in here and say "Oh, oh this is the first hearing." It is not the first hearing. The first hearing was with regard to prescription drugs. Remember, a little girl, a lady sat there . . . Her daughter died because she could not get $330 a month in insulin. That was our first hearing. Second hearing: H.R. 1, voting rights, corruption in government. Come on now. We can do more than one thing. And we have got to get back to normal. With that, this meeting is adjourned.

Cummings made a profound impression on me and it's that impression that guides me as I continue this journey, in spite of the despicable people who are eroding our democracy. It was an honor to know him. I wish that some of the members of Congress, specifically the Republicans who sat in that room while Congressman Cummings spoke, had listened and taken those words to heart. Hell, after watching the courageous Cassidy Hutchison testify before the January 6 committee, you have to wonder if anyone listened to anything I said at all. Time and again I warned them. Cummings got it. Most of the Democrats got it. The Republicans never did.

Remember when I warned Congress that Trump acted like a mob boss? Take a look at one of the tweets his team sent out to people who were subpoenaed to testify before Congress regarding the January 6 Hearings: "(A person) let me know you have your deposition tomorrow. He wants me to let you know that he's thinking about you. He knows you're loyal, and you're going to do the right thing when you go in for your deposition."

It's like something out of *The Godfather*—but that was Trump. That's how he always operated during the decade I worked for him. I suffered for it. After January 6, it was increasingly obvious the nation suffered from it as well. Without sounding too partisan, the Democratic members of the committee were truly interested in learning from me all they could about the narcissistic sociopath who occupied the Oval Office. The questions from the Democrats were poignant and relevant. For example, I had this exchange with Democratic Representative Jim Cooper of Tennessee:

> **Rep. Cooper:** Mr. Cohen, several times in your testimony, you state the bad things you did for Mr. Trump. And at some point, you apparently changed your course of action. There is a recurring refrain in your testimony that says, "And yet, I continued to work for him." At some point, you changed. What was the breaking point at which you decided to start telling the truth?
>
> **Cohen:** There are several factors. Helsinki, Charlottesville, watching the daily destruction of our civility to

one another, putting up with silly things like this, really unbecoming of Congress. It's that sort of behavior that I'm responsible for. I'm responsible for your silliness because I did the same thing you [referring to the Republican members of the committee] are doing now for 10 years. I protected Mr. Trump for 10 years . . . And I can only warn [that] people that follow Mr. Trump as I did, blindly, are going to suffer the same consequences that I'm suffering.

You may even recall three quarters through the hearing, after six hours of denigrations, badgering, nastiness, I had had enough and I said to the Republican members of the committee: "I find it interesting that not one question from you today has been about Mr. Trump. That's why I thought I was coming today."

But no, it was all about their fifteen minutes of fame, throwing themselves on the Trump flame trying to protect Donald from himself. Appease the master was their assignment for the day, and they followed like trained dogs.

Prior to my testimony in Congress, Republican members tried to postpone the hearing, claiming I had not provided a copy of my testimony in a timely fashion. That effort was derailed, so Trump loyalists had to settle on belittling me instead. In a term that became popular in the January 6 hearings, Trump loyalists did their best to "deflect and blame." In other words, on the day I testified before Congress, the Republicans tried their best to deflect from the president and blame me for his behavior.

But the best the Republicans could do that day was retreat into juvenile taunts like the one from Representative Paul Gosar of Arizona. He called me a disgraced lawyer, urged everyone to ignore my warnings and actually used a kindergarten school yard taunt: "Liar, liar, pants on fire." Then there was Matt Gaetz, who wasn't even supposed to be at the hearing—he had been turned down from joining the committee, and from being permitted to make a statement. Nevertheless, he tried his best to troll the proceedings. Not only did he send out the tweet I mentioned earlier—about my supposed "girlfriends"—for which the House had officially admonished him, but he also tweeted nasty things about me and my family.

Ohio Representative Jim Jordan, a paragon of no-virtue in the college wrestling world, tried to seize on my past false statements to Congress, which I had already admitted to. "Here we go," Jordan said smugly when the hearing began. "This might be the first time someone convicted of lying to Congress has been brought back," he said. "We are legitimizing dishonesty. We are de-legitimizing this institution." No, Gymbo. You did that yourself. That's why you were seen sniffing around for a pardon after the insurrection. It's eerily coincidental that I lied about the number of times I spoke to Donald about the failed Trump Tower Moscow project. Jordan lied about the number of times he spoke to Trump *during the insurrection.*

Remember Mark Meadows? He showed more reaction in my hearing than White House staffers say he showed during the insurrection. Meadows, who had graduated from Congress as a representative from North Carolina before becoming Trump's last chief of staff, sat playing with his cell phone doing nothing while rioters threatened the Capitol. Cassidy Hutchison testified how shocked staffers were at his detached and frankly uncaring attitude. Hey, during my testimony, he at least shook his head violently. He can't defend our democracy, he can only shake his head at those who do or ignore them completely. That's the type of person Donald Trump loves. That's who he hired and who he will easily throw under the bus.

Next up, there's Representative James Comer, a Republican from Kentucky. Capitol Hill insiders will tell you he's one of the most obsequious and ineffective congressmen in office. He tried to mousetrap me into calling myself a hero. But his efforts failed. "What would you call yourself?" he asked me.

"A fool," I answered.

Comer appeared dumbfounded and confused for a moment. He had clearly rehearsed a lengthy response, no doubt meant to denigrate me further, and not being able to spew his rehearsed speech clearly irritated him.

Mission accomplished.

At one point it got so bad with the Republicans following Trump's dicta to relentlessly badger me, that Representative Stephen Lynch of Massachusetts told the Republicans: "Your side ran away from the truth, we're trying to bring it to the American people."

That was in 2019.

That was more than two years *before* the insurrection, and the Republicans were already showing their true colors. "You don't have to take my word for it," I told the Republicans in Congress then and I repeatedly say now. "I did the same thing that you are doing now. I protected Mr. Trump for 10 years. And I will be heading to prison in a few months as a result."

How far did I go protecting Trump? Well, let's just say I may have committed my sins, but I never covered for the president when he allegedly attacked his own Secret Service detail and tried to take control of the presidential SUV. I never took the Fifth like former National Security Advisor Michael Flynn did when asked if he would support a peaceful transfer of power.

So, what did I do—that is besides paying off a woman to be quiet about her affair with the president and lying about the number of times Trump and I discussed a possible deal to open a Trump Tower in Moscow?

Jackie Speier of California asked me "What else did you do? Did you ever threaten anyone for Donald Trump?" I was honest about that too. I responded that I threatened as many as 500 people at Trump's behest—including journalists. That response to her question has become a Tik-Tok soundbite used by millions for their posts. That alone made my appearance at the hearing worth it.

But the admission was as I had admitted during my criminal sentencing, when I told judge William H. Pauley that I was blinded by misguided loyalty. "Time and time again, I felt it was my duty to cover up his dirty deeds."[27] I felt it was important that the judge, the country and the world hold the man equally accountable for the actions he directed and benefitted from; specifically the countless lies I told in order to stay on Donald's message.

During the hearing, it was Maryland Democratic Congressman Jamie Raskin who seized upon *that* fact and exposed it for what it was. Prior to asking me any questions, he made a very simple statement that he later turned into a tweet: "Our GOP colleagues aren't upset because you lied to Congress for the president. They're upset because you *stopped* lying to Congress for the president."

Truer words were never spoken, and had it not been for Raskin and the Democrats who asked me questions that actually mattered about Donald Trump, then my visit to Congress would have been a complete waste of time.

The Democrats remained focused on Donald Trump and what he could do to ruin lives. It was Congressman Cooper who gave me the opportunity to explain my most personal feelings about my time spent with Trump and how that association cost me personally. It was this answer to Cooper that Cummings later reflected upon in his closing speech:

> **Cooper:** What warning would you give young people who are tempted as you were? Would you encourage them not to wait 10 years to see the light? What advice would you give young people, in particular young lawyers, so they do not abuse their bar license, as you did?
>
> **Cohen:** Look at what happened to me. I had a wonderful life. I have a beautiful wife and two amazing children. I achieved financial success by the age of 39. I didn't go to work for Mr. Trump because I had to. I went to work for him because I wanted to. And I've lost it all. You make mistakes in life, and I've owned them. I've taken responsibility for them. I'm paying a huge price, as is my family.

Compare and contrast that against the Republicans game of infantile evasion, deflection and name calling:

> **Representative Jordan:** Mr. Cohen, how long did you work in the White House?

> **Cohen:** I never worked in the White House.

> **Jordan:** That's the point, isn't it?

> **Cohen:** No, sir.

> **Jordan:** Yes, it is.

> **Cohen:** No, it's not, sir.

> **Jordan:** You wanted to work in the White House.

> **Cohen:** No, sir.

> **Jordan:** You didn't get brought to the dance.

Jordan is an imbecile in short-sleeved shirts. Unlike him, I never needed Donald Trump. Donald Trump needed me and that's why he asked me to work for him. Gymbo made himself known to Donald by continuously going on television and repeating Trump's talking points. Jordan doesn't know the real Donald. That takes years of working with him, and experiencing all of his narcissistic, sociopathic tendencies. So, when I testified before Congress I was able to impart upon the committee my intimate knowledge of Donald and forewarned them of the danger he had and would present to the country:

> Unlike my [Twitter account] that's got 1,000 followers, [the president]'s got over 60 million people. When Mr. Trump turned around early in the campaign and said, I can shoot somebody on Fifth Avenue and get away with it, I want to be very clear: He's not joking. He's telling you the truth. You don't know him. I do. I've sat next to this man for 10 years and I watched his back. I'm the one who started the campaign, and I'm the one who continued in 2015 to promote him. So many things I thought that he can do are just great. And he can, and he is, doing things that are great. But this destruction of our civility to one another, it's out of control. When he goes on Twitter and he starts bringing in my in-laws, my parents, my wife, what does he think is going to happen? He's sending out the same message—that he can do whatever he wants. It is becoming his country, and he's becoming an autocrat. And hopefully something bad will happen to me, my family, my children, or my wife, so that I will not be here to testify—that's what his hope is, to intimidate me.[28]

Every time the Republicans on the committee pushed me, I returned the volley. But, I also tried to make them understand.

Especially guys like Jordan, Gaetz, and Gohmert. I wanted them to know: They are headed for a fall. They were either too stupid to do that, too corrupt to care, or too blinded by Trump to be able to tell the difference. I honestly suspect that most of them were, and are, delusional; suffering from all three conditions—stupidity, corruption, and delusion. So again, when I was asked about my sins by a Republican, I explained that I wasn't there to confess to the mistakes that I made. "I've already done that. And I'll do it again, every time you ask me about taxes or mistakes. Yes, I made my mistakes. I'll say it now again. I'm going to pay the ultimate price . . . The American people don't care about my taxes. They want to know what it is that I know about Mr. Trump. Not one question so far has been asked about Mr. Trump."

Time and time again, it was the Democrats who understood this wasn't a political game to be played on an uneven playing field. It was a matter of justice and it wasn't just Congressman Raskin who kept his eye on the prize. AOC stepped up and delivered a brilliant series of questions that outlined who else needed to be questioned besides me:

> **Ocasio-Cortez**: Thank you. Now, in October 2018, the *New York Times* revealed that, "President Trump participated in dubious tax schemes during the 1990s, including instances of outright fraud that greatly increased the fortune he received from his parents." It further stated [about] Mr. Trump, "He also helped formulate a strategy to undervalue his parents' real-estate holdings by hundreds of millions of dollars on tax returns, sharply reducing his tax bill when those

properties were transferred to him and his siblings."
Mr. Cohen, do you know whether that specific report
is accurate?

Cohen: I don't. I wasn't there in the 1990s.

Ocasio-Cortez: Who would know the answer to those
questions?

Cohen: [Trump Organization Chief Financial Officer]
Allen Weisselberg.

Ocasio-Cortez: And would it help for the committee
to obtain federal and state tax returns from the president and his company to address that discrepancy?

Cohen: I believe so.

The bottom line was the Democrats wanted to know everything about
Trump and his fantastic interest in becoming a dictatorial monarch,
a Caesar, a Montezuma, a pharoah. The Republicans only wanted to
cover for him.

That's why when the January 6 Commission hearings got underway the Republicans, in their arrogance, convinced themselves that if
they refused to participate in the commission, the commission would
either disappear or would have no credibility. The thought they could
cover for Trump by stonewalling the committee and make it all go
away—like sunlight or bleach would make the pandemic evaporate.

But their blind and reckless worship of Donald Trump is proving to be their undoing. Fortunately there were two Republicans who were not sniffing the ass of the big dog. Those two are Illinois Representative Adam Kinzinger and Wyoming Representative Liz Cheney, who showed themselves to be two of the very few Republicans who were willing to put country before party.

I tried to warn everyone about Trump's narcissistic, insane plans to remain in power. I rightly pointed out that he would not go gentle into that good night. And while few could have predicted the insanity Donald Trump unleashed on January 6, 2021, none of it surprises me. It does not surprise me that Donald Trump said Mike Pence deserved to be hanged. It does not surprise me that he was accused of lunging at his Secret Service driver and trying to grab the steering wheel. It does not surprise me that he didn't care that there were armed protesters—after all, as he said, they weren't there to harm him.

But it does make me wonder where we will draw the line. What does it take to hold the powerful accountable when they try to destroy our country and democracy as a whole? What do we have to do to make sure nothing like this ever happens again—for the sake of ourselves, our children, and our posterity? The ideals upon which this nation was founded are solid; however our democracy is fragile and it is not a birthright, it's a choice that needs to be protected from individuals who seek to exploit the power granted by the office for their own ends. No one said it better than Thomas Jefferson, "Eternal vigilance is the price of liberty."

In fact, from the beginning of our country, there were incidents that reinforced Jefferson's concerns for the nascent democracy in the United States. There were scandals and challenges that tested "whether that nation, or any nation so conceived, and so dedicated, can long endure," as Lincoln said in his Gettysburg address—but it wasn't just the Civil War.

In 1796, a man that was at heart not much different than Donald Trump fomented rebellion for the sake of his own bottom line. William Blount was a Continental Congressman. He was a *signatory* of the Constitution. This isn't a guy who just read it. He signed it. But he also has the dubious distinction of being the first politician to be expelled from the United States Senate. While serving as a senator in the Volunteer State (Tennessee) in 1796, Blount planned to help the British seize Spanish-held territory in what is now Louisiana and Florida. Blount called for frontiersmen and the Cherokee Indian nation to rise up against the Spanish and drive them away from the Gulf Coast. After that he planned to have the region become an English colony and open its doors to settlers thus allowing Blount— who just happened to own huge tracts of Western land—to make a killing on his investments.[29]

Sound familiar to anyone? Yeah, Donald Trump isn't unique. Maybe some of the Congressmen tied up with Trump should look to the history of this country and see what awaits them.

That's not the only scandal in American history to sound like something hatched in the rancid kitchen of Mar-A-Lago.

There is the murky Burr conspiracy, which also sounded a lot like a Trumpian scheme.

A little more than a year after former Vice President Aaron Burr killed Alexander Hamilton in a duel (okay, that part is definitely not like Trump. The Donald can barely handle himself in an argument, much less a gunfight), Burr got involved in a land-grab scheme in the American West. That's the part that sounds like Trump. The details are not fully known to this day (another feature reminiscent of The Donald—trying to get decent facts is damn near impossible), but evidence that was gathered suggests Burr planned to invade Spanish territories on the frontier and establish a new western empire with himself as its leader. (There is absolutely no truth to the rumor that he was trying to negotiate for a "Burr Tower" on the frontier.)

But that's not all. To achieve his aim, Burr may have also planned to incite a revolution to separate the western territories of the Louisiana Purchase from the United States. That plot began in 1805, when Burr traveled west and enlisted the help of U.S. General James Wilkinson, apparently the 19th-century version of Mike Flynn, a notorious intriguer who also happened to be a Spanish spy (Flynn had to settle for Russia). By the following year, Burr had assembled recruits and military equipment on an island in the Ohio River.

Whatever he planned to do, Burr never got a chance to make it happen. Wilkinson lost his nerve and told Thomas Jefferson. Burr was arrested and put on trial for treason a few months later, but was acquitted on the grounds that his plans did not constitute an "overt act" of war against his country. But the fallout from his trial left Burr's political career in ruins. He spent several years living in Europe before resettling in New York in 1812 and opening a law practice.[30]

From the time the country was running itself up to the Civil War, Congress looked then kind of like it does now, complete with divisive partisan politics, lies and threats of violence. In fact, it was so heated back then that there was an *actual* outbreak of violence on the Senate floor.

During a discussion of the Kansas-Nebraska Act—a law that allowed the citizens of those territories to vote on whether they would allow slavery—abolitionist Senator Charles Sumner gave a fiery speech in which he accused South Carolina's Andrew Butler of being a "zealot" who was enamored with the "harlot" of slavery. Ouch.

Preston Brooks, a proslavery congressman who also just happened to be Butler's nephew, didn't take too kindly to the insults. Three days later, Brooks confronted Sumner in the Senate chamber and assaulted him with a metal-topped cane, repeatedly beating him over the head until the stick splintered into pieces.

Could you see Mitch McConnell or Chuck Schumer doing that today? I don't think so. They might assault each other with pancake makeup or fake sweat, but beating each other with canes? Hey, we're a kinder and gentler nation.

The cane attack left Sumner so badly beaten that it took him more than three years to fully recover. Brooks, meanwhile, was fined for assault and put under congressional investigation, but a measure to expel him from the House of Representatives failed to gather the required two-thirds majority. He voluntarily resigned in July 1856, only to be reseated by his constituents a few days later. In a preview of the divisions that would lead to the Civil War (or a Fox News report versus an MSNBC report), the scandal saw Brooks simultaneously denounced in the North and hailed as a hero in the South. Supporters even sent him replacement canes, including one inscribed with the words "Hit Him Again."[31]

Yes, almost everything we see today has been seen before. There were also scandals in the 1870s—including an infamous one during the 1872 election season. The *New York Sun* broke a story (*Fake News*, Donald would cry!) about an infamous "very bad deal" with some "bad hombres" as Donald would say, involving several business leaders, U.S. congressmen, and even the vice president of the United States. The "Credit Mobilier" scandal involved a construction company contracted by the Union Pacific Railroad to help build the transcontinental railroad. The scandal's exposure led to a congressional investigation, but despite evidence that corruption extended to more than a dozen politicians, including Vice President Schuyler Colfax, only two representatives—Massachusetts Congressmen Oakes Ames and James Brooks—were officially censured. Neither man was expelled and no criminal charges were ever filed.

It almost seems like every 50 years or so we get a Trump-like scandal. And each succeeding scandal seemingly tops the previous one. The Aaron Burr scandal was the most infamous of its time and so was the Credit Mobilier scandal.

Just about 50 years after the Credit Mobilier scandal we reached new depths with the Teapot Dome scandal, involving President Warren G. Harding. Secretary of the Interior Albert Bacon Fall became the first presidential cabinet member to go to prison in a bribery scandal as a result of the fallout of Teapot Dome.

It was called the "greatest and most sensational scandal in the history of American politics . . ."[32] until fifty years later, in the 1970s, the Watergate scandal led to the resignation of President Richard Nixon.

John Dean, who spent a week on the stand testifying against Nixon, his former boss, today says Watergate pales in comparison to what Donald Trump has done to the nation. "Watergate was so different and mild," he told me.

Nixon could at least experience shame. He resigned
rather than put the country through an impeachment
hearing. Donald Trump put the country through two
impeachment hearings and didn't care one bit if he
ripped the country apart because of them. It's a very
different time with very different players.

That is simply an understatement by Dean. I've just outlined most
of the serious and threatening scandals this country has faced since
we kicked out King George and established our own country. They
all share similar elements with the current Donald Trump calamity
because Donald Trump is a product of this country. He was born
into the elitist upper class of the United States, and had access to
power, money, and the publicity that comes with his station. He is
the ultimate ugly American and is the synthesis of every scandal that
came before him. He sits, crying, whimpering, and throwing fits as
the king on a mountain of shitty political scandals that go back to
the founding of our country.

"I think Donald Trump is probably someone who threw tantrums
his entire life," John Dean observed, "and he's gotten away with them.
Of course he would throw tantrums as president. Of course he would
act like a spoiled child. I don't find anything surprising about that."

But what Trump brought that's new to the American history of
scandals, is the depth to which he sunk the Department of Justice.
Sure, President Harding, plagued by the Teapot Dome scandal also
had to deal with a scandal involving his attorney general Harry M.
Daugherty[33]—he was suspected of profiting from the sale of government alcohol supplies, failing to enforce prohibition statutes, and the

selling of pardons.

There have been several minor scandals involving the Department of Justice before and after Teapot Dome and Harding. But none of them compare to the level of depravity to which that institution sank under Donald Trump.

"I think the testimony certainly shows that Trump corrupted the Department of Justice," John Dean told me. "And few would dispute that fact."

That's because you can't dispute it. How low can we go? Only Donald Trump knows. I guarantee you however low you think he'll go, he will go lower. And that brings me back to the point I made earlier.

If someone will go as low as Donald Trump for his own personal gain, then how do we police that? How can we be vigilant in a world where facts are malleable, our president is corrupt, and the branch of government designed to ensure justice for every citizen cannot do its job because the attorney general is too busy acting as the president's personal lawyer?

That's the problem we face with Trump.

Sure, this country's had bad scandals before. It seems as if we cannot avoid them.

What makes this scandal truly worse than any that have come before is in the way it threatens democracy itself. What Trump has done is provide a dangerous road map for the next—probably smarter—fascist.

We need to root them out. We need to extricate them from our system. Otherwise, we're headed for madness . . . and democracy will be dead.

CHAPTER SIX

THE DEPARTMENT OF INJUSTICE

PEOPLE COME AND PEOPLE GO.

I'm not talking about the circle of life; I'm talking about the Department of Justice. While the tone of this book is critical, the purpose is far more reaching than just pointing fingers. Yes, we identified the multitude of individuals within the department who had a dirty hand in prosecuting me. However, there were many who did not. They are the agents, prosecutors, investigators and judges who are decent, honorable people who have ideals and a desire to do good and contribute to justice for all of us. These individuals should not be grouped with the ones who used the system for their own gain; threatening the end of our democracy.

The problem is, if you are associated and work for a corrupt and abusive organization, the presumption is that you are the same. It's the logical fallacy often employed when people say, if you are a MAGA Trump supporter, then you are a racist. That is not accurate.

Not all MAGA Trump supporters are racists . . . but all racists are MAGA Trump supporters. Further, don't assume because I worked for Trump that I'm like him.

In short, I mean the Department of Justice can be saved. It must be saved. Our democracy can be saved. It must be saved as well. There are more than enough good people currently working at the DOJ to pass down the proper way to conduct business; to behave in a manner consistent with the ideals to which the department was established; to stand for justice.

If I were to only speak and write of the decent individuals, then the dangers that lurk in the shadows of the Department of Injustice will never be revealed. The same miscarriage of justice that was committed against me can and will happen to you. No one said it better than George Santayana when he declared, "those that fail to learn from history are doomed to repeat it."

Or, if you prefer, there's the maxim offered to us by Dr. Martin Luther King Jr.: "Justice denied anywhere diminishes justice everywhere."[1]

The justice system as it exists today seems incapable of serving its purpose—even at the most basic level. I'm not talking about creating a "perfect" system. I'm merely talking about making sure our government is responsible to its citizens, acknowledges its mistakes and tries to do better. It has been argued, notably by historians, political scientists and authors, that the United States has historically embraced this ideal. "The founding of America, its government and its institutions have been uniquely constructed to expect and tolerate human fallibility. Instead of demanding perfection, we are 'a country made great by disagreement and error.'"[2]

Today our government has become numb and bitter. Those in government believe themselves to be above reproach. If a mistake is made, then tough shit. Live with it. I have the badge, so it's my way or the highway to the federal correctional facility. The result: Ineptitude and self-interest are rampant and threaten the crash and fall of the entire system.

This is the United States we live in today.

If justice is to prevail, then those who can must stand up and speak truth to power. Despite all that I have gone through, and put my family through, I remain steadfast in this effort to do so and I refuse to quit. I refuse to accept what was done to me, bury my head in the sand, and allow these bastards to do it to anyone else.

In pursuit of the documentary proof needed to hold those responsible accountable for their actions, I have sought information for the last year and a half that I know the government has relating to my case. I want and need this information, so I once again filed several Freedom of Information Act requests for it. As of this date, like my previous FOIA requests, I still have not been provided the requested information.

In the first filing, the government incredulously denied that *any* information existed. In the denial letter, the government stated, "The OIG (Office of the Inspector General) has completed its search and identified no responsive documents."[3] I knew this was shit. So, I went to the James Madison Project, which took up my case and filed suit against the U.S. Department of Justice.

Still, we received nothing!

I knew they were completely disingenuous when they said they had "no responsive documents."

They were just stonewalling me.

For fuck sake, I had copies of letters from Michael Horowitz, the Inspector General of the Justice Department, about me and my case. Only after I provided members of the DOJ with copies—*from their own office*—did they admit they were wrong.

They knew they had been caught.

Let me be clear, this wasn't an innocent mistake. This wasn't a case of government forgetting, or failing to find some single piece of information hidden away in some vast complex with people toiling away for months trying to find it. This wasn't the final scene of Indiana Jones where a box is stored in an enormous warehouse, essentially hidden from view with no one able to retrieve it.

This is a case that required a simple computer search. Input the keywords and the system identifies the documents that match the query. I don't want to oversimplify it, but it's literally as simple as typing my full name in the search bar and pressing enter. Thanks to the James Madison Project initiating litigation, on March 10, 2022, the OIG provided another response to our request. It stated, "Prior to the parties' last status report, Plaintiffs provided additional information to the OIG to consider and the OIG provided Plaintiffs with its response to that additional information."[4]

And that response? After we informed the government that *we knew* they had information including providing a copy of a letter proving it, the DOJ suddenly had a change of heart. I nearly fell off my chair when I received their letter, stating that the DOJ "had identified over 450,000 pages of potentially responsive material, and the parties had begun discussing ways to narrow the scope of the search and review for this case."[5]

That's right. Soak that shit in for a minute. The U.S. government went from telling me it had nothing (after I confronted them with evidence to the contrary) to admitting they actually had in their possession more than "450,000 pages" of documents.

That's like 400 copies of Tolstoy's *War and Peace*. If you believe for a second this was an innocent oversight, then oh do I have a bridge to sell you. In truth this was an attempt to cover up information that I believe will lead to the conclusion that the DOJ acted irresponsibly and corruptly in its prosecution of me.

To add salt to the wound, these stalwart lackeys claim that due to the amount of the documents requested they wanted me to narrow the parameters of my search to make their job easier. If that isn't a cherry on top of the cake, they then claimed they would have to converse and receive authorization from other agencies before releasing any of the documents. It is their farcical assertion that they can only provide no more than 500 documents per month. You don't have to be a math genius to calculate that you won't receive the last batch of documents until 2112. With my co-morbidities there's a slim chance I'll be around to collect the final package.

Knowing the difficulties of obtaining the FBI 302s, forms used by agents to report or summarize the interviews they conduct for the grand jury, I elected to remove them from the request. As a result that reduced the number of documents to approximately 47,000. So, I guess I only have to wait nine years for my request to be fulfilled. I have a good chance of surviving that time period; but does our democracy?

If the DOJ really had any intention of filling my request they don't have to dole it out piecemeal. They could easily download it to a thumb drive and send it to me. But they won't.

"Delay. Delay. Delay." That should be the motto of the Department of Justice instead of "Qui Pro Domina Justitia Sequitur" (Who prosecutes on behalf of justice). The former is certainly more applicable.

They just don't want to do anything—especially if my name is attached to it.

I can't even obtain my First Step Act earned time credits I am statutorily entitled to for work and programming courses I completed while in prison. Those credits are designed to allow eligible federal inmates, non-violent offenders with a low chance of recidivism, to get a reduction in their sentence. The First Step Act was designed so those inmates can earn up to a year off of their prison term—including any time spent in home confinement and on supervised release.

While the First Step Act was signed by Trump just before Christmas Day 2018, the law as written gave the Federal Bureau of Prisons three years to *fully* implement the act—by no later than January 13, 2022. Maybe Trump had amnesia the day he signed it, or didn't realize the act would benefit me. Of course, there is also the possibility he signed it thinking ahead to his or one of his children's future incarceration.

While on home confinement I reached out to the Bureau of Prisons and FCI Otisville to find out about my earned time credits. The goal was to get off of home confinement, placed on supervised release, thus bringing me closer to completing my sentence.

That request still hasn't been answered.

With plenty of time on my hands, no pun intended, I elected to file pro se a writ of habeas corpus in hopes that a federal judge would step in and interpret the First Step Act as it related to my case. I based my writ on a United States District Court, District of New Jersey case, "Goodman v. Ortiz," decided August 2020, four months before I filed my own.

By coincidence, my attorney Danya Perry represented Goodman in that. It's too bad I didn't have the same judge as in that case; United States District Judge Renee Marie Bumb. In the Goodman case, Judge Bumb concluded,

> the BOP's position that a prisoner can complete the PATTERN [the Prisoner Assessment Tool Targetting Estimated Risk and Needs] program before January 15, 2022 with no benefit to the prisoner is *contrary* to the statutory language, not to mention the unfairness of such a result. Therefore the court concludes that Petitioner is entitled to habeas relief. The Court will direct the BOP to immediately apply Petitioner's Earned Time credit of 120 days in an accompanying Order.

I'm not superstitious by nature, but I believed that since my case closely mirrored Goodman, and the Goodman case was decided on my birthday, I'd get essentially the same result.

As it turned out, good for Goodman. Not so good for me, as the judge in my case, the honorable U.S. District Court Judge John G. Koeltl, didn't see it the same way.

I filed the writ on December 21, 2020, exactly two years after Trump signed the First Step Act into law. I pointed out I had pleaded guilty and was sentenced to 36 months, and I outlined the act's purpose and how as a low risk prisoner the act applied to me. I walked the judge through the history of the act and how "Congress aimed to enhance public safety by improving the effectiveness and efficiency of the federal prison system with offender risk and needs assessment, individual risk reduction incentive and rewards, and risk and recidivism reduction."

I guess the judge didn't buy my cogent, well thought-out argument—or he didn't care about public safety as much as Congress did. Judge Koeltl dismissed my writ April 20, 2021. He said my case wasn't "ripe" for consideration until January 2022.

Here's something that should not surprise you; as of July 2022, I *still* haven't heard anything from the government. More than a year and a half has passed since I initially filed the writ and the government has yet to provide me with any earned time credit for my work or programming credits. I also asked in the writ for the Bureau of Prisons to just *calculate* the proper credits that could reduce the time I needed to serve.

To this day, after 32 emails back and forth with Darrin Howard, the Northeast Region Regional Counsel of the Bureau of Prisons, not only have I not received the requested credits information, I haven't even been told how all my work and programming will apply to any potential sentence reduction. Howard just continuously says he just doesn't know. Would it surprise anyone if I told you that they still apparently have not figured out *how* to apply the credits toward pre-release custody or supervised release? No one seems to know. After four years, the government apparently can't even tell me *how much* earned time credit I am entitled to!

How can Congress pass a law, how can the Bureau of Prisons institute a policy, and have no means of figuring out how to implement it?

Seriously?

I've said it before: Delay. Delay. Delay. The BOP, through the DOJ, will delay this to the point that the request means squat and I've served my full time or, using my newly-learned prison lingo, they ran me door to door.

If justice delayed is truly justice denied, the DOJ and by extension the BOP are the valedictorians of injustice.

Let's not criticize *only* the government. Government does not stand alone in what we endured during the Trump administration. Every guilty actor has an accomplice, or, as I once described Donald, a co-conspirator. Accordingly, we need to hold the media accountable as well. Who can forget the endless hours of televised Trump rallies being aired on all national media, and then covered on the front pages of major newspapers. As if we hadn't had enough of the Mandarin Mussolini, every news panel and pundit would then offer their opinion on the Trump chaos of the day. Why wouldn't they? As Trump demonstrated, the media are all driven by ratings and money and don't give a shit about the gathering of facts and information, as romance would have it. Journalists today, as H. L. Mencken put it, have slipped "supinely into the estate and dignity of a golf player."[6]

Too hard to understand? Well, then let's let Mencken, the pre-eminent media critic of the 20th century, be blunt:

> He prints balderdash because he doesn't know how to
> get anything better—perhaps in many cases, because
> he doesn't know that anything better exists . . . it is not

that he is dishonest, but that he is stupid—and, being stupid, a coward. The resourcefulness, enterprise, and bellicosity that his job demands are simply not in him.[7]

That lazy intellect and cowardice leads us to where we are today as consumers of what passes for news. It is easy to sit in our favorite chair in the comfort of our home, pointing a finger at an individual on television that you despise. That raw emotion is often predicated on news you've seen from your favorite news channel, newspaper, or app. What if that information is truly misinformation, disinformation or (in the new term of the day) *malinformation?* No one said it better than my former friend and bullshit spreader, Fox television's Sean Hannity, when he stated, "I'm not a journalist, I'm a talk show host."[8]

Let me break this down. Misinformation is the easiest to define. It is when unintentional mistakes are made, such as inaccurate photo captions, dates, statistics, translations, or even when satire is taken seriously.[9] Disinformation? Well that's a lot of what's on Fox News and other even more questionable so-called news venues, like News Max and OANN. That's fabricated or deliberately manipulated content. Then there's "malinformation"—that's the deliberate publication of private information that doesn't serve any public interest or the deliberate change of context, date or time of genuine facts.[10]

Regrettably this is the new normal.

In my case, I have had to deal with all three being used against me by members of the media either too stupid or too lazy to get the real story. There were tens of millions of articles that were wrong, wrong to the core, but they were publicized hour after hour and day after day for at least the last three years. No wonder I was so despised.

Truth be told, if the only way I learned about Michael Cohen was from those news articles and reports, I'd despise me too.

Let us briefly go over some of the mistakes that have been made in the media about me and my case. This is not done for a self-serving purpose. The bigger point is that my experience reinforces the opinion that people on both the left and the right say when they claim there's something wrong with journalism. Too often, they are right. Media corporations, driven by profit and shareholders' distributions, could care less about the facts—so long as the revenue spigot remains open. In essence they go where the advertising money is, based on the size of their audience. Next up, we have the reporters who simply want to get "the scoop" and ignore well-established journalistic standards to get it. They don't verify facts and they don't reach out for comment. They just want to be first. As a result they become unwitting partners with the corrupt DOJ and others providing the often-inaccurate source material.

For example, the DOJ typically doesn't speak on the record about ongoing investigations. "We can neither confirm nor deny" such investigation exists, is the standard response to any press inquiry at the DOJ about most investigations, right up until the point where there are indictments. But that doesn't stop reporters from working their DOJ sources—who often supply prurient details on investigations as long as it is done "on background," meaning that the reporter will use the information but not attribute it to anyone. (Trump commonly referred to such sources as "the leakers.") The danger of relying on background information is that it cannot be vetted. It's childish, it's lazy, and it's the kind of innuendo you might remember from the fourth grade when you learned little Bobby had a crush on Mary.

Wait. It gets worse. Journalism today is controlled by a very small number of companies that, motivated solely by profit, save money by hiring fewer and less experienced (i.e. less expensive) reporters. That's part of the profit strategy. It's one of the ways these companies control expenses. It is a well-established dicta that if you reduce expenses, then you generate greater profitability. And profitability is what these companies are all about. What's more, the bigger they get, the *more* that's what they're about.

These large corporations have thrown out the belief that complex news stories require years of experience to understand. Sorry, Walter Cronkite and Barbara Walters. You're out.

Instead of news today, what we get are talking heads on panel shows taking up our time espousing their personal opinions while passing on rumors they've heard, have not verified and never even thought to verify.

How about we just all agree—no more *innuendo.*

My case, in particular, was fraught with lies based upon unverified facts, misinformation, malinformation and pure, bullshit propaganda. As a result, I got the living shit kicked out of me—not only by the Justice Department and the courts, but in the court of public opinion. And what were these lies predicated upon? Rumor, conjecture, speculation, and insinuation.

One such example is the persistent rumor that when you stepped into my office that a recording device immediately switched on and I taped you. If that seems patently false to you, then congratulations you can join reality. Because it was and is a *lie.* So was the rumor that I taped Trump during hundreds of conversations. Wrong. I taped Trump *once.* I've already explained in this book when and why. Yet, due to lies promoted by Trump's inner circle and spewed across various news platforms, millions of people *to this day* believe I have dozens if not hundreds of taped recordings of Donald Trump.

Here are just a few of the additional lies about me that metastasized in the press:

- I wanted to go to DC and work in the administration.

- I went to Prague.

- All of the allegations raised against me in the Steele Dossier.

- I paid hackers to hack HRC and DNC computers.

- I managed to have the two SARS reports deleted from the FINCEN system.

- I laundered money through my LLC, Essential Consultants.

- The Avenatti claim that I sent a thug to threaten Stormy Daniels in Nevada.

- The FBI obtained 16 pages of shredded sensitive documents during the raid.

- I sold access to the White House.

- Gene Friedman, the Taxi King, was my business partner.

- I wired $60 million overseas to ???.

- I was indicted and fined $1 million for kiting titles in Chicago.

- Rudy Giuliani's contention that "this has nothing to do with POTUS . . . it's all about Cohen's businesses."

- 20 of my electronic devices were seized.

- The Andre Artemenko Ukrainian peace plan.

- I received $400,000 from Petro Poroshenko to arrange access to Trump.

- I have multiple passports and must have used one of them to enter the Czech Republic to get to Prague.

- I paid Karen McDougal $150,000.

While these lies wound their way through social and mainstream media, I wanted to reply the way Jack Nicholson does in *A Few Good Men*, and say, "You want the truth? You can't handle the truth." Nobody can pull it off like Jack. I'd probably just shout it at the top of my lungs.

Let me do it this way instead:

Remember what the Buddha taught—"Three things cannot be long hidden: the sun, the moon, and the truth." Donald Trump remains the kind of guy who would beat his head against a wall long enough to prove the Buddha wrong and keep the truth hidden. With a frequency and ferocity, Donald Trump lies—about damn near everything. He only tells truths if they'll further his lies. But even he can't avoid certain facts—like the fact that I *never* wanted to go to D.C and work in the Trump administration. What I wanted I got. It was the best of both worlds. I had the power without being trapped in government. I was the personal attorney to the president of the United States of America. Damn fine title if you can get it. It was exactly what I asked for and exactly what I received.

I told Jim Jordan that very fact when I testified before Congress. Not that he listened. There are those who still don't. On a CNN panel, *after I testified before Congress,* reporters continued to doubt my word. "I think the issue there is that one sentence: 'I did not want to go to the White House.' All of our reporting suggests that's not true," Jake Tapper said.[ll] The problem is, nobody asked me. They asked people who were sworn to spread Donald Trump's lies. Journalists and others took those people at face value. Some reasoned that the powerful Wizard of Trump was omnipotent and therefore if he wanted me at the White House then it would magically happen. Since I wasn't there, he must not want me there—free will be damned. The failure in logic is amazing.

As for going to Prague; I won't bore you. There is no point in responding further. Go back to Chapter One. Reference the Mueller and the FBI report. It's all there.

The same holds true regarding the allegations raised in the fictional Steele Dossier, including hacking Clinton's and the DNC computers. As for the source of that report, Christopher Steele, I still hold him in the highest minimum regard.

Another player I hold in the same regard as Steele is Michael Avenatti. He beats Steele for being the worst offender of all in spreading tales about me. Thankfully he will be spending years behind bars; so there is still some measure of justice in our system. Avenatti would often end his tweets with "#Basta." Well, basta to you pal. Enough. He lied about me from the very beginning for his benefit as he attempted to extort money from Nike while simultaneously stealing money from his client, Stormy Daniels. Again, it's all about the money.

He held press conference after press conference deriding me. During one appearance on the "The Beat with Ari Melber," he claimed I was in sole possession of secret tapes about Trump. "Just like the Nixon tapes, years ago, we now have the Trump tapes . . . and now they are under lock and key," Avenatti claimed. Then he urged me to "Go ahead and release the recordings."[12] It sure caused a caustic shitstorm. One thing Avenatti was good at was sensationalism—making bold statements on matters he had no knowledge of—other than knowing that what he was saying was utterly false. No different than when he provided a photo of an open safe with a computer disc, claiming he was in possession of information that would take Trump apart. With what? A blank CD disc?

Every news outlet featured so-called experts and pundits chiming in on Avenatti's constant lies—treating them as gospel. It was all made up by a narcissistic sociopath (Avenatti) looking to take advantage of and make money off of another narcissistic sociopath (Donald Trump). The networks believed him, until they couldn't and then had their so-called experts and pundits chiming in on the same lies—this time defending their coverage of the lies. Let's just hope they all become cellmates.

And here is where we must hold media accountable. Not one news organization vetted Avenatti's statements to determine their veracity. Rather, they continued to put him on television where he could openly spout his falsehoods.

On another occasion, while he was on with Jake Tapper, Avenatti continued promoting these claims. Pressed by Tapper on why the American people should have access to my private conversations, Avenatti responded, "I know for a fact that one or more of these conversations do describe things that are inappropriate." Really? The only inappropriate thing I did was pay off Stormy Daniels at the direction and benefit of Donald J. Trump. Perhaps Avenatti was referring to his own inappropriate actions, including stealing money from Stormy. He did, after all, plead guilty to it.

"People are allowed to have conversations," Avenatti said, "but they're not allowed to tape or record those conversations unless they have permission, unless you're in a single party state. A number of these recordings were made illegally. They should be disclosed now to the American people."

Avenatti added that "our understanding is there are countless hours of recordings of conversations between Michael Cohen and others," and "the conversations include conversations with Mr. Trump."[13]

Again, let me be blunt. This was pure crap. And while individually these indiscretions don't add up to much, when you consider the lies told cumulatively about me over the years—along with my prosecution at the hands of the federal government—it's like a bomb going off every day with someone pointing a finger at you saying, "Michael Cohen did this . . . Michael Cohen did that."

Blaming Michael Cohen for anything that went wrong became so popular, and my name was mentioned so often, that I wouldn't be surprised if it became a college drinking game.

The extremes this blame game took on were never more ridiculous than when the United States became embroiled in the Ukrainian/Russian conflict. Let's start with Ukrainian lawmaker Andre Artemenko. I met with him in late January 2017. Why, you may ask? At the request of Felix Sater, a former Trump confidant and someone I had casually been acquainted with since I was a teen. The press, of course, falsely turned Felix into my best friend growing up. In reality we crossed paths five or six times socially as young adults. It wasn't until I began working at the Trump Organization that I became reacquainted with Sater. He was a principal in Bayrock Group, a real estate conglomerate that was a licensee of the Trump Organization in the proposed Trump SoHo property.

One day in early 2017, he asked me for a favor. He asked if I could meet a friend of his at the Regency in one of the conference rooms. I did. I had no idea why I was going there or who I was to meet. When I got there Sater introduced me to Artemenko, who said he was a member of the Ukrainian parliament.

"What can I do for you?" I asked him.

He handed me a manilla envelope. Inside was a one-page document. A third of the document was some kind of hyperlink explaining who he was.

As he handed me the document, he asked me to give it to Trump and Mike Flynn, because, he said "Tens of thousands of Russians and Ukrainians are dying over Crimea." He spoke relatively decent English.

I took the document and said, "Well, nobody wants to see anybody die, what can I do?"

That's when they said they would like for me to speak to Trump about getting Russia to lease Crimea for 50 to 100 years.

Boy, was this guy barking up the wrong tree.

"Not going to happen," I told him. "What you are asking me is out of my wheelhouse." I smiled, said it was a pleasure meeting him and then told him he'd have a better chance of mailing the letter to 1600 Pennsylvania Ave. in care of whoever he wanted to send it to.

That was my testimony to five different congressional committees, the Mueller team and the FBI, but that's not the way the media told the story. I have to admit the media's version is definitely more exciting and salacious; it's just not true.

But what is true is that the outcome of my meeting with Artemenko ended up with international consequences. As *Business Insider* reported, "Andrey Artemenko was expelled from Ukraine's Radical Party and has been accused of treason by Ukrainian prosecutors for meeting with Michael Cohen, Trump's lawyer, and businessman Felix Sater in New York on January 27 to discuss a plan that would allow Russia to lease Crimea for either 50 or 100 years in return for Russia's withdrawal from eastern Ukraine."[14]

The reports made it sound like I was in Putin's hip pocket trying to negotiate a Ukrainian real estate deal. It makes no sense. I told everyone "No." I had no desire to be involved in that kind of international intrigue. I didn't even bring up the letter to Trump.[15]

I actually thought I had thrown that letter in the garbage, but I didn't. I found it three years later in a pile of papers. As I stated I never took it to D.C., never gave it Trump, never gave it to Flynn, and never discussed this with them either. When I found the letter, I tweeted out a picture of the document to show the absurdity of the allegation, as well as the absurdity of Artemenko's proposal. That concept, as a peace plan, is as stupid as the notion of Jared Kushner creating peace in the Middle East by moving the U.S. embassy from Tel Aviv to Jerusalem. Who thought creating peace could be so easy. If only Henry Kissinger knew this trick.

An attempt at a "back-channel deal," that's what the *New York Times* called the letter. The *Times* also reported, "American experts say offering Russia any alternative to a two-year-old international agreement on Ukraine would be a mistake."[16]

That newspaper also noted that I denied any illicit connections to Russia, which everyone else promptly and conveniently forgot as they started painting me as a rogue operative trying to wheel and deal internationally. Artemenko came to me, not the other way around. And it would be more than three years before the media set the record straight—and I had to find the letter to do it. Artemenko got his citizenship stripped for what he did, but the media took his word over mine.

The same thing also happened in a May 2018 story that the BBC printed and later retracted before having to pay damages to Ukraine President Petro Poroshenko. That story alleged that Poroshenko paid me $400,000 to secure access to President Donald Trump. Never mind I had my own problems at that time—what with trying to weather the FBI raid of my office and hotel suite. Just exactly how was

I supposed to have made such a deal? The BBC never bothered with accurate details or facts in that piece of news. Whoever supplied the story to the BBC made it up and the BBC never bothered to check its sources. The result: Hundreds of U.S. publications picked up the story too. In the end the BBC issued a statement saying it agreed to pay damages to Poroshenko for its "since-retracted report" and also issued a statement saying that it "accepts its report was untrue."[17]

Poroshenko got an apology "for any distress caused," while today there are some who still believe I sold access to Donald Trump.

One last lie to briefly mention: my trip to Prague that never occurred. I've covered it extensively, but in the same February 2017 *New York Times* article about Artemenko my trip that never happened to Prague was mentioned—almost as an aside. When it came to claims I had met with a Russian official in Prague, the *Times* was skeptical. "The Russian official named in the report told the *New York Times* that he had never met Mr. Cohen. Mr. Cohen insists that he has never visited Prague and that the dossier's assertions are fabrications."[18]

But the truth got buried under a mountain of press misinformation that helped to destroy my reputation, so that when I appeared before Congress and warned them about Donald Trump—many didn't take me seriously—and I'm referring to every Republican member sitting there that day.

The rest of the lies on that list, and many more told about me, have been repudiated *continuously* even as Trump and his acolytes spew them. That's what it takes to push back—you have to knock every lie down every time it's told.

Again, I'm not complaining. I'm not asking anyone to feel sorry for me or try to understand what it feels like to walk in my shoes.

Sure, Atticus Finch in *To Kill a Mockingbird* said, "You never really understand a person until you consider things from his point of view—until you climb into his skin and walk around in it," but I don't think you have to do *that* to understand the truth of what I and many others are saying about the dangers to our country *because of* Donald Trump.

Millions of Americans, in fact, do understand the ramifications of the facts at hand. Granted, those are rational, cogent people who aren't either held hostage in Donald Trump's circle or in the echo chamber of Fox News.

So, now that I've established my bona fides, through my past actions and hopefully cleared up any misunderstandings about my credibility or my intention, here's the Cuba Gooding Jr. (Rod Tidwell) moment of truth from Jerry McGuire; remember when I said earlier that it was all about money, well . . . "Show me the money!"

Donald Trump ran for the presidency seeking to make money. The campaign was designed to be the greatest infomercial in the history of politics and to increase the value of the Trump brand. I know. I was there. I helped orchestrate it. And not only was Donald Trump only about the money (and continues to be), but everyone else with their finger in the pie is guilty of this too. Newspapers, television networks, Cable news operations, radio networks, and social media all made bank on Donald Trump. Every politician, every financier, banker, Middle Eastern leader, OPEC nation, shysters, and the assorted con men attracted to the Donald's act on center stage made money; and lots of it.

You know who didn't? Donald's supporters. They continue to

this day to buy his commemorative golf balls, hats, shirts and assorted cheaply manufactured swag. They're paying, and the rich are eating it up. After Donald Trump took over the presidency the distance between the richest and the poorest American hit a record high. Household wealth remained flat while billionaires became richer. In fact, the number of billionaires in this country skyrocketed under Donald Trump's administration. U.S. billionaires got $1 trillion richer during Trump's term. Fifty of the country's top billionaires collected 80 percent of that gain, and even some of the president's biggest critics gained the most from him.[19] All of the billionaires circulated around Trump's corpulent, morbidly obese body just lapping up the money while others who couldn't afford it paid for all of it. The politicians who went along for the ride did so for the money too—the revenue stream was deep and rich, made so on the backs of working Americans. As long as we allow dark money in politics it will *always* be that way.

They are all just stealing from what's left of the middle class. Trump, the rotund ringmaster, directed them to the riches while "the suckers," as Trump often called the middle class, freely gave away their hard-earned money. They still don't realize the thing they fear most (poverty) was being delivered to their doorstep by the man who they thought would give them pride and save them from it—Donald J. Trump.

That is ultimately why he lies and why he tries to discredit those who stand against him. He needs you to question the truth and believe his lies—so he can keep making money. That's the Trump grift. After I began my government cooperation, his campaign of disinformation turned on me—because I knew the truth about him and he knew I wouldn't hesitate to tell everybody the deepest truth; Our way of life is threatened by Donald Trump.

I'm not being dramatic, or hyperbolic.

In my attempt to make amends for my own mistakes, I have to sound the alarm about Donald Trump. And I need to do more. I want to try to frame the argument so everyone else understands exactly what occurred within the Department of Justice and how we can fix the problem. That's my mission. I want people engaged. Only if we work together can we make meaningful changes to the system that benefits justice for all.

In the last chapter I outlined changes I believe need to take place within the Department of Justice. I've cited facts backing up these assertions. So, let me take the last few pages to do what was done on the old "America's Most Wanted," television show when John Walsh asked for your help. This was a "call to action."

Consider *this* my call to action.

First, we must overhaul our national media. We must encourage healthy competition, ensure good pay for working reporters (the anchors are doing just fine) and return traditional guardrails on journalism that helped, in the past, to ensure the credibility of the free press. We need a greater number of better, more experienced reporters as well as a greater diversity of news ownership. Enough of the bullshit talking heads taking up our valuable time arguing just for the sake of arguing. Enough of the Michael Avenattis talking out of their ass. Do the job right. Journalism done right leads to critical thinking. Journalism done wrong opened the door to Donald Trump.

Once Donald Trump got in the door, he drove the news coverage, including about me. The media hounds, thinking they smelled blood often fell for the chum Donald Trump laid down. In fact, most of the major lies told about me initially started with Donald Trump himself. The epitome of his rancid, lying behavior is seen in a variety of tweets that led to multiple erroneous stories about me. Trump: "He lied! Additionally, he directly asked me for a pardon. I said NO. He lied again! He also badly wanted to work at the White House. He lied." He sent that tweet on March 8, 2019.

And, as I pointed out earlier, Donald Trump's manipulation of the media was also done to try and keep me in prison. If you work for the Department of Justice, were appointed by Trump, worked for Trump and were loyal to Trump, how would you react to a tweet from your overlord that said I should serve as much time in prison as possible? "He lied . . . and should, in my opinion, serve a full and complete sentence," Trump tweeted on December 3, 2018.

Many people have speculated this is why the late Judge William H. Pauley III disproportionately sentenced me to 36 months plus another 36 months of supervised release. Unfortunately we will never know why he did this.

Trump directly manipulated social media with lies which led to endless stories about me that were also lies. This could happen to anyone who Trump is angry with, and many people fit that description. The power of the presidency and the ability to shape news cannot be denied or dismissed. So, to that end, I know some in the news industry would like to see a presidential blue-ribbon commission made up of reporters, independent media, social media, and industry leaders convened to find ways to break up media monopolies, and reinstate the fairness doctrine. Doing that will provide accountability in some fashion and will help put some of the guardrails back on journalism that were destroyed by politics and corporate ownership during the last 40 years.

Secondly, we must fix the Department of Justice and hold those who are responsible for its corruption accountable for the same.

In March of 2021, the American Bar Association published an article by Robert N. Weiner called "Fixing the Department of Justice." It directly points the finger at the DOJ and holds those who run it responsible for its turgid miasma. Are you listening, Bill Barr?

"The Department of Justice (DOJ) is a mess. Its morale is low. Its independence is compromised. And its integrity is suspect. The cleanup will be hard," Weiner wrote.[20]

He noted that in October 2020, a respected federal prosecutor who served for 36 years resigned because of Bill Barr's "slavish obedience" to the whims of Donald Trump.

No amount of Barr's protestation against Trump after the January 6 insurrection should be able to wash away that stain. We must insist that Bill Barr answer for his corruption. We must implore Congress to act.

In May of 2021 the top prosecutor in the Michael Flynn case quit after Barr ordered the case's dismissal. This is the very same Michael Flynn who took the Fifth when Congresswoman Liz Cheney asked him if he supported a peaceful transfer of power after the election. Flynn, a stalwart defender of Trump simply couldn't accept the single greatest feature of our democracy—peacefully transferring power. Of course, I warned everyone when I testified before Congress two years earlier that Trump wouldn't accept it either, and

I was castigated for that comment until Trump himself said as much in a September 22, 2022 press briefing at the White House. That's another story.

In February 2021 all four attorneys handling the prosecution of Roger Stone, a friend of Trump, resigned when the DOJ rescinded and lowered their recommended sentence—apparently on the insistence of Bill Barr.

"The attorney general," wrote *American Bar*,

> justified this unprecedented interference by attacking career prosecutors, who, he claimed, lack the political legitimacy to make important law enforcement decisions. As he acidly summarized his point, "Letting the most junior members set the agenda might be a good philosophy for a Montessori preschool, but it's no way to run a federal agency." Neither is attacking its employees. It is no surprise that morale at the department is in the tank.[21]

What Bill Barr did was put politics *ahead* of law and policy.

That's exactly what he did for the *entire time* he served as the attorney general of the United States *both times* he held the post. He was the chief law enforcement officer in this country and there's little doubt that he manipulated his office and allegedly broke the law—all to support Donald Trump. And it wasn't that Barr loved Trump—he eagerly threw The Donald under the bus when it became inconvenient to support him any longer. No. Barr acted as Donald's personal attorney (remember that was my old job) so Barr could use Donald to further his own agenda. That's the real reason many who know better supported Trump—they got something out of the deal. They are all as corrupt as Donald and some, because of their long experience in government, were able to use Donald better than he used them. Senator Mitch McConnell, dozens of Congressmen, White House officials like Stephen Miller and AG Bill Barr, all used Donald to their own ends. They must all be held accountable for everything they did to the people of the United States, just as I was.

And while Trump, Barr, and the clown show have thankfully left 1600 Pennsylvania Avenue, "Trumpism" remains imbedded in our culture and politics. We're seeing the Republicans who remain loyal to the country and the Democrats in Congress trying to take steps in the January 6 Committee Hearings to dislodge those seditionists who swear fealty to the peculiar brand of Trump fascism.

To further those efforts in Congress, we not only need to adopt the actions I suggested in Chapter Five, but we must hold Bill Barr accountable for the things he did to subvert justice while he was the attorney general of the United States. And we have to hold every Republican who was complicit in the insurrection, and knowingly lied for Trump accountable as well.

Inasmuch as Donald Trump is responsible for the insurrection, Barr is responsible for the abomination of the Justice Department. In legal terms he's, in my opinion, guilty of aiding and abetting Trump. And remember, being Trump's attorney general wasn't Barr's first rodeo, it was easy for him to walk into that office and pull the lever—he installed many of them. He'd been there before. In his first tour of duty during the George H. Bush administration, Barr oversaw the largest single manpower shift in the history of the department as he took on street gangs and pushed the case for more incarceration."[22]

And while he tried to put gang members in jail he also launched a surveillance program to gather records of innocent Americans' international phone calls. The DOJ inspector general concluded that it had been launched without a review of its legality. *USA Today* reported that the program "provided a blueprint for far broader phone-data surveillance the government launched after the terrorist attacks of September 11, 2001."

In short, Bill Barr's tenure as a public servant is a blueprint for corruption.

When he told the January 6 Committee that Trump was full of bullshit and the DOJ wasn't his personal attorney, that was only because Bill Barr didn't want to go down with Donald Trump. His experience with corruption, along with his experience in government, gave him the perfect venue to use Donald Trump to his own ends and then spit him out when the time was right.

We cannot allow Barr to get away with what he's done—and it will take years to clean up the mess in the DOJ he has caused by twice heading up the department.

Finally, in addition to fixing the media and fixing our justice department, we need to branch out and address the rest of the corruption, not only among the Trump apologists seated in Congress, but everywhere else in government.

That leads us to the IRS.

The IRS and the federal government railroaded me into an income tax evasion charge to get me to plead guilty so that my wife wouldn't have to get dragged through the mud. I know many people think I deserved everything I got. Fine. Thank you. You may think that. But it's a short walk from me to anyone else—especially those who have limited means. You could be the next to become a political prisoner tortured by the IRS with an audit or continued scrutiny in order to get you to say "Uncle."

Donald Trump once famously said "only suckers" pay taxes. Is that justice? Can he get away with that while the rest of us are dealt with differently? Hell, when I was forced to sign a plea deal I had never even been served a letter from the IRS claiming I owed money. Worse, I wasn't even told how much I owed when I pleaded. It was like signing a blank check and being forced into prison to boot.

The IRS was used as a weapon against me and that could happen to us all. And though at the time it's doubtful Trump himself orchestrated this weaponization of the IRS, he certainly learned from it and apparently used that knowledge to go after his other enemies.

The *New York Times* broke a story July 6, 2022, that showed the IRS, under Trump appointed IRS Commissioner Charles Rettig, conducted extensive audits of both former FBI directors James Comey and Andrew McCabe—men who drew Trump's ire on more than one occasion. As the article noted, "Mr. Trump, as president, attacked Mr. Comey regularly, calling him a "dirty cop" who "should be tried for treason" and "should be arrested on the spot!"[23]

And Trump spared no criticism of McCabe either. "Was Andy McCabe ever forced to pay back the $700,000 illegally given to him and his wife, for his wife's political campaign, by Crooked Hillary Clinton while Hillary was under FBI investigation, and McCabe was the head of the FBI??? Just askin'?" Trump tweeted in September 2020.

At a minimum, some lawyers said, Trump's public statements about Comey and McCabe indicate a political vendetta. Couple that with the fact that the man Trump appointed to head up the IRS was running it at the time of the audits, and you can certainly create a perception that the IRS might have been used to carry out a political vendetta, the *Times* reported. Really? You think so? "When something like that happens, the president's involvement inevitably casts a shadow over an otherwise routine government function and harms the public's confidence in the fair administration of taxes," said Scott D. Michel, a longtime lawyer who specializes in tax disputes.[24]

The day after the *Times* broke the Comey and McCabe case, July 7, 2022, the head of the IRS asked the Treasury Department's internal watchdog to investigate the agency's extensive audits. Trump had no statement, and Trump supporters claimed it was all just an unfortunate coincidence. According to the IRS data book "for all returns filed for the tax years 2011 through 2019, just .55 percent of individual returns were audited."[25]

Still think it's a coincidence? Could lightning strike twice on two of the most vocal opponents to Donald Trump's attempt to destroy the rule of law? "If you think the audit of Donald Trump's purported enemies was a random act of God then I have a bridge in North Jersey I'd like to sell you," said Representative William Pascrell, chairman of the House Ways and Means Subcommittee on Oversight. "There may be no group on the face of this earth that deserves the benefit of the doubt less than Donald Trump and his government enablers," the lawmaker said. "The IRS under Donald Trump's handpicked commissioner Charles Rettig has been one catastrophe after another."[26]

"It just defies logic to think that there wasn't some other factor involved," McCabe said, referring to the idea that audit targets are selected randomly. Both McCabe and Comey were told in letters that their returns were selected in that manner.[27]

I agree with Pascrell that Rettig should be fired. The IRS targeted Comey and McCabe. People capable of rational thought can do the math on that one—and there is no doubt the IRS did the same with me. That's how Trump learned how to do it to Comey and McCabe. Again, this is evidence of government corruption that existed long before Trump, but was seized, manipulated and perfected by Don the Con.

In that respect Donald Trump is the mirror into the depths of the soul of government corruption. He is the standard bearer for corrupt dictator wannabes. He is the poster boy for fascism.

From the day Donald tweeted out I was just one of his lawyers who worked for him, I knew where I stood—out in the cold. And I knew part of the reason the government went after me was to go after Trump. But I also know Trump very well, and knew he'd find a way to use the government's own avarice, arrogance, and corruption to his own benefit.

That is who he is. That is what he does. That is what he has always done.

There's no more need for conjecture and innuendo as so much information has been provided from the plethora of hearings and investigations into Donald, his family, his inner circle and others in his orbit. By now, reality is obscenely obvious to anyone who cares to look at the facts.

Facts matter. Trump's manipulation of his personal financial statements was placed on full display during my House Oversight

Committee hearing. That is a fact. But that was just the start. The last four years have been one extremely long ongoing investigation into Trump's monumental attempt to screw over the country. Investigations into Rudy Giuliani, Michael Flynn, and Jeffrey Clark regarding their association with Donald Trump, have been—as of this writing—ongoing for months, while other new investigations continue to open. Meanwhile, those involved in the insurrection continue to come forward to say they showed up because The Donald wanted them to do so.

But, the *piece de resistance* is Jared Kushner securing a $2 billion investment from a fund led by the Saudi crown prince suspected of having journalist Jamal Khashoggi murdered.

That's not the worst of it. The fact is that a panel that screens investments for the Saudi fund advised against making the deal! Apparently, Kushner's newly formed private equity firm, Affinity Partners, doesn't have what it takes. The oversight panel had a lot of objections to Kushner, according to a *New York Times* article:

> Those objections included: "the inexperience of the Affinity Fund management"; the possibility that the kingdom would be responsible for "the bulk of the investment and risk"; due diligence on the fledgling firm's operations that found them "unsatisfactory in all aspects"; a proposed asset management fee that "seems excessive"; and "public relations risks" from Mr. Kushner's prior role as a senior adviser to his father-in-law, former President Donald J. Trump, according to minutes of the panel's meeting last June 30."[28]

The article goes on to note that ethics experts say that such a deal creates the "appearance of potential payback" for Kushner's actions when he worked at the White House. Appearance? Really? That's not *appearance*; that's reality.

And it's par for the course from the Donald Trump Wild West Show. Going back to the sage of Baltimore, H. L. Mencken again: He never met Donald Trump, but he knew what Trump looked like. "A good politician, under democracy, is quite as unthinkable as an honest burglar," Mencken wrote.[29]

That's what they were, a group of burglars.

If what I've just laid out doesn't show you the thesis of this book is sound, then no one will ever be able to convince you of reality. That, as it turns out, is more of a problem than we realized—until Donald Trump came around and made it painfully obvious. We are disconnected from our government and many of us do not realize how desperate our times have become. And because we have sacrificed our daily involvement in government, for a variety of reasons both big and small, we have left our democracy to the whims of those we elect. When we manage to elect someone decent like Elijah Cummings, we may do well, or at least we don't do as badly as we have when we fall into the clutches of a narcissistic sociopath like Donald Trump.

In speaking with a long-time Department of Justice investigator who was familiar with my case, he summed up what happened to me very succinctly, but in doing so he gave a warning to which we should all listen. He said, "You fell through the cracks. At first those who thought they were doing their job right pursued you because you were aligned with Trump and they thought you could provide them with information—if you were squeezed."

But, I never had the information they thought I had. What I had was a roadmap to finding it, which I provided willingly.

As I went through the system, this source told me, Trump saw and took advantage of several opportunities to make me suffer. Except for the concerns of my family, a few friends and concerned members of Congress, I was forgotten. "Your reputation was destroyed by Trump and the press. That made it easier for Trump to use the system against you," it was explained to me.

"In essence they were able to torture you—up to the point that they nearly killed you. They damn near got away with it."

I can't begin to express the pain and anguish I wake up to and go to sleep to each and every day. I suffer from this mental torment, as I look at my wife, my daughter, and my son's faces each day, realizing how much pain and suffering I have put them through due to my association with Trump. Those feelings are compounded when I take walks in the city and I see the faces of my neighbors, men, women, children walking and oblivious to the depth of the perils we all still face.

Roe v. Wade, Obergefell, Bivens (where the court threw out protection against Federal agencies overstepping—it's simply the very beginning of the erosion of our personal freedoms. That is Donald Trump's legacy.

It is straight out of the fascist playbook.

I heard testimony from White House staffers in the seventh January 6 hearing that's also straight out of the fascist playbook. Donald Trump left the outer Oval Office door open so he could listen to the sound of the crowd screaming his name, all in his honor. That mob represented the pinnacle of his power. Of course, when he heard the crowd, staffers said, Trump was in a good mood. I watched the expression on the faces of the members of Congress when that was reported. They were in disbelief. Not me. I could envision that smug face with his lips pursed; his eyes squinting like he had just sucked on a lemon.

That's certainly not the image I want to see on the front of U.S. currency or Mount Rushmore. And that's not the ideal version of the United States we were taught about in our history books.

We are truly at a precipice in the survival of American democracy. I remember the countless times my father, a Holocaust survivor, praised the United States of America as being the land of the free—the greatest country in the world.

I thought of that again as I heard Representative Stephanie Murphy of Florida talk about her experience coming to the United States as a small child after the Vietnam War, and how much this country means to her and to anyone around the world who values self-government and democracy. I have imparted the same words and heartfelt sentiment to my children. Damn if I'm going to let Trump and his family take that away from all of us for generations to come.

But as someone wiser than me once said, there's nothing wrong with the United States that can't be fixed by what's right with the United States.

We must recognize that Trumpism is fascism. We must destroy it and erase it from our body politic.

AFTERWORD

NORMAN EISEN AND E. DANYA PERRY

AS THIS VOLUME GOES TO press, the country continues to deal with one of the core themes this book has taken on: Donald Trump's sense of impunity and his utter disregard for the rule of law. He has been indicted or faces indictment in multiple federal and state cases. Michael Cohen warned us all that Trump's pattern of conduct would inevitably result in exactly this kind of situation, and now Trump—and the nation—confront the consequences.

One of the most serious of the cases is the former president's prosecution for wrongly retaining classified documents and obstructing justice. In August 2022, investigators searched Mar-a-Lago—Mr. Trump's Florida residence and private club—pursuant to a warrant signed by a federal magistrate judge. Those investigators recovered items that alarmed us to a degree akin to if bomb-grade uranium were found on the property. Highly classified documents were recovered, including many marked as Top Secret/SCI, "Sensitive Compartmented Information"—some of the most closely held secrets in our nation's intelligence system. In our former roles as a United States ambassador and as a federal prosecutor, we gained an appreciation for the gravity of mishandling such files. Those documents have the potential to identify intelligence community sources and operations. Mr. Trump also allegedly retained and, in at least one case showed, highly sensitive documents containing potential military attack plans concerning a foreign nation. Mr. Trump's recklessness and willfulness in taking, improperly storing, and even reportedly sharing these items has the potential to damage our country's national security and intelligence capabilities in ways most of us cannot even imagine.

Then, as we went to press, there is breaking news that Trump has received a target letter in Special Counsel Jack Smith's investigation of the events of—and leading up to—January 6. We were among the co-authors of a model prosecution memo analyzing the substantial evidence against Trump and predicting that he was likely to be charged. In our memo, we explained just how close the constitutional framework of our country came to failing, and just how close Mr. Trump came to succeeding in his attempted coup. In addition to Mr. Trump's pressuring state officials (such as in the now infamous phone call to Georgia Secretary of State Brad Raffensperger asking him to "find" 11,780 votes for him) we now have more information as to just how extensive his campaign was to develop and deliver fabricated slates of electors to Congress, and to pressure Vice President Mike Pence to overrule the democratic will of the voters. We have also learned more about the events of January 6 itself, including that Mr. Trump reportedly stood idly by (other than the occasional tweet to urge on his supporters) for 187 minutes as the rioters stormed the Capitol.

In both cases, the Department of Justice's handling of its investigations has been consistent with the law, precedent, and its own institutional norms. Indeed, the appointment of Special Counsel Jack Smith by Attorney General Merrick Garland demonstrated a desire to remove even a hint of any appearance of improper motives. As Michael Cohen chronicles in this book, this stands in contrast to the disregard for the rule of law shown by Mr. Trump and former Attorney General William Barr, and to their abuse of the criminal justice system.

But the consequences of Trump's heedless disrespect for the rule of law do not stop there. He has been charged in connection with his 2016 election interference by Manhattan district attorney Alvin Bragg—a matter in which Michael Cohen is a critically important witness. The charges are for falsifying business records to cover up hush money payments made to avoid another scandal at the end of the 2016 campaign—one which, on the heels of the infamous Access Hollywood tape, could have changed the outcome of that race.

In retrospect, that misconduct represented a gateway drug for the 2020 election interference. That later and more elaborate alleged electoral misconduct is, in addition to Jack Smith's federal investigation, also under review by the Fulton County, Georgia district attorney, Fani Willis. As we go to press, she is widely expected to bring charges as soon as August 2023, targeting Trump and others for his sweeping national schemes as they impacted the state of Georgia. That includes Trump's notorious call to Mr. Raffensberger to "find" votes that did not exist.

Moreover, the criminal cases triggered by Trump go beyond these four current or anticipated cases charging him. In the very first prosecution relating to his plan to fob false electoral slates off on the country in the aftermath of the 2020 election, Michigan Attorney General Dana Nessel has charged all 16 of the false electors in that state. Each faces eight charges for forgery and related crimes, with penalties ranging from 5 to 14 years in prison for each count. Other states are also investigating the fake electors and related matters in their jurisdictions. These investigations are not remotely a "witch hunt," as Mr. Trump so frequently claims. Take for example the federal Mar-a-Lago documents case. Aware of the likely incendiary ramifications of any public action by the DOJ against Mr. Trump, Mr. Garland—and the executive branch generally—gave the former president every opportunity to avoid criminal consequences related to his mishandling of classified documents. Throughout the year following Mr. Trump's departure from the White House, the National Archives and Records Administration attempted to arrange the return of what it believed were missing records. In January 2022, Mr. Trump returned fifteen boxes containing 184 unique documents with classification markings. Those were haphazardly mixed with miscellaneous other items, including newspapers, magazines, and photos.

The FBI subsequently obtained evidence that many additional boxes remained at Mar-a-Lago that likely contained classified material. In May 2022, Mr. Trump's counsel accepted service of a DOJ subpoena demanding production of any remaining classified documents. If Mr. Trump were to have complied at this stage of the investigation, no further action likely would have been taken—despite the grave harm Mr. Trump already had done to our country's security capabilities. Instead, several weeks later, Mr. Trump produced a single

Redweld folder of additional material along with a certification from his counsel that "a diligent search" had been performed and that no further documents remained. That woefully deficient production led directly to the warrant and the search of Mar-a-Lago.

During the search, the government recovered thirteen more boxes containing over 100 classified documents. It appears that either a diligent search had not been performed or that Mr. Trump or others willfully refused to relinquish these highly sensitive materials.

It is worth noting that the attorney general likely wanted to do everything possible to avoid both a search warrant and a criminal indictment of Mr. Trump. Mr. Garland has attempted to restore the DOJ's stature and credibility, in part by avoiding the appearance of any political influence in the department's operations and charging decisions. Rather than being the political "witch hunt" Mr. Trump repeatedly decries, the investigation (and now prosecution) has instead been a model of restraint and caution. Time and again, the DOJ tried to give Mr. Trump an out. In a characteristically contemptuous response that by now will be familiar to readers of this book, Mr. Trump repeatedly refused to take it. The subsequent indictment in fact demonstrates the DOJ's commitment to the rule of law over politics.

Compare that with the DOJ as it existed under Mr. Barr—an institution decidedly less concerned with the rule of law. Mr. Barr was appointed in early 2019, at the tail end of the investigation by Special Counsel Robert Mueller. Prior to his appointment, Mr. Barr had publicly described the investigation concerning possible obstruction of justice by Mr. Trump as "asinine" and said it risked "taking on the look of an entirely political operation to overthrow the president." Those comments were made during the earliest stages of Mr. Mueller's investigation, long before Mr. Barr knew what evidence the special counsel had uncovered.

Mr. Barr took extraordinary steps after assuming office to protect then-President Trump. Shortly before the Mueller Report was released, Mr. Barr sent what he described as its "principal conclusions" to Congress. Mr. Barr accurately reported that the special counsel had concluded that it was outside his purview to determine whether Mr. Trump should ultimately be prosecuted for obstruction of justice: quoting one of the report's most consequential lines, the summary stated, "while this report does not conclude that the president committed a crime, it also does not exonerate him."

Nevertheless, Mr. Barr decided to announce his own office's determination that Mr. Trump had not committed any crime. According to Mr. Barr, no crime had been committed because "no actions that, in our judgment, constitute obstructive conduct, had a nexus to a pending or contemplated proceeding, and were done with corrupt intent."

Prior to the announcement, two of the most senior members of the DOJ authored a memo analyzing Mr. Trump's actions that were detailed in the report. It served as the legal justification for Mr. Barr's summary to Congress. Because of the seniority of the authors, it is likely that the memo was drafted at the direction of, and perhaps also with input from, Mr. Barr himself. At any rate, he signed it, agreeing with its conclusions.

Two federal District Court judges, a Republican appointee and a Democratic one, have noted Mr. Barr's dishonesty in connection

with the Mueller Report, with the latter stating that the former attorney general's treatment of the memo is further confirmation of his
"disingenu[ity]." Perhaps the most egregious aspect of the memo is
its suggestion that prosecution for obstruction is appropriate only if
the conduct at issue involved "(i) inherently wrongful acts to destroy
evidence, to create false evidence, or to tamper with witnesses or jurors, and (ii) an effort to prevent the investigation or punishment of
a separate, underlying crime."

You don't need to be a former prosecutor to understand how
wrong this is. The logic of the memo suggests that any person who
successfully obstructs justice cannot be charged with obstruction because the proof of the underlying crime would be unavailable. Even at
the time the memo was drafted, that was an incorrect interpretation
of the law—and prior cases had indeed been prosecuted where proof
of the underlying crime was not established. (Martha Stewart's conviction is one of the more high-profile examples of this phenomenon.)

Moreover, Special Counsel Robert Mueller *did* find compelling
evidence of efforts by Mr. Trump to create false documents and to
tamper with witnesses. For example, Mr. Trump's pattern of obstruction included urging his own White House counsel to create a false
document relating to the Mueller investigation—and his witness
intimidation included targeting none other than the author of this
book, Michael Cohen.

The contrast between the two attorneys general could not be more
stark. Whereas Mr. Garland has taken steps to avoid political con-
siderations and to hold Mr. Trump accountable, Mr. Barr appears to
have deliberately misconstrued the law to insulate Mr. Trump from
accountability for political reasons.

These events are not unrelated. It is this type of enabling behavior by Mr. Barr that helped create the sense of impunity that ultimately required the execution of the search warrant at Mar-a-Lago. There are chapters in that narrative yet to be written. But regardless of the final outcome, it serves as a reminder of the danger a potential re-election of Mr. Trump presents to the country: the specter of a president who places himself above the law.

APPENDIX

Donald J. Trump
@realDonaldTrump

Bad lawyer and fraudster Michael Cohen said under sworn testimony that he never asked for a Pardon. His lawyers totally contradicted him. **He lied!** Additionally, he directly asked me for a pardon. I said NO. He lied again! He also badly wanted to work at the White House. **He lied!**

March 08, 2019

Donald J. Trump
@realDonaldTrump

Virtually everything failed lawyer Michael Cohen said in his sworn testimony last week is totally contradicted in his just released manuscript for a book about me. It's a total new love letter to 'Trump' and the pols must now use it rather than his **lies for sentence reduction!**

March 03, 2019

Donald J. Trump
@realDonaldTrump

'Michael Cohen asks judge for no Prison Time.' You mean he can do all of the **TERRIBLE**, unrelated to Trump, things having to do with fraud, big loans, Taxis, etc., and not serve a long prison term? He makes up stories to get a GREAT & ALREADY reduced deal for himself, and get.....

December 03, 2018

Donald J. Trump
@realDonaldTrump

....his wife and father-in-law (who has the money?) off Scott Free. He lied for this outcome and should, in my opinion, serve a full and complete sentence.

December 03, 2018

Donald J. Trump
@realDonaldTrump

....which it was not (but even if it was, it is only a CIVIL CASE, like Obama's - but it was done correctly by a lawyer and there would not even be a fine. Lawyer's liability if he made a mistake, not me). Cohen just trying to get his sentence reduced. WITCH HUNT!

December 10, 2018

Donald J. Trump
@realDonaldTrump

Remember, Michael Cohen only became a 'Rat' after the FBI did something which was absolutely unthinkable & unheard of until the Witch Hunt was illegally started. They BROKE INTO AN ATTORNEY'S OFFICE! Why didn't they break into the DNC to get the Server, or Crooked's office?

December 16, 2018

Donald J. Trump
@realDonaldTrump

Michael Cohen's book manuscript shows that he committed perjury on a scale not seen before. He must have forgotten about his book when he testified. What does Hillary Clinton's lawyer, Lanny Davis, say about this one. Is he being paid by Crooked Hillary. Using her lawyer?

March 01, 2019

Donald J. Trump
@realDonaldTrump

If anyone is looking for a good lawyer, I would strongly suggest that you don't retain the services of Michael Cohen!

August 22, 2018

These are the Freedom of Information requests.

IN THE UNITED STATES DISTRICT COURT
FOR THE DISTRICT OF COLUMBIA

THE JAMES MADISON PROJECT, *et al.*,)

)

   Plaintiffs,   )

)

   v.   ) Case No.1:22-

          cv-00092-JMC

)

U.S. DEPARTMENT OF JUSTICE,)

)

   Defendant.   )

JOINT STATUS REPORT AND PROPOSED SCHEDULE

The parties, by counsel, respectfully submit this Joint Status Report and Proposed Schedule in response to the Court's May 26, 2022 Minute Order.

Plaintiffs seek records under the Freedom of Information Act ("FOIA"), 5 U.S.C. § 552, from the Federal Bureau of Investigation ("FBI") and the DOJ Office of the Inspector General ("OIG") related to the investigation and prosecution of Mr. Michael Cohen.

The OIG has completed its search and identified no responsive documents. On March 10, 2022, the OIG provided its final response to Plaintiffs' request. Prior to the parties' last status report, Plaintiffs provided additional information to the OIG to consider and the OIG provided Plaintiffs with its response to that additional information. Plaintiffs are presently considering OIG's response.

The FBI has completed its search and is still in the process of loading the potentially responsive records into the system used for review and processing. As reported in the parties' last JSR, the FBI had identified over 450,000 pages of potentially responsive material, and the parties had begun discussing ways to narrow the scope of the search and review for this case. Through these discussions, Plaintiffs have agreed to waive the search for and processing of any grand jury material. Since the last JSR, the FBI has worked to separate out the grand jury material from other potentially responsive materials identified and, as a result, the approximate volume has dropped to 47,000 pages of potentially responsive pages in need of review. This approximate page count may still change as the FBI loads the remaining potentially responsive materials.

The FBI's searches have identified over 5,000 pages of prior, publicly available FOIA releases of Special Counsel Mueller's investigation records, which includes material that is at least partially responsive to the subject matter of Plaintiffs' FOIA request. *See* FBI FOIA Vault, available at https://vault.fbi.gov/special-counsel-mueller-investigation-records.

Also, at Plaintiffs' request, the FBI has agreed to prioritize the processing of FD-302s, the forms used by the FBI to record investigative activity, without prioritizing at this point the attachments or media associated with FD-302s, and to begin processing the FD-302s that are identified while the FBI continues its work gathering potentially responsive material. As to the rest of the potentially responsive documents, Plaintiffs have agreed to postpone FBI's processing of all attachments and media, with the plan to revisit the processing of attachments and media after the parties have a better sense of what those records might contain.

The FBI anticipates it will process the prioritized FD-302s on a rolling basis at a rate of 500 pages per month and it expects to have completed its review of the first 500 pages by August 22, 2022. The FBI expects that some of these pages will require consultation with other entities with equities in the records before it can make a final decision regarding the release or withholding of the pages. After the FBI has completed processing the prioritized FD-302s and finished gathering the full set of potentially responsive material, the FBI anticipates it will review non-prioritized material at the same rolling rate of review and expects those pages may require additional consultation before it can make a final decision regarding the release or withholding of the pages.

The parties have discussed the FBI's proposed processing of the potentially responsive materials. Plaintiffs object to the FBI's processing rate of 500 pages per month, particularly on a topic that has received a great deal of news attention, and are willing to provide the Court with caselaw where the FBI (as well as other agencies) have been required to process far more than 500 pages per month. The FBI is likewise willing to support its proposed processing rate with caselaw authority. However, given that the FBI continues to gather potentially responsive records, the parties will address this issue in their next joint status report.

In light of the current circumstances and a mutual desire to continue forward movement of this litigation, the parties respectfully propose that their next joint status report be due on or before August 26, 2022.

Dated: June 30, 2022   Respectfully submitted,

BRIAN M. BOYNTON

Principal Deputy Assistant Attorney General

ELIZABETH J. SHAPIRO

Deputy Branch Director, Federal Programs Branch

UNITED STATES DISTRICT COURT
SOUTHERN DISTRICT OF NEW YORK

```
USDS SDNY
DOCUMENT
ELECTRONICALLY FILED
DOC #:
DATE FILED: 4/20/21
```

MICHAEL D. COHEN,

                Petitioner,

    -against-

UNITED STATES OF AMERICA;
MICHAEL CARVAJAL, Director of
the Federal Bureau of Prisons,

                Respondents.

20-CV-10833 (JGK)

MEMORAUNDUM OPINION
AND ORDER

JOHN G. KOELTL, United States District Judge:

The petitioner, Michael D. Cohen, brought this petition for
a writ of habeas corpus pursuant to 28 U.S.C. § 2241,
challenging the execution of his sentence, specifically the
calculation of earned time credits ("ETCs") towards his sentence
in accordance with the First Step Act of 2018, P.L. 115-391 (the
"FSA" or the "Act"). For the reasons explained below, the
petition is **dismissed**.

I

Mr. Cohen pleaded guilty to five counts of tax evasion in
violation of 26 U.S.C. § 7201, one count of making a false
statement to a financial institution in violation of 18 U.S.C.
§ 1014, two counts of making unlawful campaign contributions in
violation of 52 U.S.C. § 30109(d)(1)(A), and one count of making
a false statement to the Congress in violation of 18 U.S.C.
§ 1001(a)(2), and was sentenced to 36 months' imprisonment and 3

Michael D. Cohen

1399 Franklin Avenue, Suite 200
Garden City, New York 11530

April 12, 2021

The Honorable John G. Koeltl
United States District Judge
500 Pearl Street
New York, New York 10007

Re:　Cohen v. United States of America, et al., No: 20-cv-10833 (JGK)

Dear Judge Koeltl,

Petitioner respectfully submits this letter to Your Honor in furtherance of Petitioner's Reply to Respondent's Answer for a Writ Of Habeas Corpus, submitted on March 25, 2021.

Specifically, Petitioner requested and continues said request that this Honorable Court and Your Honor act upon this Petition with genuine urgency as each day that this matter is pending is a day that Mr. Cohen is incarcerated unlawfully. Petitioner therefore asked, and continues to ask; (i) that the Court order his release pending adjudication of this statutory question to immediately abate the ongoing and irreparable harm of his excessive confinement, and (ii) that the writ be granted for the reasons stated in Mr. Cohen's Petition... (page 8).

The impetus for said request stems from the well-known fact that The Bureau of Prisons conspicuously slow walks these petitions to moot the determination; especially in matters like the one before Your Honor where Petitioner will be released from home confinement in 7 months.

Supplementarily, I wish to respectfully bring to this Court's attention Government's reply to the petition of Bains v. Quay (21-cv-00353). Government appears to have finally acknowledged and abandoned their misguided and flawed defenses of ripeness and exhaustion of administrative remedy. Rather, Government allocates, albeit without explanation, a 62.5-day reduction of sentence for Bains' productive activity at LSCI Allenwood. Government's reply states, "At most, however, the work yields 500 hours of EBRR credit. (Id.) Thus, again assuming that Bains' work with FPI is not otherwise disqualifying, he accrued 500 hours EBRR credit with FPI, or another 62.5 days." (Page 14)

It is for these reasons that I beseech Your Honor to prevent Government from impinging on my constitutional rights (again) by granting the relief sought in my petition or, in the alternative, removing me from home confinement pending a hearing or the disposition of this matter.

Respectfully submitted,

/s/ Michael Cohen

Michael D. Cohen
Pro Se Petitioner
1399 Franklin Avenue, Suite 200
Garden City, New York 11530

PETRILLO KLEIN & BOXER LLP

655 Third Avenue
22nd Floor
New York, NY 10017
Telephone: (212) 370-0330
www.pkbllp.com

Guy Petrillo
Direct Dial: (212) 370-0331
Cell: (646) 385-1479
gpetrillo@pkbllp.com

CONFIDENTIAL
BY EMAIL

Robert Khuzami
Deputy U.S. Attorney
U.S. Attorney's Office
    for the Southern District of New York
One St. Andrew's Plaza
New York, NY 10007

Re: Michael Cohen

Dear Deputy U.S. Attorney Khuzami:

I write on behalf of Michael Cohen to request a meeting with you and your colleagues to discuss the charge(s) the Office is prepared to present to the grand jury and an opportunity in short order (ten days or less) to return to the Office to present points relevant to the Office's discretionary decision to seek an indictment.

On Tuesday, August 14, 2018, we were told by the Assistants assigned to the case that the Office would only accept a meeting on or before Friday of this week, and in substance that we should already know what the charges will be based on the public nature of the investigation. With all respect, the press concerning the referral from the Special Counsel and the Office's investigation, the search warrants, and the materials seized in the searches of Mr. Cohen's residence, temporary residence, office and bank safe deposit box in April 2018, do not manifestly announce the charge(s) the Office is actually prepared to seek. To take one example, over more than a decade, no financial institution that has dealt with Mr. Cohen has lost any money as a result. Many of the search warrant specifications refer to evidence pertaining to financial institutions, loans, etc. We are not presuming that the Office would seek a charge where no losses were incurred, but if it is, it would be fair to permit Mr. Cohen's counsel to be heard on more than a few days' notice.

The son of a Holocaust survivor, Mr. Cohen, 51, has no prior convictions. He is married and has two children. He presents no risk of flight. Furthermore, Mr. Cohen has voluntarily presented himself for a full day's interview by the Office of the Special Counsel, and understands that his interview may continue on a date to be scheduled.

In the circumstances, and so that we, as counsel, may consider options including available alternatives to indictment, we request a confidential explanation of the charge(s) to be sought from the grand jury, and an opportunity, on a short but reasonable schedule, to discuss the same with the Office.

Sincerely,

Guy Petrillo

Amy Lester

cc: AUSA L. Zornberg

        Chief, Criminal Division

        AUSA Carbone

        Chief, Public Corruption Unit

        AUSA   A. Griswold

        AUSA R. Maimin

        AUSA T. McKay

        AUSA   N. Roos

U.S. Department of Justice
Federal Bureau of Prisons

Northeast Regional Office
U.S. Custom House
2nd & Chestnut St., 7th Floor
Philadelphia, PA 19106

October 6, 2020

E. Danya Perry
Perry Guha LLP
35 East 62nd Street
New York, NY 10065   Request Number: 2021-00096

Dear Ms. Perry:

We received the above referenced Freedom of Information Act (FOIA) request wherein you seek expedited processing. A copy of the first page of your request is attached.

The Department of Justice requires all requests for records be processed on a first-in, first-out basis. The four exceptions to this requirement are: "(i) Circumstances in which the lack of expedited processing could reasonably be expected to pose an imminent threat to the life or physical safety of an individual; (ii) An urgency to inform the public about an actual or alleged Federal Government activity, if made by a person who is primarily engaged in disseminating information; (iii) The loss of substantial due process rights; or (iv) A matter of widespread and exceptional media interest in which there exist possible questions about the government's integrity that affect public confidence." 28 C.F.R. § 16.5(e).

Your request meets the requirement to be processed on an expedited basis and will be expedited to the best of our ability. This request will be placed on the processing track ahead of other requests and processed as soon as practicable. Processing this request may take up to six months.

If you have any questions, please contact the undersigned or BOP's FOIA Public Liaison, Mr. C. Darnell Stroble at (202) 616-7750; 320 First Street NW, Suite 936, Washington, DC 20534; or ogc_efoia@bop.gov. You can also check the status of your request at http://www.bop.gov/PublicInfo/execute/foia.

Sincerely,

Frank A. Bruno
Paralegal Specialist

UNITED STATES DISTRICT COURT
SOUTHERN DISTRICT OF NEW YORK
-- X
MICHAEL D. COHEN,   :
                                                          :
                                    Petitioner,   :   **ORDER GRANTING**
                          v.   :   **PRELIMINARY INJUNCTION**
                                                          :
WILLIAM BARR, in his official capacity as   :   20 Civ. 5614 (AKH)
Attorney General of the United States, MICHAEL   :
CARVAJAL, in his official capacity as Director of   :
the Bureau of Prisons, and JAMES PETRUCCI, in   :
his official capacity as Warden of the Federal   :
Correctional Institution, Otisville,   :
                                                          :
                                    Respondents.   :
-- X
ALVIN K. HELLERSTEIN, U.S.D.J.:

Upon the findings and conclusions stated on the record at oral argument

conducted telephonically on July 23, 2020, Petitioner Michael D. Cohen's motion for injunctive

relief, *see* ECF No. 4, is granted as follows.

The Court finds that Respondents' purpose in transferring Cohen from release on

furlough and home confinement back to custody was retaliatory in response to Cohen desiring to

exercise his First Amendment rights to publish a book critical of the President and to discuss the

book on social media. Accordingly, Respondents are hereby enjoined from any continuing or

future retaliation against Cohen for exercising his First Amendment rights. Respondents are

directed to provide Cohen with a COVID-19 test at his place of detention no later than tomorrow

morning, July 24, 2020, to report the results of that test to Cohen and to his Probation Officer

promptly when they become available, and to release Cohen from custody to any member of his

immediate family at the place of his detention at or before 2:00 p.m. tomorrow, July 24, 2020.

Upon Cohen's release, the parties agree, and I so order, that Cohen will be subject

to the eight conditions of release set forth in the Federal Location Monitoring Agreement, *see*

ECF No. 7-2, provided, however, that adherence to condition one, except for the last sentence, is temporary, subject to the parties' renegotiation of said temporary condition.[1] The condition shall

be consistent with the First Amendment and legitimate penological limitations on conduct to

which the parties mutually agree or the Court subsequently orders. The parties shall have one

week to conduct their negotiations and will, unless an extension has been granted, file a proposed

order to the Court by July 31, 2020. I reserve continuing jurisdiction to resolve any disputes in

settling an order and enforcing same.

This order, which codifies my extemporaneous ruling at argument, is intended to

be final. A written decision providing a fuller statement of my findings and conclusions will

follow when ready. The Clerk is instructed to terminate the open motion (ECF No. 4).

SO ORDERED.

Dated: July 23, 2020   _____/s/_____
            New York, New York   ALVIN K. HELLERSTEIN
                                                  United States District Judge

UNITED STATES DISTRICT COURT
SOUTHERN DISTRICT OF NEW YORK
- -x
                                                    :
UNITED STATES OF AMERICA   :
                                                    :
        -   v.   -   :   18 Cr. 602 (WHP)
                                                    :   18 Cr. 850 (WHP)
MICHAEL COHEN,   :
                                                    :
                Defendant.   :
                                                    :
- -x

**SENTENCING MEMORANDUM
ON BEHALF OF MICHAEL COHEN**

PETRILLO KLEIN & BOXER LLP

655 Third Avenue, 22nd Floor
New York, New York 10017
Telephone: (212) 370-0330

Attorneys for Michael Cohen

Dated: November 30, 2018

NOTES

CHAPTER ONE: THE BULLSHIT BEGINS

1 Twitter feed, Michael Cohen, Jan. 10, 2017.
2 Buzzfeed, January 10, 2017.
3 *New York Times*/Buzzfeed.
4 https://www.nytimes.com/2017/08/28/us/politics/trump-tower-putin-felix-sater.html
5 https://www.youtube.com/watch?v=HHckZCxdRkA
6 https://www.businessinsider.com/carter-page-congressional-testimony-transcript-steele-dossier-2017-11
7 Ibid.
8 https://en.wikipedia.org/wiki/Carter_Page
9 Stephanie Kirchgaessner; Spencer Ackerman; Julian Borger; Luke Harding (April 14, 2017). "Former Trump adviser Carter Page held 'strong pro-Kremlin views', says ex-boss." *The Guardian*. Retrieved April 14,2017.
10 Zengerle, Jason (December 18, 2017). "What (if Anything) Does Carter Page Know?" *New York Times*.
11 Iskoff, Michael (September 23, 2016). "U.S. intel officials probe ties between Trump adviser and Kremlin." Yahoo! News. Retrieved September 24, 2016.
12 https://www.nytimes.com/2018/07/13/us/politics/trump-russia-clinton-emails.html

13 https://www.mcclatchydc.com/news/nation-world/national/article160622854.html

14 https://www.nytimes.com/2020/01/23/us/politics/carter-page-fbi-surveillance.html

15 https://www.mcclatchydc.com/news/nation-world/national/article160622854.html

16 https://reason.com/2017/07/16/mccain-and-the-trump-russia-dossier/

17 https://www.wsj.com/articles/intelligence-dossier-puts-longtime-trump-fixer-in-spotlight-1484178320

18 Buzzfeed, May 5, 2017 "This is the inside of Trump's lawyer's passport"

19 Ibid.

20 Tom Porter and Reuters 4/14/2018 https://www.newsweek.com/mueller-has-evidence-back-russia-dossiers-claims-about-trump-attorney-cohen-886152

21 https://www.vox.com/2018/4/13/17236660/michael-cohen-prague-trump-steele-dossier

22 https://www.newsweek.com/mueller-has-evidence-back-russia-dossiers-claims-about-trump-attorney-cohen-886152

23 https://www.buzzfeednews.com/article/jasonleopold/here-are-the-documents-recovered-from-michael-cohens

24 Ibid.

25 Ibid.

26 https://www.washingtonpost.com/news/politics/wp/2018/04/14/michael-cohen-visiting-prague-would-be-a-huge-development-in-the-russia-investigation/

27 https://www.thenation.com/article/politics/trump-russiagate-steele-dossier/

28 https://www.mcclatchydc.com/news/politics-government/white-house/article208870264.html

29 https://www.mcclatchydc.com/news/investigations/article219016820.html

30 https://www.thenation.com/article/politics/trump-russiagate-steele-dossier/

31 https://www.bbc.com/news/world-us-canada-41419191

32 https://thehill.com/homenews/administration/384249-trump-denies-cohen-will-flip

33 https://www.vox.com/2019/2/28/18243151/michael-cohen-testimony-mueller-russia

34 The Mueller Report. Pg 39.

35 https://www.axios.com/michael-cohen-timeline-events-plea-deal-donald-trump-53baca63-9662-4116-910e-5f3404e18576.html

36 *New York Post*, February 9, 2019

37 H&R Block, "Statistical Overview of Tax Fraud and Client Base," October 2016, HRB.com

38 https://thehill.com/blogs/blog-briefing-room/402972-attorney-cohen-would-not-accept-a-pardon-from-trump/

39 https://www.vice.com/en/article/pajdb9/william-barrs-been-accused-of-a-presidential-coverup-before

40 https://www.wired.com/story/ag-nominee-william-barr-no-friend-telecom-competition/

41 https://thehill.com/opinion/criminal-justice/527121-redeeming-justice-the-next-attorney-general/

42 https://www.washingtonpost.com/politics/2020/05/11/latest-allegation-william-barrs-malfeasance-explained/

43 https://thetriallawyermagazine.com/2021/07/bill-barr-is-the-master-of-covering-up-political-scandals/

44 https://www.usatoday.com/story/news/politics/2019/03/28/review-finds-phone-data-dragnet-dea-doj-began-without-legal-review/3299438002/

45 https://www.nytimes.com/1992/11/12/opinion/essay-1st-global-political-scandal.html

46 https://billmoyers.com/story/bill-barr-and-the-ghost-of-fascism/

47 https://www.thedailybeast.com/yes-attorney-general-bill-barr-is-incredibly-corrupt-but-hes-also-incredibly-inept

48 https://www.politico.com/news/2020/07/22/bill-barr-bar-association-probe-377272

49 https://www.cnn.com/2022/02/14/politics/trump-mazars/index.html

50 https://www.justice.gov/usao-sdny/pr/michael-cohen-pleads-guilty-manhattan-federal-court-eight-counts-including-criminal-tax

51 https://thehill.com/homenews/administration/403097-timeline-how-michael-cohen-turned-on-trump

52 Ibid.

53 https://www.cnbc.com/2018/08/23/national-enquirer-david-pecker-told-prosecutors-trump-knew-of-cohen-payments-report.html

54 https://nymag.com/intelligencer/2021/07/steele-dossier-was-case-study-in-journalistic-manipulation.html

55 https://www.thenation.com/article/politics/trump-russiagate-steele-dossier/

56 Ibid.

57 https://thehill.com/opinion/white-house/453384-fbis-spreadsheet-puts-a-stake-through-the-heart-of-steeles-dossier

CHAPTER TWO: THE "SOVEREIGN DISTRICT" OF NEW YORK

1 Ibid.

2 https://www.pbs.org/newshour/politics/records-show-fbi-was-investigating-michael-cohen-long-before-raid (03/19/19)

3 https://www.cnsnews.com/news/article/emilie-cochran/judicial-watch-sues-doj-records-related-fbi-raid-michael-cohen (07/03/2018)

4 FBI official record (19cv1278).

5 Ibid.

6 https://www.nybooks.com/articles/2014/11/20/why-innocent-people-plead-guilty/

7 Ibid.

8 https://abovethelaw.com/2018/04/the-best-and-worst-lawyering-at-the-cohen-hearing/

9 https://nypost.com/2021/07/24/bizarre-arrest-of-fbi-agent-spotlights-accusations-of-bureau-corruption/

10 https://en.wikipedia.org/wiki/List_of_FBI_controversies

11 Ibid.
12 https://www.politico.com/news/2021/12/12/fortenberry-indictment-524107
13 https://www.fincen.gov/what-we-do
14 Ibid.
15 https://www.courthousenews.com/irs-worker-who-leaked-cohen-docs-sentenced-to-five-years-probation/
16 https://www.washingtonpost.com/national-security/irs-analyst-pleads-guilty-to-leaking-michael-cohens-financial-records/2019/08/14/17e25d0c-bed4-11e9-a5c6-1e74f7ec4a93_story.html
17 https://www.nytimes.com/2020/05/17/business/media/ronan-farrow.html
18 https://www.nytimes.com/2020/05/17/business/media/ronan-farrow.html

CHAPTER THREE: TO OTISVILLE I GO!

1 https://apnews.com/article/tax-evasion-donald-trump-us-news-ap-top-news-crime-8b9d39ea54374ae296a9a8401bf58cb8
2 https://www.cny.org/stories/prisoners-arent-beyond-gods-grace-cardinal-says-at-otisville-correctional,13356
3 Ibid.
4 https://en.wikipedia.org/wiki/Federal_Correctional_Institution,_Otisville
5 https://people.com/tv/jersey-shore-mike-sorrentino-otisville-prison-det
6 Ibid.
7 https://www.justice.gov/usao-sdny/pr/dean-skelos-former-new-york-state-senate-leader-sentenced-51-months-son-adam-skelos#:~:text=%C2%A7%20515%2C%20announced%20today%20that,his%20son%2C%20ADAM%20SKELOS%2C%20in
8 https://www.nytimes.com/2015/05/05/nyregion/dean-skelos-new-york-senate-leader-and-son-are-arrested-on-corruption-charges.html
9 https://time.com/6133336/jan-6-capitol-riot-arrests-sentences/

10 https://people.com/tv/jersey-shore-mike-sorrentino-otisville-prison-details/

11 https://www.cnn.com/2019/12/11/politics/cohen-prison-request/index.html

12 Ibid.

13 https://grandjurytarget.com/2019/12/13/michael-cohens-sentencing-reduction-request-reveals-the-minuscule-bargaining-power-of-a-cooperating-defendant/

14 https://www.cnn.com/2019/12/11/politics/michael-cohen-jail-request/index.html

15 Private interview with members of the DOJ.

16 NPR, March 7, 2022.

17 Ibid.

18 https://www.courthousenews.com/michael-cohen-wants-to-stay-home-too-to-avoid-covid-19/

19 https://www.courtlistener.com/docket/7709849/53/united-states-v-cohen/

20 https://www.themarshallproject.org/2020/05/21/michael-cohen-and-paul-manafort-got-to-leave-federal-prison-due-to-covid-19-they-re-the-exception

21 Ibid.

22 Case 1:20-cv-05614-AKH Document 28 Filed 07/22/20.

23 Letter via electronic mail from Dany Perry to Thomas McKay and Nicolas Roos. 7/14/2020.

24 Letter via electronic mail to Thomas McKay and Nicolas Roos, 7/13/2020.

25 Case 1:20-cv-05614 Document 8 Filed 07/20/20 Page 3 of 4.

26 https://www.washingtonpost.com/national-security/government-says-michael-cohen-was-returned-to-prison-because-he-was-antagonistic-with-probation-officials-not-because-of-trump-book/2020/07/22/cd1b2790-cc56-11ea-b0e3-d55bda07d66a_story.html

27 Document 24, Michael Cohen vs. William Barr, Michael Carvajal and James Petrucci. Pg 3-9.

28 https://www.cnbc.com/2021/07/02/trump-lawyer-michael-cohen-moves-to-sue-us-over-prison-return-and-book.html

29 Ibid.
30 https://www.cnbc.com/2020/07/23/michael-cohen-judge-orders-former-trump-lawyers-release-from-prison.html

CHAPTER FOUR: HOW MANY ACCOUNTANTS DOES IT TAKE TO SCREW IN A LIGHTBULB?

1 Ibid.
2 Letter from Jeffries and Lieu to Michael Horowtiz, OIG, dated 7/24/2020.
3 Letter to Ted Lieu and Hakeem Jeffries, 1/19/22 from Michael Horowitz.
4 Ibid.
5 Ibid.
6 https://www.latimes.com/politics/la-na-pol-house-cohen-trump-hearing-partisan-clash-20190227-story.html
7 https://www.usatoday.com/story/news/politics/2019/02/27/michael-cohen-testimony-change-voter-attitudes-trump/3001704002/
8 https://www.cnn.com/2019/02/27/politics/michael-cohen-donald-trump-oversight-committee-russia/index.html
9 https://www.playboy.com/read/confessions-of-a-trumpaholic
10 Ibid.
11 https://nypost.com/2020/06/03/accountant-accuses-michael-cohen-of-extortionist-cash-grab/
12 "Just Ask the Question" podcast. 5/17/2022.
13 https://www.npr.org/2022/05/23/1099690649/john-legend-progressive-prosecutors-district-attorneys-activism
14 https://www.nytimes.com/2018/07/11/nyregion/dean-skelos-trial-corruption-son.html
15 https://www.wsj.com/articles/skelos-gets-over-4-years-in-prison-1540401553
16 https://www.nytimes.com/2022/03/23/nyregion/mark-pomerantz-resignation-letter.html
17 Ibid.

18 https://thedailybeast.com/manhattan-das-star-witness-michael-cohen-indict-trump-now-or-im-out

19 https://lawandcrime.com/objections-podcast/i-call-bullst-michael-cohen-doesnt-buy-manhattan-das-claim-that-donald-trump-investigation-is-still-alive/

20 https://thedailybeast.com/manhattan-das-star-witness-michael-cohen-indict-trump-now-or-im-out

21 https://www.esquire.com/news-politics/politics/a39842477/manhattan-district-attorney-trump-investigation/

22 https://www.nydailynews.com/new-york/manhattan/ny-michael-cohen-da-bragg-allen-weisselberg-trump-investigation-20220605-undicy33fng6plukdxdezjo6om-story.html

23 https://www.salon.com/2022/05/24/manhattan-da-tells-hes-ready-to-move-ahead-with-org-case-felony-charges-against-exec_partner/

24 https://www.cnn.com/2021/08/11/politics/weisselberg-lied-federal-prosecutors-suspect/index.htm

CHAPTER FIVE: DEMOCRACY IN PERIL

1 https://www.washingtonpost.com/national-security/2022/06/21/ruby-freeman-shaye-moss-jan6-testimony/

2 Ibid.

3 https://pagesix.com/2022/02/21/michael-cohen-rudy-giuliani-have-awkward-run-in-at-nyc-hotspot/

4 https://apnews.com/article/tax-evasion-donald-trump-us-news-ap-top-news-crime-8b9d39ea54374ae296a9a8401bf58cb8

5 Ibid.

6 https://www.thetrumparchive.com/?results=1&searchbox=%22michael+cohen%22

7 https://www.washingtonpost.com/national-security/2022/06/21/ruby-freeman-shaye-moss-jan6-testimony/

8 Ibid.

9 https://rollcall.com/2020/08/21/gaetz-admonished-by-ethics-committee-for-threatening-tweet-directed-at-michael-cohen/

10 https://www.washingtonpost.com/politics/2022/01/27/sex-trafficking-allegations-matt-gaetz/

11 https://rollcall.com/2020/08/21/gaetz-admonished-by-ethics-committee-for-threatening-tweet-directed-at-michael-cohen/
12 https://rollcall.com/2020/08/21/gaetz-admonished-by-ethics-committee-for-threatening-tweet-directed-at-michael-cohen/
13 https://www.businessinsider.com/gaetz-proud-republicans-work-january-6-capitol-rioters-patriotic-2022-1
14 Ibid.
15 https://www.newsweek.com/matt-gaetz-pardon-december-trump-jan6-1718777
16 https://www.cnbc.com/2019/02/27/shame-on-you-mr-jordan-michael-cohen-battles-gop-committee-leader.html
17 https://www.cnn.com/2022/02/04/politics/jim-jordan-trump-january-6/index.html
18 https://www.newsweek.com/matt-gaetz-pardon-december-trump-jan6-1718777
19 https://www.washingtonexaminer.com/news/louie-gohmert-michael-cohen-needed-a-colonoscopy-from-lawmakers
20 https://www.rollingstone.com/politics/politics-news/michael-cohen-trump-was-a-mobster-1056098/
21 https://www.nytimes.com/2022/06/13/us/barr-trump-jan-6-election-2020.html?action=click&pgtype=Article&module=&state=default&region=footer&context=breakout_link_back_to_briefing
22 https://www.newsweek.com/bill-barr-laughs-over-trump-saying-he-sucked-says-hed-expect-attacks-1714964
23 https://www.hrblock.com/tax-center/irs/tax-responsibilities/prision-for-tax-evasion/
24 https://constitutioncenter.org/interactive-constitution/blog/the-executive-and-the-rule-of-law
25 Ibid.
26 Ibid.
27 https://www.usatoday.com/story/news/politics/2019/02/27/ex-trump-lawyer-michael-cohen-testify-house-oversight-committee/2995659002/
28 https://www.theatlantic.com/politics/archive/2019/02/big-moments-michael-cohen-testimony-congress-trump/583750/

29 https://www.history.com/news/8-early-american-political-scandals

30 https://www.history.com/news/8-early-american-political-scandals

31 https://www.history.com/news/8-early-american-political-scandals

32 https://web.archive.org/web/20100709015531/http://www.gilderlehrman.org/historynow/historian5.php

33 https://www.u-s-history.com/pages/h1378.html

CHAPTER SIX: THE DEPARTMENT OF INJUSTICE

1 https://heller.brandeis.edu/news/items/releases/2020/weil-madison-justice.html#:~:text=Martin%20Luther%20King%20Jr.,and%20respect%20for%20every%20individual

2 https://www.theatlantic.com/national/archive/2010/07/what-makes-america-great-mistakes/340412/

3 Case No. 1:22-cv-00092-JMC The James Madison Project v. U.S. Department of Justice/ joint status report 6/22/22.

4 Ibid.

5 Ibid.

6 H. L. Mencken, *The American Scene* (New York: Alfred A. Knopf, Inc., 1965) pg. 254.

7 Ibid.

8 https://www.huffpost.com/entry/sean-hannity-not-a-journalist_n_570fc4f3e4b0ffa5937e6cd2

9 https://libguides.pace.edu/fakenews

10 Ibid.

11 https://freebeacon.com/politics/cnn-panel-cohen-lied-when-he-told-congress-he-never-wanted-white-house-job/

12 https://www.youtube.com/watch?v=4LKdSraZA7M

13 https://www.cnn.com/2018/05/30/politics/michael-avenatti-cohen-trump-recordings/index.html

14 https://www.businessinsider.com/andrey-artemenko-michael-cohen-trump-ukraine-2017-5

15 https://twitter.com/michaelcohen212/status/14146407402784563
24?lang=en
16 https://www.nytimes.com/2017/02/19/us/politics/donald-trump-
ukraine-russia.html
17 https://www.businessinsider.com/bbc-damages-over-cohen-
poroshenko-trump-report-2019-3
18 https://www.nytimes.com/2017/02/19/us/politics/donald-trump-
ukraine-russia.html
19 https://www.bloomberg.com/news/articles/2020-10-30/u-s-
billionaires-got-1-trillion-richer-in-trump-s-first-term
20 https://www.americanbar.org/groups/crsj/publications/
human_rights_magazine_home/the-next-four-years/fixing-the-
department-of-justice/
21 https://www.americanbar.org/groups/crsj/publications/
human_rights_magazine_home/the-next-four-years/fixing-the-
department-of-justice/
22 Barr, William P. (October 28, 1992). The Case for More
Incarceration (PDF). Office of Legal Policy, United States
Department of Justice (Report).
23 https://www.nytimes.com/2022/07/06/us/politics/comey-
mccabe-irs-audits.html
24 https://www.nytimes.com/2022/07/06/us/politics/comey-
mccabe-irs-audits.html?
25 https://www.cnbc.com/2022/07/07/irs-chief-asks-watchdog-to-
probe-rare-tax-audits-of-trump-foes-comey-and-mccabe.html
26 https://www.cnbc.com/2022/07/07/irs-chief-asks-watchdog-to-
probe-rare-tax-audits-of-trump-foes-comey-and-mccabe.html
27 Ibid.
28 https://www.nytimes.com/2022/04/10/us/jared-kushner-saudi-
investment-fund.html
29 H. L. Mencken, The American Scene (New York: Alfred A.
Knopf, Inc., 1965)

ABOUT THE AUTHORS

MICHAEL COHEN is the principal of Crisis-X, a crisis management company. He acted as personal attorney to the former president of the United States, Donald. J. Trump, and before that was executive vice president for the Trump Organization and special counsel to Donald J. Trump. Since his release from the Otisville Federal Correctional Institution, he has authored the *New York Times* number one best-selling book, *Disloyal: A Memoir*. He also hosts the top-rated news podcast, *Mea Culpa With Michael Cohen*, and has become a political commentator regularly seen on major news outlets. He lives in New York City with his wife and two children.

BRIAN J. KAREM is an award-winning journalist and author who writes a weekly column on the White House for *Salon*, and hosts the podcast *Just Ask the Question*. He served as senior White House correspondent for *Playboy* magazine during the Trump administration, and successfully sued the president when Trump tried to take away his White House press pass because he didn't like Karem's questions.

NORMAN EISEN was an ambassador and ethics czar for President Barack Obama and counsel to the House Judiciary Committee in Donald Trump's first impeachment. He first met Michael Cohen when he was investigating impeachment and is a frequent guest on Mr. Cohen's podcast, *Mea Culpa*.

E. DANYA PERRY is the founding attorney at Perry Law in New York, as well as a former federal prosecutor in the Southern District of New York and New York State deputy attorney general. Ms. Perry represented Mr. Cohen in his successful habeas corpus complaint against William Barr and others after Mr. Cohen was unlawfully remanded to federal custody in violation of his First Amendment rights.